Promise Unfulfilled

Promise Unfulfilled

Unions, Immigration and the Farm Workers

PHILIP L. MARTIN

Cornell University Press   *Ithaca and London*

First published 2003 by Cornell University Press
First printing, Cornell Paperbacks, 2003

Printed in the United States of America

Library of Congress Cataloging-in-Publication Data

Martin, Philip L.
  Promise unfulfilled : unions, immigration, and the farm workers /
Philip Martin.
     p. cm.
Includes bibliographical references and index.
  ISBN 0-8014-4186-2 (cloth : alk. paper) — ISBN 0-8014-8875-3 (pbk. :
alk. paper)
  1. Agricultural laborers—Labor unions—California.   2. Agricultural laborers—Labor unions—Law and legislation—California.
3. Agricultural laborers, Foreign—California.   I. Title.
  HD6515.A29M37 2003
  331.88′13′09794—dc21

                                                          2003007774

Cornell University Press strives to use environmentally responsible
suppliers and materials to the fullest extent possible in the publishing
of its books. Such materials include vegetable-based, low-VOC inks
and acid-free papers that are recycled, totally chlorine-free, or partly
composed of nonwood fibers. For further information, visit our
website at www.cornellpress.cornell.edu.

Cloth printing   10 9 8 7 6 5 4 3 2 1
Paperback printing   10 9 8 7 6 5 4 3 2 1

Contents

Acknowledgments

This book evolved from two decades of teaching University of California, Davis, students about farm labor. UC Davis began a farm labor course in the 1970s, when Cesar Chavez and the UFW were in the news daily, and UC Davis, the major agricultural university in California, was the focus of many farm labor protests. The farm labor course began as an effort to teach modern personnel economics and evolved with the farm labor market into an effort to teach history and law as well as economics.

This book was made possible through the generous support of the Rosenberg and Giannini Foundations, as well as the Farm Foundation and the UC Institute for Labor and Employment. I have also benefited from interacting with the relatively small community of farm labor scholars, including Daniel Carroll, Elias Lopez, Bert Mason, Rick Mines, and Ed Taylor. Land-grant universities have a remarkable system of regional committees that permit researchers around the United States to exchange ideas about topics of interest. Since 1987, I have been privileged to work with the WCC-076 group of twenty-five farm labor researchers, including Wally Huffman, Will Rochin, Jack Runyan, and Dawn Thilmany. I thank Kim Brobeck for organizing the manuscript, and several referees for their careful reviews.

PHILIP MARTIN

Davis, California

Prologue: What Went Wrong?

> The greatest accomplishment of my administration was the enactment of a farm labor relations law.
>
> Jerry Brown, California governor, 1975–83

A few American youth may still dream of growing up to be cowboys, but dreams of becoming a migrant and seasonal farm worker would be scarcely imaginable. Migrant and seasonal farm workers bring to mind the Joad family of John Steinbeck's *The Grapes of Wrath*, or the young black and Mexican men who "shaped up" seeking jobs with contractors in the CBS documentary, "Harvest of Shame." Some of the people who read *The Grapes of Wrath* in 1940, or saw "Harvest of Shame" in 1960, identified with the migrants portrayed because they remembered the farm work they or their parents had done. Most of them, and most of their parents, were Americans.

America's farm workers have changed. At least 75 percent of U.S. farm workers are immigrants, and most are not authorized to work in the United States (NAWS, 2000, 14). In the nonfarm economy, by contrast, 12 percent of workers are immigrants, and 3–4 percent are unauthorized.[1] The farm workers of tomorrow are growing up today outside theUnited States, raising a major public policy issue—how easy should it be for farmers to import foreign workers? What should the government do to help improve the lives of farm workers? Farmers say that Americans will not do farm work, and so foreigners eager to fill U.S. farm jobs should find it easy to enter the United States and work. Since these migrants are better off in the United States than they were at home, there should be little worry about them, even if their wages are low by U.S. standards.

Worker advocates are divided. Most recognize that slowing immigration would put upward pressure on wages and working conditions, so they want high hurdles between farm employers and foreign guest workers, who they often refer to as indentured servants. However, other worker advocates, including the current leaders of the United Farm Workers union founded by Cesar Chavez, say they are not worried about the presence of unauthorized workers, only legal guest workers. They say it is not the number of farm workers that depresses farm wages, but rather their fear of joining unions and negotiating higher wages. Federal and state governments could, they argue, do more to help workers join unions, and thus push up farm wages despite continued immigration.

This book examines a quarter century of experience with farm worker unions, immigration, and wages in California. Readers will learn that California's farm workers have been newcomers without other U.S. job options for more than a century. The federal government has followed a contradictory policy, acceding to farmer demands for additional farm workers, but embarrassed by farm worker poverty, developing a variety of assistance programs to help farm workers and their children. In 1975, California took an historic step to help farm workers to help themselves by granting farm workers the right to organize into unions. The hope was that, with unions, farm workers would be able to lift themselves out of poverty.

Helping Farm Workers

Farm workers are poor. On average, they earn a quarter as much as nonfarm workers. This great discrepancy has two causes: lower wages per hour and fewer hours of work. In 2002, farm workers earned an average eight dollars an hour, versus fifteen dollars an hour for nonfarm workers. Most U.S. workers are employed forty hours a week, fifty weeks a year, and this two thousand hours of work a year generates earnings of thirty thousand dollars. But most farm workers are employed only a thousand hours a year and earn only eight thousand dollars a year—a fourth as much. The earnings gap is widened by the fact that nonfarm workers are much more likely than farm workers to receive employer-paid benefits such as health insurance, pension benefits, and paid vacations.

What should be done to help farm workers raise their earnings and overcome their poverty? During the 1950s and 1960s, when the number of farmers and farm workers was shrinking rapidly, agricultural economists argued that low farm earnings resulted from the presence of too many farm workers—supply exceeded demand—and that the government could best help farm workers by encouraging faster rural to urban migration (Bishop, 1967). More farm workers would become nonfarm workers, the reasoning went, if the United States were at full employment, making nonfarm jobs easier to find. Agricultural economists, in short, argued that farm workers were a reserve labor supply for the nonfarm economy, and that most would never be able to increase their earnings in agriculture. Moving from the lower-wage primary sector to the higher-wage industrial sector was considered a normal part of economic development (Taylor and Martin, 2001).

During the 1930s, when there was very little immigration, the United States enacted laws that aimed to level the playing field between workers and employers by giving workers the right to organize into unions. To provide a floor for workers, a minimum wage was established, and social security and unemployment insurance programs were created to provide benefits to retired and jobless workers. Farm workers were excluded from these labor laws because, it was argued, farming is different. Most farms, the argument went, are family operations, and labor laws would be inappropriate for a hired hand or two who worked and lived alongside the farm employer. Furthermore, most hired hands were aspiring farmers, so they wanted the government to raise commodity prices, the same thing that farmers wanted.

In reality, most hired farm workers did not become farmers. Most learned that upward economic mobility required geographic mobility, moving from the fields, where there were few labor protections but many workers from the Caribbean and Mexico, to factory jobs, where there was year-round work at higher wages and with fringe benefits. Many of these ex-farm workers had joined protests of low farm wages, prompting government and private studies of farm worker protest and poverty. Each house of Congress had a subcommittee on migrant farm workers in the 1950s and 1960s, and the economists, unions, churches, and worker advocates who testified before them agreed that the top priorities for the federal government were to end the importation of foreign workers and to extend labor law protections to farm workers, in short, to treat farming like other industries and to treat farm workers like other workers.

Farmers countered that "farming is different," that agriculture needed both foreign guest workers and exemptions from labor laws. Farmers succeeded on both counts, and the pressure to "do something" about farm worker poverty was redirected during the 1960s war on poverty to federally financed assistance programs. Beginning with subsidized health care for farm workers and their children in 1962, the federal government created ten programs that today spend about $1 billion a year, one-seventh of annual farm worker earnings, to provide education, health care, and job training for farm workers and their children. These assistance programs have helped some individuals get out of farm work, but because exiting farm workers are replaced by even poorer farm workers, they have not eliminated farm worker poverty (Martin and Martin, 1994).

Farm Workers Helping Themselves

Self-help is an alternative to government assistance programs, and it was preferred by most worker advocates throughout the twentieth century. In 1975, Cesar Chavez and the United Farm Workers (UFW) union persuaded California to enact the Agricultural Labor Relations Act (ALRA), which granted farm workers the right to organize into unions and bargain with employers. When the ALRA was enacted, political leaders said that California had fulfilled its promise to level the playing field between farm workers and farmers and end the violence between unions and growers in the fields. There were predictions that the UFW would soon become one of the nation's largest unions, and that collective bargaining would close the gap between farm and nonfarm wages while the UFW served as an example of a new kind of self-help organization for the growing Latino work force.

The promise that the ALRA would put farm workers on a path to higher wages and improved working conditions has not been fulfilled. A quarter century of organizing and bargaining has not raised farm worker wages above its historical 50-percent-of-nonfarm-wages mark. The UFW lost members and contracts in the 1980s and 1990s, and unions such as the Service Employees International Union and the International Brotherhood of Teamsters have far more Hispanic members than the UFW. Union density—the percentage of workers in an industry or occupation represented by unions—is very low in California agriculture: fewer than 35,000 of the 800,000 persons employed for wages sometime during a typical year on California farms work under union contracts, less than 5 percent. By contrast, about 10 percent of private sector workers are represented by unions.

Why did the ALRA fail as a self-help tool for farm workers? Four major explanations are put forward by those who have observed farm labor in California: poor union leadership, larger political changes, farm employer changes, and immigration. All these explanations have merit. Those who lay responsibility on the UFW say that Cesar Chavez was a charismatic leader who could articulate the hopes of farm workers, but was not capable of the vital task of administering the contracts signed on behalf of its members. For example, UFW-run hiring halls could not efficiently deploy seasonal workers who were shifting from farm to farm, and union-run health and pension plans were unable to pay doctors and workers in a timely fashion, prompting worker dissatisfaction and reducing support for the union (Barr, 1985; Bardake, 1993). The political change explanation is that the ALRA was enacted and administered under pro-worker Democratic appointees between 1975 and 1982. However, between 1983 and 1999 progrower Republican governors appointed their ideological allies to the agency administering the ALRA, the Agricultural Labor Relations Board (ALRB); this argument makes the success of unions dependent on who is making appointments to the ALRB (Schilling, 1992; Majka and Majka, 1995).

The other two explanations for the failure of the ALRA and unions to transform the farm labor market are empirical, based on what happened in the farm labor market in the 1980s and 1990s. Employers changed in the 1960s and 1970s. Unions were most successful when they were dealing with the farming subsidiaries of nonfarm conglomerates, such as Shell Oil, Seven-Up, and Tenneco. Many of these conglomerates sold their farming operations in the 1980s, and their land was taken over by farmers who did not have to worry as their predecessors did about union threats to boycott their nonfarm products. Instead of hiring workers directly, as the conglomerates had done, many farmers had farm labor contractors bring crews of workers to their farms to prune or harvest crops (Villarejo, 2000). Contractors select their crews, and thus know their workers. They also know that, if they develop a reputation for bringing prounion crews to a farm, farmers will select a different contractor.

The final explanation for the failure of the ALRA to transform the farm labor market is increased legal and illegal migration. Two numbers tell the story. In 1987–88, when there were about 6 million adult men in rural Mexico, the United States legalized 1 million Mexican men under the Special Agricultural Worker (SAW) program, which granted immigrant status to unauthorized foreigners who asserted that they had done at least ninety days of U.S. farm work in 1985–86. The fact that many of these men did not do the qualifying farm work but nonetheless became immigrants taught rural Mexicans that being an unauthorized worker in the United States can bring immigration benefits and encouraged more rural Mexicans to migrate to the United States, as indicated by the rising number of apprehensions: 1.6 million during the 1960s, 8.3 million during the 1970s, 12 million during the 1980s, and 14 million during the 1990s. The period from the late 1960s, after the *bracero* program ended, to the early 1980s, when peso devaluations sent Mexicans streaming north, is often thought of as the golden age for American farm workers. The ALRA was enacted in the middle of that golden age.

Outline of This Book

This book explores these explanations for the failure of unions and collective bargaining to transform the California farm labor market. Part I lays out the key features of the California farm labor market, the history of farm labor, and the evolution of farm worker unions. Part II examines the activities of the ALRB in implementing the ALRA by reviewing allegations of labor law violations in farm worker organizing and bargaining, and the remedies ordered to ensure that the promises of the ALRA would be fulfilled. Part III reviews the economics of the farm labor market and immigration and focuses on the impacts of immigration on U.S. agriculture and farm workers.

My goal is to present the facts of what happened in the fields of California during the past quarter century. I have concluded that, if society continues to stint on its rewards to farm workers, we will have slightly cheaper food than we would have with better-paid workers, but this cheap food will come at high price—the price of integrating poor farm workers and their children. There are alternatives to the farm labor status quo that would make farming profitable, raise farm worker wages, and still keep strawberries and lettuce affordable. I conclude that we should pursue these alternatives, which would improve wages and working conditions for farm workers and strengthen agriculture's long-run competitiveness in the global economy.

I FARM LABOR AND UNIONS

In chapter 1, I focus on the employers who create farm jobs, the characteristics of the workers who fill them, and the market in which workers exchange their effort for wages. I review the waves of newcomers who formed the core of the seasonal work force in California agriculture in chapter 2. Closely examined is the way in which low wages paid to seasonal farm workers helped to raise land prices, which gave land owners an economic incentive to keep immigration doors open to maintain their wealth. In chapter 3 I show how farm workers often protested the low wages they received but were unable to form durable unions that could develop lasting collective bargaining agreements with employers.

1

California Farm Labor

For the great bulk of farm work, procedures of job-getting and hiring are
as miscellaneous as the labor force is heterogeneous.

Varden Fuller and Bert Mason, "Farm Labor"

Farms that produce food and fiber are defined in the U.S. Census of
Agriculture (COA) as places that sell at least a thousand dollars worth
of farm commodities a year. Most of the 2 million U.S. farms are considered family farms, a term that is not defined officially. The U.S. Congress, in the Food Security Act of 1985, defined a family farm as one
using less than 1.5 person-years of hired labor and having no hired manager; other definitions are that the farmer and his or her family members must do more than half of the work on the farm.[1]

Most family farms are diversified crop and livestock operations, providing work for farmers and family members who plant crops such as
corn and wheat in the spring, harvest them in the fall, and tend livestock
in the winter. The mechanization of many farm tasks has enabled most
farm families to include one or more persons employed in nonfarm jobs.
The farms on which farm workers are employed in California are different. Instead of producing field crops such as wheat or corn, California
farms tend to specialize, to produce only lettuce, peaches, or grapes. Instead of year-round work for a few hired hands, fruit and vegetable
farms often employ large numbers of workers seasonally, which means
that hundreds of thousands of workers must be matched with hundreds
of thousands of jobs that may last from several days to several weeks.

Most U.S. farms do not specialize in the production of labor-intensive
fruits, nut, and berries; vegetables and melons; and horticultural specialties (abbreviated as FVH crops) that range from nursery and greenhouse crops to Christmas trees, mushrooms, and sod. In 1997, the

193,000 U.S. FVH farms were 10 percent of U.S. farms, but they accounted for over 80 percent of seasonal jobs on farms, those that lasted less than 150 days on one farm. FVH commodities occupy less than 3 percent of the nation's 350 million acres of crop land, but they generate one-sixth of the U.S. crop sales. In California, FVH commodities are far more important—they occupy a third of the state's irrigated crop land and account for half of the state's farm sales.

Three *C*s of Farm Labor

There is a farm labor market transaction every time a farmer hires a crew of twenty to thirty workers to prune, hoe, or harvest, or every time a crew leader hires a worker to join his crew, so there are many farm labor markets. Perhaps the easiest way to summarize the California farm labor market is with three words that begin with C—concentration, contractors, and conflict:

- *Concentration* highlights the fact that most FVH commodities are produced by, and most farm workers are employed on, the largest farms.
- The word *contractors* means that most workers are matched with jobs by intermediaries, people who profit from the difference between what a farmer pays to have a job done and what the contractor or intermediary pays to workers.
- *Conflict* refers to the stormy history of farm workers protesting low wages and poor working conditions. Collective efforts to obtain better wages and benefits generally failed, so most farm workers individually exited the farm labor market for upward mobility rather than staying in agriculture and voicing their protest via unions and bargaining.

The 1997 Census of Agriculture reported that 36,450 California farms hired 549,265 workers, implying that the "average farm employer" hired 15 workers. However, this average obscures the concentration of farm jobs. The 9,000 farms that each hired 10 or more workers accounted for over 80 percent of total hires, an average of almost 50 per farm.[2] At the small end of the spectrum, three-quarters of the farm employers hired fewer than 10 workers—they collectively accounted for 20 percent of total hires, an average 4 each. The fact that there are many farm employers makes "average employment" low, but when farmers are ranked from small to large, and their share of total employment is added to the distribution, the result is an X, with the left part of the X that slopes

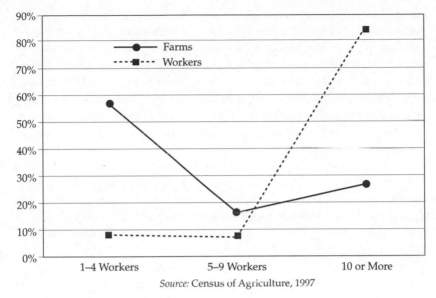

Source: Census of Agriculture, 1997

Figure 1.1. California Farm Employers and Workers: 1997

down and to the right showing that most farm employers are small, and the right or upward to the right line showing that most workers are hired by the largest employers. The average in an X-distribution can be misleading, since it is akin to having one hand in fire, and another on ice, and having an "average temperature" of 98.6.

Many large FVH farms call themselves "family farms." Three examples illustrate employment and earnings on FVH farms. The Zaninovich table grape farm in California's San Joaquin Valley provides an example of long-season employment. In the late 1990s, Zaninovich sold about 5 million twenty-one-pound boxes of table grapes a year for ten dollars per box and hired one thousand farm workers to help generate $50 million in annual sales.[3] Most of these workers were employed five hundred to one thousand hours between May and October and, at seven to eight dollars an hour, workers averaged thirty-five hundred dollars to eight thousand dollars for four to eight months of farm work. If these workers only pick grapes, their incomes are below the poverty level.

Dole Food Company is the world's largest producer of fresh fruit, vegetables, and flowers, with sixty thousand employees worldwide. Dole's farming operations in California are divided into several separate businesses. For example, Dole's Bud of California subsidiary in Salinas hires an average thirty-eight hundred farm workers, represented by the Teamsters Union, to harvest lettuce and other vegetables; most work six to nine months a year, and earn ten thousand to twenty thousand dollars, some of the highest wages earned by seasonal workers.[4]

Fresno-area raisin farms epitomize employment and earnings on smaller labor-intensive farms. Some forty thousand to fifty thousand workers are hired each August through September to cut bunches of green grapes and lay them on paper trays to dry into raisins. Most raisin vineyards are small—twenty to fifty acres—and raisin growers often recruit harvest workers by placing a sign at the entrance to the vineyard that says, in Spanish, "workers wanted." Workers are paid about one cent a pound for picking green grapes, and the contractor that recruits and supervises a crew receives a small fee to cover his supervision costs, payroll taxes, and other business expenses. If raisin harvesters are employed ten hours a day for eight weeks, they work 560 hours and, at seven dollars hourly, a raisin harvester would earn thirty-nine hundred dollars a season.

Dole is the preferred employer for most seasonal workers, and Zaninovich would be a preferred employer to most raisin farm workers because table grapes offer more hours of work with one employer. Seasonality that requires workers to shift from job to job helps to explain why contractors, the second C, are often called the glue that matches workers and jobs. One function of labor market "intermediaries" such as farm labor contractors (FLCs) or crew bosses is to arrange a series of farm jobs for workers, so that they can work instead of looking for jobs. Contractors or intermediaries have a long history in California: Chinese and Japanese farm labor "gangs" in the late 1800s included a bilingual crew member to arrange jobs for the crew. However, contractors in the twentieth century evolved into independent businesses whose profits reflected the wedge between what a farmer pays to have a job done and the wages received by workers.

Since the ALRA was enacted in 1975, contractors have increased their share of total employment; they now account for almost half of average employment on California farms, and 60 to 80 percent of employment in seasonal harvesting. Most farm worker advocates decry the rising market share of contractors, associating them with abuse of workers and pushing for legislation that would, for example, require a farmer to pay the fines levied on contractors who abuse the workers they bring to his farm—many contractors disappear, leaving workers and fines unpaid. Farmers counter that contractors are independent businesses and should be regulated by the state, not by the farmer who uses them to obtain workers.

When they hire a contractor, farmers say they are acting like a non-farm business that turns to a temporary help firm such as Manpower or

Labor Ready for additional workers.[5] An employer utilizing workers from a temporary help firm is not normally liable for the labor law violations committed by the temporary help firm, and thus farmers say they should not be liable for contractor violations. Worker advocates counter that the analogy is misleading because many farm labor contractors are not truly independent businesses. Manpower and Labor Ready are typically in a stronger position than the companies to which they send workers, while farmers tend to be in a stronger position than contractors. For this reason, contractors sometimes make what appear to be money-losing deals with farmers, but then make a profit by not paying required taxes, or by unlawfully charging workers for housing or rides to work. Under most tax, labor, and immigration law, contractors are considered employers, and farmers are not usually liable for contractor violations of these laws.

Cesar Chavez believed that contractors and unions were mutually exclusive, with each competing for the loyalty of workers. Chavez insisted that contractors could not be considered employers under the ALRA.[6] This means that a contractor crew can vote for the union, and the farmer on whose farm they are working can be obliged to recognize the union and bargain, even if the crew was on his property only one week and never returns. Contractors do not leave a string of union elections in their wake—any contractor who did would have little business. Chavez failed to anticipate contractors obtaining equipment such as forklifts and trucks and becoming "custom harvesters," who are considered to be employers in their own right under the ALRA. If contractors/custom harvesters bring workers and equipment to the farm and assume some managerial risk and judgement by making decisions about when and how to harvest independent of the farmer, farm workers would have to vote to have a contract with the contractor/custom harvester, not the farmer who owned or leased the land where they happened to be working.

The third C is conflict. Employment is the exchange of effort for reward, and there is an inevitable conflict between employers and workers over the appropriate wage and the level of effort required to keep one's job. Labor market conflict can be resolved in three major ways:

- by employers unilaterally, as when the employer says, the wage is eight dollars an hour—take it or leave it;
- through collective bargaining, which produces a two- or three-year agreement spelling out wages, benefits, and work rules, and a mechanism for resolving disputes during the agreement;
- by having government regulate wages and benefits, such as setting

за

minimum wages and requiring the provision of unemployment insurance and pension benefits for jobless and retired workers.

Over the past quarter century, employer unilateralism and collective bargaining have declined, and the role of government has increased—the decline of collective bargaining tends to produce more government regulation, not a return to employer unilateralism. Employers unilateralism is often associated with "exit responses" to workplace dissatisfaction, as especially younger and more mobile workers quit jobs they do not like and employer personnel policies become oriented toward hiring replacements, who also tend to be young and mobile (Freeman and Medoff, 1984). Collective bargaining, by contrast, is often a voice response to worker dissatisfaction and tends to involve older workers whose wages reflect their skills with the firm and who may have a harder time finding a job paying comparable wages. By collectively voicing their dissatisfaction via a union, older workers and those with firm-specific skills try to change wages and conditions.

Conflicts in the farm labor market have unique characteristics. Farm employers sometimes band together to set wages and benefits, producing what is called employer monopsony—a group of farmers acting as the only employer of workers can hold down wages. Many farm worker advocates are nontraditional; many have been radical outsiders who have not been welcomed in often conservative rural communities. The stakes may be high in a seasonal labor conflict, since the farmer's annual income, and much of the worker's income, may depend on whether a perishable crop gets harvested. If farm workers live on the farm where they work, a strike can mean loss of housing, which raises the stakes in the conflict.

Factories in the Fields

Farm workers are often compared to factory workers because most are employed in open-air enterprises that turn raw materials into finished products. A nonfarm factory brings together people and machines to transform inputs such as steel, rubber, and glass into cars; a farm factory brings together people, land, water, and machines to transform seeds into fruits and vegetables. The agricultural production process is biological—farm factories face unique pest and weather risks that do not arise in manufacturing, where production processes are governed by engineering relationships. Farm and nonfarm factories also differ in other dimensions. Farming requires land, so agriculture is dispersed over wide geographic areas. The supply of good farmland is fixed, so farmers who want to expand must bid against each other to acquire more land. Land is the major asset of farmers—the value of farmland in 2000 represented about 85 percent of the $1 trillion in assets of U.S. agriculture—and the value of farmland serves as a barometer of the economic condition of farmers, an agricultural stock market.

Farming differs in other ways. Farming is often considered a "way of life," not simply a job. Many Americans believe that there is a special virtue in producing food on family-sized farms, so family farmers are celebrated as the independent yeomen who are living links to the nation's founding fathers. The Midwestern farmer who works hard every day, while being subject to the vagaries of weather and markets, evokes enough sympathy so that U.S. taxpayers provided about half of U.S. farmers' net income of $50 billion in 2000.[7]

California agriculture never evoked images of farm families producing crops and livestock. Instead, farming in California has been dominated for the past 150 years by specialized enterprises that hire hundreds of seasonal workers to produce one or two commodities. Unlike Midwestern farmers who do most of the farm's work with their hands, California farm owners and managers rarely do "farm work" themselves and, due to language barriers, they are generally not able to communicate with the workers who do. A familiar adage captures the difference: California agriculture is a business, not a way of life (Fisher, 1953, 1).

California has led the nation in farm sales since 1950. California has only 2 percent of U.S. farmland, yet the state accounts for 12 percent of the nation's farm sales because it produces high-value FVH commodities, from artichokes to zucchini. California farmers obtain far more revenue per acre, and have far higher production costs, than other farmers. For example, California harvested 222,000 acres of lettuce in 2000 and had lettuce sales of $1.5 billion, or $6,700 an acre. Wisconsin farmers, by contrast, tilled 10 million acres but had the same farm sales (CDFA, COA). As farmland becomes more valuable, and water more expensive, many California farmers are switching from lower-value field crops, such as cotton and alfalfa, to higher-value FVH commodities: California fruit and vegetable production, measured in millions of tons, doubled between 1974 and 1998.

United States farmers had cash receipts from the sale of farm products of $209 billion in 1997, when the Census of Agriculture was conducted (see box 1.1). About $96 billion, or half of these farm sales, came from the sale of livestock products, such as cattle, dairy products, and chickens, and $112 billion resulted from the sale of crops that ranged

Box 1.1. Farming and Food Expenditures

A farm is "any place from which $1,000 or more of agricultural products were produced and sold or normally would have been sold during the census year[s]" that end in 2 and 7. There were 1.9 million farms in 1997, including 20 percent of the national total located in Texas, Missouri, and Iowa. The 1920 census was the first to find that more Americans lived in cities than on farms and in small towns; the number of farms peaked in 1935 at 6.6 million.

The largest 28,000 U.S. farms—about 1 percent of U.S. farms—each sold farm products worth $1 million or more in 1997, and they accounted for 41 percent of farm sales. The smallest 960,000 farms each sold farm products worth less than $10,000—they were half of all farms, and they accounted for 1 percent of farm sales.

Most farmers are older white men; most farm workers are young and minority men. The average age of farm operators was fifty-four in 1997, and almost one-third were sixty-five or older—many considered themselves retired. Both large and small farms are included in calculations of average household income, which was $52,347 for farm households in 1997, 5 percent more than the $49,692 of all U.S. households. Farm household incomes included an average $6,000 from farming and $46,400 from off-farm sources, that is, 89 percent of the average farm household's income came from nonfarm sources. Farming households are, on average, about twice as wealthy as nonfarm households—they had an average net worth of $560,000 in 1999.

There were 24 million Americans—17 percent of U.S. workers—employed in the $1 trillion food and fiber industry in 1996, making the food and fiber sector about one-eighth of the U.S. economy (Lipton, 1998). The food and fiber sector includes:

- Input industries that supply inputs to farmers, such as banks, chemical companies, and equipment manufacturers (5 million employees);
- Farming, or producing crops and livestock on farms (1.5 million employees);
- Output industries that transport, pack, and process; and distribute and sell farm products, including grocery stores and restaurants (17 million employees).

The size of the food and fiber system varies across countries with the level of income, not how much food is produced in the country. This explains why city states such as Hong Kong and Singapore have large "food systems" despite small farm sectors.

The U.S. Bureau of Labor Statistics reported that there were 109 million "consumer units," or households, in the United States in 2000, with

an average of 2.5 persons, 1.4 earners, and two vehicles. The average
consumer unit or household spent $38,000 on all items during the year,
including $5,200 for food (14 percent). Some 58 percent of these food ex-
penditures were for food eaten at home, and the $58 a week spent on
food at home included $6.20 for fresh fruits and vegetables.

from wheat and corn to fruits and vegetables. In most U.S. states, livestock sales exceed crop sales. For example, in New York, livestock sales
were 55 percent of total farm sales. However, in states that specialize in
the production of fruits and vegetables such as California, crop sales
were three times livestock sales.[8]

Crop sales are often subdivided into field crops and FVH commodities. In 1997, field crops such as soybeans, cotton, wheat, and corn accounted for about two-thirds of U.S. crop sales. FVH commodities
worth $32 billion accounted for one-third of U.S. crop sales, and 44 per-
cent of FVH commodities came from California.[9] The FVH sector has
three major components:

- 86,000 U.S. farms produced fruits, nuts, and berries worth $12.7 bil-
  lion in 1997—California accounted for 62 percent of fruit and nut
  sales.
- 53,600 U.S. farms produced vegetables and melons worth $8.4 bil-
  lion in 1997—California accounted for 48 percent of vegetable and
  melon sales.
- 67,800 U.S. farms produced horticultural specialties—nursery and
  greenhouse crops, Christmas trees, mushrooms, and sod—worth
  $11 billion in 1997. California accounted for 20 percent of these spe-
  cialty crops.

California began producing labor-intensive fruits and vegetables and
shipping them long distances a century ago, but much of the expansion
of California's FVH agriculture occurred after World War II, when rising incomes increased consumer demand for fruits and vegetables, irrigation projects expanded the amount of land that could be farmed
intensively, and the interstate highway system made it possible to ship
fresh fruits and vegetables cheaply to distant consumers. California produces more than 250 commodities commercially—most of these are various kinds of fruits and vegetables—but a few fruits and vegetables
account for most farm sales. For example, grapes—raisin, wine, and
table—accounted for about half of California's $6 billion in fruit and nut
sales in 1998, and lettuce sales were 20 percent of the state's $4 billion in

vegetable and melon sales.[10] Most of California's fruits and vegetables are consumed outside the state, including in Canada, Mexico, and Japan.[11]

The land used to produce fruits and vegetables is valuable. In 2000, land used to grow vegetables in Monterey County sold for an average fifteen thousand dollars an acre, while vineyard and orchard land in Fresno County was worth an average eight thousand dollars an acre. A conservative indicator of the value of the land used for grow fruits and vegetables in California can be derived as follows. If the 1.2 million acres of land used to grow vegetables in 1997 was worth an average fifteen thousand dollars an acre, its total worth is $18 billion, while if 2.6 million acres of land with fruit and nut trees and grape vines was worth an average eight thousand dollars an acre, its total worth would be $21 billion. The wages paid to farm workers are a key determinant of whether this fruit and vegetable land continues to be worth almost $40 billion.

Farm Worker Employment

Farm worker employment has been rising. In 2000, an average 408,000 workers were employed on California farms, with a peak 486,000 farm workers employed in September, and a low 312,600 employed in February. There were more than 486,000 individuals employed on farms— at least 800,000, according to state unemployment insurance records.[12] However, table 1.1 shows that average annual employment—employment each month summed and divided by twelve—has been stable for farm production, or for workers hired directly by crop and livestock farms, and rose sharply for farm services, mostly farm labor contractors who assemble crews of workers and bring them to farms.

One way to measure employment fluctuations is with a peak-trough ratio, employment in the peak month divided by employment in the trough month. A peak-trough ratio of one indicates no seasonality— employment is the same each month of the year, while higher peak-trough ratios indicate more seasonality. In 2000, the peak-trough ratio for employment in California agriculture was 1.6, meaning that 160 workers were employed in September for each 100 employed in January. The peak-trough ratio for workers brought to farms by farm service employers such as contractors is higher, 1.7, than for workers hired directly, 1.5.

During the 1960s, the employment of hired workers fell as a result of mechanization. Farm worker employment was expected to continue falling as machines replaced workers in the 1970s and 1980s, practically eliminating unskilled seasonal farm workers by 2000, according to most

Table 1.1. Average Annual Wage and Salary Employment in California Agriculture

Employer	1985	1990	1995	2000	1985–2000
Farm Production	232,700	229,700	228,400	228,500	−2%
Farm Services	102,700	133,800	145,100	179,500	75%
Total	335,400	363,500	373,500	408,000	22%
Farm Services Share	31%	37%	39%	44%	

Source: http://www.calmis.ca.gov/file/indhist/cal$haw.xls

predictions (Cargill and Rossmiller, 1969-70). A world of few seasonal farm workers seemed plausible at a time when the harvesting of cannery or processing tomatoes was mechanized and fork lifts and bulk bins were brought into the fields to replace workers.

The mechanical tomato harvester exemplifies 1960s labor-saving farm mechanization. University of California, Davis, plant scientists developed tomatoes that ripened uniformly and had an oblong shape amenable to mechanical harvesting and bulk handling. Engineers from UC Davis developed a machine capable of harvesting these tomatoes in one pass through the field, and then conveying harvested tomatoes to processing plants in twin 12.5 ton tubs mounted on tractor trailer trucks. The keys to transforming the processing tomato harvest included state-run stations that took random samples of tomatoes to determine their quality and an agreement among processors to switch from accepting 60-pound lugs to 12.5 ton tubs, that is, processors had to invest to switch to facilities that handled mechanically harvested tomatoes. Cooperation between researchers, farmers, processors, and the government transformed the processing tomato industry within five years after the *bracero* program ended in 1964.

There were many consequences of tomato harvest mechanization, and some of them curtailed mechanization research. The number of farm workers hired for the harvest fell by 90 percent, and the number of farms growing tomatoes dropped 70 percent—tomato harvesting machines were costly, and only farmers with large acreages could justify purchasing them. These impacts on farm workers and small farmers prompted suits against the University of California that alleged that taxpayer monies, whose purpose was to help all rural residents, were instead spent on mechanization that displaced farm workers and small farmers (Martin and Olmstead, 1985). The UFW and worker advocates reached a settlement with the University of California in the early 1980s

Table 1.2. Monthly Employment in California Agriculture

	2000 Max	2000 Min	2000 Difference	2000 Ratio	1993 Max	1993 Min	1993 Difference	1993 Ratio
Farm Production	266,400	179,600	86,800	1.5	267,200	175,500	91,700	1.5
Farm Services	219,900	133,000	86,900	1.7	176,700	103,500	73,200	1.7
Total	486,000	312,600	173,400	1.6	443,900	279,000	164,900	1.6

Source: http://www.calmis.ca.gov/htmlfile/subject/indtable.htm

that led to worker and small farmer representatives on committees that reviewed research priorities. Although these review committees did not stop mechanization research, scientists and engineers turned from mechanization to problems for which there was funding support from private industry; funding for mechanization research dropped because workers were readily available.

During the 1960s, some observers of agricultural technology predicted that fruit would be shaken off trees rather than be picked by workers climbing ladders, and fresh vegetables would be harvested by once-over-the-field machines rather than workers making several passes through the field to cut heads of lettuce or bunches of broccoli,[13] and that mechanically harvested vegetables and fruits would move in large bins and trucks to packing and processing plants (Cargill and Rossmiller, 1969-70). This mechanized fruit and vegetable agriculture did not materialize, largely because farm wages stopped rising in the 1980s and 1990s, dulling interest in mechanization, and consumer demand for fresh fruits and vegetables increased.

Was labor-saving mechanization simply delayed, so that there will be a sharp drop in farm worker employment in the twenty-first century rather than in the 1970s and 1980s? Most observers do not expect a sharp drop in farm worker employment because they see few economic signals that would encourage mechanization. There is some additional labor-saving mechanization driven by international competition, as some growers of raisin grapes and olives switch to machines to compete with cheaper imports, but there is little 1960s-style mechanization prompted by rising wages.

Labor-intensive crops are often described as high-risk and high-reward. To produce most fruits and vegetables, farmers must invest two thousand dollars to four thousand dollars an acre. By the time crops are ready to be harvested, pruning, planting, and other costs are fixed or sunk—farmers will harvest their crops as long as the price they receive exceeds the cost of harvesting. Harvesting is usually the most labor-intensive activity on fruit and vegetable farms, accounting for half or more of the labor costs of producing the crop. However, "labor-intensive" can be a misleading adjective—labor costs range from 15 percent to 35 percent of the costs of producing most fruits and vegetables, about the same as labor's 20 percent share of production costs in manufacturing, but much less than labor's 70 to 80 percent share of production costs in many services.[14] Farm wages are not very important determinants of retail prices, since farmers receive only 15 to 20 percent of the retail price of lettuce and strawberries. Thus, for a dollar head of lettuce, farmers receive twenty cents, and farm labor costs are five to six cents.

Seasonal farm work has traditionally been associated with harvesting fruits and vegetables, as workers cut heads of lettuce or climb ladders to pick peaches or pears into bags. Harvesting occurs year-round in California. Vegetables are harvested during the winter months in southern California deserts (Imperial Valley) and navel oranges are harvested in the San Joaquin Valley between December and March.[15]

Harvesting activities shift to the coastal plains in March and April, as workers harvest lemons and oranges in the Ventura area and vegetables in the Salinas area; camps for migrant families usually open for six months in April or May. By May, farm workers are picking strawberries and vegetables, and these harvesting activities continue throughout the summer. June marks the beginning of fruit thinning activities in the San Joaquin Valley, as workers move through orchards of peaches, plums, and nectarines to remove some of the buds so that those that remain develop larger fruit. Harvest activities continue to require large numbers of workers in July and August, as vegetables are harvested in the coastal valleys and tree fruits, cantaloupes, melons, tomatoes, and Valencia oranges are harvested in the San Joaquin Valley.

September is the month in which farm worker employment reaches its peak. A series of harvests, symbolized by the raisin harvest, brings employment on California farms to almost 500,000, exceeding the number of state government employees (450,000). Fruit, grape, and olive employers often complain of "labor shortages," which may mean that they want a harvest crew of forty workers, but have a crew of only twenty working in the field or orchard. Harvesting winds down in October, and most migrant camps close. Some farm workers return to homes in Mexico, but most stay in the area where they worked.

The fact that harvesting activities move around the state suggests that farm workers could migrate from one harvest to another. Most do not—there are far fewer migrants than assumed, in part because of the variety of definitions. A migrant worker crosses a geographic boundary to do farm work, but there is no uniform definition of the border to be crossed or of farm work. Each assistance and statistical program develops its own definition of migrant, so that a migrant under the federal Migrant Education Program (MEP) is not the same as a migrant under a USDA statistical definition. For example, the MEP defines a migrant as a person who crosses school district lines in search of farm or farm-related nonfarm work. Since there are sixteen hundred U.S. school districts, including one thousand in California, and MEP allows migrants to search for (but never hold) farm or nonfarm food processing jobs, MEP casts a far wider net for migrants than USDA, which defined migrants for statistical purposes as persons who cross county lines and stay away from a usual U.S. home overnight to do farm work for wages. There are thirty-one hundred U.S. counties, and USDA required earnings from a farm job away from home, so the USDA migrant definition covers fewer people. Some of the very different estimates of the number of migrant farm workers—from 100,000 to 1 million—reflect these different definitions.

Regardless of definition, migrancy has been declining. A 1965 survey found that 30 percent of California's farm workers moved from one farming region to another and stayed away from home overnight, the USDA definition, and a 1981 survey of Tulare County farm workers found that 20 percent had to establish a temporary residence away from a usual U.S. home because a farm job took them beyond commuting distance, a similar definition (Peterson, 1969; Mines and Kearney, 1982). USDA analyses found that about 11 percent of U.S. farm workers were migrants in the 1950s and 1960s, and only 7 percent were migrants in the 1970s and 1980s (Olivera, 1989, 4; Smith and Coltrane, 1981). USDA attributed the drop in follow-the-crop migration to the expanded availability of unemployment insurance (UI) benefits, which provides an alternative source of income when there is no farm work, to farmers staggering their plantings in order to stretch out of harvesting for marketing and processing reasons, and to scarce temporary housing for migrants, which made many workers reluctant to move in search of farm jobs. Many migrants also heeded the pleas of assistance agencies and stopped migrating, or stopped taking their children with them when they traveled, especially when labor laws were tightened to limit the employment of children on farms.

Farm Worker Characteristics

The two major sources of farm labor data paint very different pictures of farm workers. The Current Population Survey (CPS), the source of most socioeconomic data, is based on the assumption that each of the 108 million housing units in the United States has an equal probability of being among the 60,000 households that are asked employment and other questions. Between 1945 and 1990, USDA had questions added to the December CPS, when migrants were presumed to be at home, that asked if anyone in the household did farm work for wages during the previous twelve months. About 1,500 of the CPS households included a farm worker and each was considered representative of 1,667 who were not interviewed, that is, the hired farm work force was estimated to be 2.5 million.

Farm worker households were asked a series of questions about their farm and nonfarm jobs, including their major activity during the previous twelve months and whether any family members migrated to do farm work. The responses indicated that hired workers did an average one hundred days of farm work a year, and earned thirty to forty dollars a day in the 1980s, which came to three thousand to four thousand dollars a year. USDA analysts emphasized that the farm work force was diverse and reported much of the data on worker characteristics by the days of farm work done, so that workers were grouped by whether they did less than 25 days of farm work a year, as 37 percent did in 1983; 25–149 days, as 34 percent did; or 150 or more days, as 28 percent did—long-season farm workers did about three-quarters of all days of farm work, and had the highest farm earnings (Oliveira, 1989). The CPS data supported a "salvage view" of farm workers—farm workers were workers who did low-wage farm work with time that would otherwise not be compensated (Fuller and Mason, 1977).

As immigration increased in the 1980s, many analysts expressed skepticism about the CPS data, largely because most of the farm workers they observed were Hispanics, but the CPS continued to find that most farm workers were non-Hispanic whites. For example, in the early 1990s, the CPS found that hired farm workers were 78 percent white, 14 percent Hispanic, and 8 percent black and other races (Ilg, 1995). The administrators of migrant assistance programs, as well as union leaders and worker advocates, concluded that CPS data missed many farm workers who were in Mexico in December, and their dissatisfaction with CPS data, as well as immigration reform in 1986, set the stage for a new approach to surveying farm workers—interviewing them at work. Given the responsibility to determine how many farm workers entered and exited the farm work force each year, the U.S. Department of Labor created a new at-work survey, the National Agricultural Worker Survey (NAWS). However, the NAWS did not have funds to interview systematically throughout the United States, so its sample cannot be expanded to report the number or distribution of farm workers, although most analysts believe that the NAWS reliably portrays the characteristics of the 1.8 million workers employed on U.S. crop farms.[16]

Legal Status

The NAWS has been conducted since 1989, and it interviews mostly Mexican-born men: 75 to 85 percent of U.S. crop workers were born outside the United States, usually in Mexico.[17] The NAWS asked workers a series of questions about their place of birth and legal status, and inferred from the answers whether the worker was authorized to work in the United States. When the NAWS began interviewing workers in 1989, after legalization programs in 1987–88, over 90 percent of the workers interviewed were legally in the United States. However, the unauthorized share of workers interviewed rose rapidly in the 1990s, so that, by the late 1990s, over half of the workers were unauthorized. The most recent survey, based on 1997–98 interviews, found that 48 percent of the crop workers interviewed were authorized to work in the United States and 52 percent were not.

Demographics, Migration, and Earnings

Farm workers are unlike other U.S. workers. In 1998, about 54 percent of U.S. workers were male and 39 percent were under thirty-five years of age. By contrast, 80 percent of crop workers were men and 67 percent were under thirty-five. Despite their youth, 52 percent of crop workers were married, and half had children, but half of the married farm workers left their families in Mexico while doing U.S. farm work; other farm workers left their families in places such as South Texas as they migrated north to Michigan or Ohio to do farm work. About 84 percent of the farm workers interviewed speak Spanish, and 85 percent, compared to 11 percent of all U.S. workers, have not completed high school; the median years of schooling completed was six. Less than 5 percent of foreign-born farm workers reported that they could read or speak English well. Many farm workers are in poor health, and few are covered by employer-provided health insurance.[18]

As Fuller and Mason observed in the 1970s, "hired farm labor is not dominated by migrants," especially migrants who following the ripening crops from south to north (1977, 68). About 60 percent of the workers interviewed by the NAWS had only one farm job. The NAWS defined a migrant as a worker who had a farm job at least seventy-five

Table 1.3. SAW and Unauthorized Workers: 1989–98
(percentage of U.S. crop workers)

	SAWs	Unauthorized
1989	37	8
1990	30	17
1991	27	19
1992	23	33
1993	12	44
1994	20	38
1995	19	40
1996	16	50
1997	17	51
1998	15	52

Source: U.S. Department of Labor. 2000

miles from his usual (United States or Mexican) residence; an overnight stay away from home was not required. The largest group of workers interviewed, 44 percent (which would represent 792,000 of 1.8 million crop workers) were not migrants. Another 39 percent (702,000) were shuttle migrants—their usual homes were in Mexico, and they traveled more than seventy-five miles from their Mexican homes to their U.S. farm jobs. Only 17 percent (306,000) were follow-the-crop migrants who had at least two U.S. farm jobs at least seventy-five miles apart.[19]

The NAWS asked workers about how they found jobs, what they were paid, and what they did when they were not doing farm work. Recruitment was mostly by word of mouth—70 percent of workers found their current job through a friend, relative, or work mate; 25 percent applied on their own, and 1 percent used the Employment Service, the no-fee federal-state job matching service available in every U.S. state. Workers earned an average $5.93 an hour and worked thirty-eight hours a week in 1997–98,[20] yielding average weekly earnings of $225 at a time when average weekly earnings for all private sector workers were $442.[21] About 77 percent of the 7,697 farm jobs held by the workers NAWS interviewed paid hourly wages and 20 percent paid piece rate wages.

Workers averaged 24.4 weeks of farm work, for farm earnings of fifty-five hundred dollars in 1997–98. They also averaged 4.6 weeks of non-farm work, for nonfarm earnings of one thousand dollars, 10 weeks of unemployment in the United States, and 12 weeks abroad. During the 1990s, weeks of farm and nonfarm work in the United States declined while weeks abroad increased. Unemployment is pervasive, even during the summer months. NAWS recorded the status of workers on a month-by-month basis, and the percentage of workers doing farm work peaked in the summer months at 55 to 60 percent; even in summer, the unemployment rate was at least 15 percent. During the winter months, the percentage of workers doing farm work was 35 to 40 percent, and the percentage who were unemployed was 20 to 25 percent.

Farm work is often described as a job, not a career. Workers had an average eight years of U.S. farm work experience, a potentially misleading indicator because authorized workers—half of the total—had an average of thirteen years of U.S. farm work experience, while unauthorized workers had an average of four years of U.S. farm work experience. Half of the workers interviewed said that they intended to remain farm workers as long as possible; the other half intended to exit the farm work force within five years. About 60 percent of the workers interviewed had relatives or friends with nonfarm U.S. jobs.

The NAWS has been interviewing farm workers for a decade, and the data suggest three trends. First, the percentage of unauthorized workers rose as the unauthorized workers who were legalized in 1987–88 got out of agriculture and were replaced by newly arrived unauthorized workers. Second, slowly rising wages, few benefits, and more unemployment speeded up the revolving door through which workers enter the United States from abroad, do farm work for five to ten years, and then move on to nonfarm jobs. Third, tomorrow's farm workers are growing up and being educated in rural areas of Mexico and Central America.

The Farm Labor Market

Labor markets match workers and jobs by performing recruitment, remuneration (or motivation), and retention functions. These three *R*s are handled in unique ways in agriculture. For example, farmers rarely place ads in newspapers to recruit workers or send recruiters to high school or college campuses in search of workers. More typical is how one farmer described his recruitment strategy—"when we need X amount of workers, we call up the contractor, and they supply the workers."

Recruitment matches workers and jobs. In seasonal industries such as agriculture, a central clearinghouse for farmers to list vacancies and for workers seeking jobs should be the most efficient way to match hundreds of thousands of workers with a similar number of jobs. A clearinghouse could be operated by employers, unions (hiring halls), or the federal-state Employment Service (ES, called EDD in California). The logic of a job-worker clearinghouse to minimize uncertainty for growers and unemployment for workers is clear, but there are few examples of their successful operation in agriculture. Until the early 1970s, the Employment Service and employer associations were the major clearinghouses. However, DOL curtailed its farm job-matching to settle lawsuits that charged the ES discriminated against farm workers by not telling them about nonfarm jobs (Goldfarb, 1981). Many employer associations that served as clearinghouses disbanded after their workers voted for union representation in the 1970s.

The UFW tried to become an alternative clearinghouse with union-run hiring halls, but most farmers who did not have contracts requiring them to obtain workers via UFW-run hiring halls did not do so, and many workers objected to having to pay dues to the UFW before being sent to farm jobs. The UFW tried to operate hiring halls in the 1970s without the benefit of computers, and deployed those seeking jobs on the basis of their seniority with the UFW, which sometimes split families and workers who wanted to work together; with the loss of contracts in the 1980s, most of the UFW-run hiring halls closed. Today job-worker matching in California agriculture is decentralized, with contractors and other intermediaries matching most seasonal workers and jobs (see box 1.2).[22] The key intermediary is a foreman or crew boss in charge of one or more crews of twenty to forty workers; this foreman is responsible for hiring and disciplining his crew. In this decentralized system, there can be simultaneous shortages and surpluses, as farmers complain of labor shortages even when crews are idle.

The second function of labor markets is to remunerate or motivate workers. There are two major wage-motivation systems: hourly and piece rate. According to the NAWS, about 75 percent of farm jobs paid hourly wages in the 1990s, and 25 percent paid piece rate wages or a combination of hourly and piece rate wages. Piece rates were most common in fruit harvesting jobs, while nursery workers and supervisors tend to be paid hourly wages. Employers pay hourly wages when:

- they want slow and careful work, such as pruning trees and vines,
- the employer can easily control the pace of the work, as when a crop such as broccoli is packed in the field with a system that has the workers walking behind a machine whose speed is controlled by the driver/employer.

Piece rates are common when it is hard to regulate the pace of work, as when workers climb trees to pick fruit (and are thus often out of sight), when quality is less important (as for picking oranges that will be processed into juice), and when an employer wants to keep labor

Box 1.2. Farm Labor Contractors

Farm labor contractors are the intermediaries who, for a fee, match farm workers with jobs. Intermediaries are common in labor markets where workers are hired in crews of twenty to forty for short-duration jobs, and the employer does not speak the language of the workers (Thilmany, 1994).

Contractors in western agriculture were originally bilingual members of the crew. Chinese crews in the 1870s and 1880s included a bilingual "head boy" who arranged seasonal farm jobs for his twenty to thirty compatriots and worked alongside them. During the 1920s, contractors became independent businesses, and contractor profits were the difference between what a farmer paid to have a job done and what the contractor paid the workers. Some of the first farm labor strikes involved workers protesting farmers who hired workers only via contractors.

The federal government began to regulate contractors in the 1960s, first by requiring them to register and thus identify themselves, and later requiring them to pass tests on labor laws and post bonds so that workers could receive unpaid wages. Today, contractors must be fingerprinted, pass a test of labor and pesticide laws, and post bonds. The intent of ever-stricter regulation was to drive out of business the "bad apples." However, enforcement data suggest that labor law violations remain common—inspections usually find that the majority of contractors are violating at least some labor, immigration, and/or tax laws.

Most contractors evade effective enforcement of labor laws for a simple reason: they know the workers they hire. As the U.S. Industrial Commission explained in the early 1900s, contractors can "drive the hardest kinds of bargain" with the immigrant workers they employ because they "know the circumstances from which farm workers come" (quoted in Fisher, 1952, 43). It is hard to get immigrant farm workers, who may be from the same village as the contractor, and dependent on the contractor for a job as well as housing and rides to work, to complain of violations of U.S. laws. When there is enforcement against contractors, it is often hard to prove violations, since written contracts are rare, and it is costly to obtain evidence of violations from often illiterate and non-English speaking workers.

costs constant with a diverse work force—note that it costs the employer one hundred dollars to have a thousand pounds of table grapes picked if the piece rate is ten cents a pound whether one fast picker or three slow pickers do the work. However, average worker earnings are very different if there is one or three workers. If workers are paid piece rate wages, labor laws require employers to record the units of work and hours worked of each worker. If a piece rate worker does not earn at least the minimum wage, the employer must provide "make up" pay, so the worker gets at least the minimum. As the minimum wage has risen, more farm employers switched to hourly wages to reduce record keeping.

The U.S. minimum wage has been $5.15 an hour since September 1, 1997; the California minimum wage has been $6.75 since January 1, 2002. Most farm employers pay the minimum wage or $0.50 or $1 an hour more, and increase their entry-level wage when the minimum wage rises. When reviewing farm wage data, it is important to remember that most data sources report earnings, which is what workers who are employed under a variety of wage systems—hourly, piece rate, and others—actually earn, not the wage rate that would be announced to a newly hired worker.[23]

The average hourly earnings of field and livestock workers in the USDA Farm Labor Survey, $7.56 an hour in 2000 in California, have traditionally been about half the average hourly earnings of private sector production workers, $14 to $15 an hour. The ratio of average farm to nonfarm earnings rose in the 1990s, so that California and U.S. farm workers earned 56 to 58 percent as much as nonfarm workers in 1998, up from about 50 percent in the late 1960s. One reason the gap narrowed in the 1990s was because nonfarm employers maintained and added benefits for workers, including health insurance, while farm employers eliminated health, housing, and other benefits in favor of higher cash wages; the rising minimum wage in California also helped to close the gap.[24]

Piece rate workers tend to earn more per hour than workers who are paid hourly wages, but to work fewer hours a week. Piece rate workers can earn eight to ten dollars an hour, while hourly workers get seven to eight dollars an hour, but most piece rate workers cannot sustain their typically faster pace of work for more than six to seven hours a day. The weekly earnings of piece rate and hourly workers are similar because the hourly workers tend to be employed more hours.

The cost of employing workers includes wages and mandatory and voluntary fringe benefits. Mandatory benefits are those that the employer must provide to workers—social security, unemployment and disability insurance, and workers compensation. Voluntary fringe benefits include health insurance, paid vacations and holidays, and extra pension benefits. The U.S. Bureau of Labor Statistics computes the cost of wages and fringe benefits, and in March 2000 reported that the total cost of employing workers in the U.S. private sector was $21 an hour, including $15 an hour in wages and salaries (73 percent) and $6 an hour in benefits (27 percent). The cost of mandatory fringe benefits was $1.67 an hour, or 9 percent of total compensation, and employers provided voluntary fringe benefits worth $4.33, or 19 percent of total compensation, including $1.42 an hour for paid leave (vacation and holiday pay) and $1.36 for health and other insurance.

Fringe benefits can be expensive for farm workers with low earnings, since benefits such as health insurance for workers and their families that cover off-the-job injuries and illnesses require monthly payments that are independent of earnings. A low-cost $160 a month, or dollar-an-hour, health insurance premium for a full time worker adds 16 percent to the cost of a worker earning six dollars an hour and 7 percent to the cost of a fourteen-dollar-an-hour worker.[25] Only 5 percent of the workers interviewed in the NAWS had health insurance provided by their employers.

Farmers in the past often provided housing in order to attract and retain good workers. However, poor farm worker housing led to higher standards and, because farmers are not required to provide housing, many responded to tougher housing rules by closing their housing. Farm workers were thus pushed into cities and towns in agricultural areas, where they competed with other tenants for housing, sometimes living in rented houses or sheds that were no better than the on-farm housing that was closed. However, the cost of living in cities was usually more than what farmers charged—often fifty to hundred dollars a week—and workers living away from the fields must usually pay for rides to work, which add another twenty to twenty-five dollars a week to their costs of working. The government, which used to regulate farmer-provided housing, today primarily makes grants and loans to provide subsidized housing for farm workers, often families with children.[26]

Since most farm workers do not live on the farms on which they are employed, there are special issues associated with transporting farm workers between homes and jobs, usually in areas without public transportation. There have been tragedies when poorly regulated *raiteros* use vans to transport workers to far-flung fields for jobs that often start very early or end very late. The processing tomato harvest normally runs twenty-four hours a day, and thirteen tomato sorters who had worked all night were killed in Fresno County on August 9, 1999, when the van in which they were riding collided with a tractor-trailer truck making a U-turn in the early morning hours on a remote farming road. The farm-labor contractor who hired the workers was fined $21,500 for allowing them to be transported in an illegally operated vehicle, and the California legislature responded to the tragedy with a law requiring all vans that charge farm workers fees for transportation, usually three to six dollars a day, to have regular seats with seat belts. In many farm labor vans, including the one involved in the Fresno accident, the regular seats are removed, and wooden benches were installed along the sides of the van in order to accommodate more workers.

The third key labor market function is retention—identifying and keeping the best workers, or encouraging the best seasonal workers to return next year. Most U.S. employers have formal evaluation systems under which supervisors evaluate each worker, and these evaluations are used to determine promotions and wage increases. Few farm employers have formal personnel systems. Instead, there are two methods of recruitment and worker evaluation that illustrate agricultural extremes in personnel practices. Some farmers, especially those who work closely with one or a few year-round workers in dairies and similar operations, treat hired workers "as part of the family," selecting workers carefully and providing them with housing near the farmer's home (Billikopf, 2001). The other extreme is exemplified by a grower who hires a crew of workers through a contractor or a foreman, and never deals directly with them.

Crew-based hiring explains why recruitment and retention are often part of the same labor market function in agriculture. Indeed, an analogy to obtaining irrigation water may be helpful to understand the recruitment and retention options. There are two major ways to supply irrigation water to crops: a field can be "flooded" with water so that some trickles to each tree or vine, or fields can be irrigated with a drip system that involves laying plastic pipes on or under the rows and dripping water and nutrients to each tree or vine. If water is cheap, farmers flood fields with water; if water is expensive, farmers may invest in drip irrigation systems. The analogy to recruitment and retention is clear: farmers more often work collectively to flood the labor market with workers, usually by getting border gates opened or left ajar, instead of recruiting and retaining the best farm workers for their operation, the drip irrigation model. The best way to ensure plenty of irrigation water is to invest in more dams and canals; the best way to flood the labor market is to invest in politicians willing to ease access to foreign workers.

2

History of Farm Labor

All my life, I have been driven by one dream, one goal, one vision: To overthrow a farm labor system in this nation which treats farm workers as if they were not important human beings.

Cesar Chavez, Commonwealth Club, November 9, 1984

American literature during the twentieth century called attention to the problems of farm workers in books with self-explanatory titles, such as *The Slaves We Rent* and *Sweatshops in the Sun*. These books and countless government reports made most Americans aware of farm worker poverty, but there were few reforms, and those that were enacted did not lead to lasting structural changes in the farm labor market. Instead of waiting for changes in the farm labor market that would push up their poor pay, farm workers and their children who wanted to get ahead deserted farm labor for nonfarm jobs. The immigrants who replaced them have become ever more different from mainstream Americans.

This chapter focuses on three farm labor questions. First, why did the United States develop elaborate agricultural policies to support farmers in the 1930s, but few policies to assist farm workers? Second, why did most Californians in the late nineteenth century agree that the large farms inherited from the Mexican-Spanish era should be broken up into family-sized units? Third, how did the availability of newcomer farm workers hold down farm wages, increase land values, and set in motion an agricultural system that "needed" a constant infusion of new workers? Brief answers to these questions are that hired farm workers were considered to be primarily future farmers whose interests were the same as farmers, so labor protections were not needed; most Californians wanted "vibrant rural communities" based on family farms, not large and specialized enterprises that required migrants who came with the wind and went with the dust; and land owners developed an economic incentive to maintain the influx of newcomer farm workers to hold down their labor costs. Since they succeeded in finding newcomers willing to accommodate to seasonality, it was unnecessary to break up large farms to get a seasonal work force.

Farm labor reform was a popular cause during the twentieth century, as churches, unions, and government reformers tried to change a system in which newcomers took seasonal farm labor jobs because they were the only jobs available and wound up among the visible poor. The goal of most reformers was to enact laws that would make the farm labor market more like factory labor markets, which were enabling many factory workers to become middle-class Americans. Reformers failed to make farm work comparable to factory work in wages, benefits, and status during the twentieth century. In the twenty-first century, the farm labor is more different from nonfarm labor markets than it has ever been, but the gap may narrow as some nonfarm labor markets acquire farm labor market characteristics, including hiring workers through intermediary contractors. This chapter outlines the progressive isolation of the California farm labor market in the twentieth century.

Three Responses to Seasonality

The first U.S. Census of Population in 1790 found that 90 percent of the 4 million U.S. residents lived in rural areas, where most adults were farmers or farm workers (U.S. Census, 1976). Family farming was "a way of life" as well as a business that supported farmers and their families and was, in the view of so-called agrarian fundamentalists, both an essential business and a virtuous way of life, to be fostered and encouraged.

Thomas Jefferson, the third president, was an agrarian fundamentalist who considered family farmers to be the backbone of American democracy. In his *Notes on Virginia*, Jefferson wrote: "Those who labor in the earth are the chosen people of God . . . corruption of morals in the mass of cultivators is a phenomenon of which no age or nation has furnished an example."[1] Jefferson believed that rural life was superior to urban life and that self-sufficient family farmers would preserve fledgling American democracy.[2] European peasants immigrating to the United States wanted to be family farmers, and the availability of land reinforced American "exceptionalism," the idea that America was uniquely endowed with natural resources and that Americans were a uniquely favored people.

Family farms were the ideal as well as reality for most of American agriculture in the early 1800s. The model family farm included a hard-working farmer, his family, and perhaps a hired hand—typically a young man who was a temporary addition to the farmer's family, living and eating with the farmer's family and perhaps marrying the farmer's daughter. For this reason, reports about farm labor drew no distinctions between farmers and farm workers, considering both to be "land workers" who labored alongside each other (Daniel, 1981, 17). Family farms had peak seasonal labor needs—there was more work to be done during some months of the year, which meant that everyone worked in the busy harvest season, and children went to school when there was less farm work. Seasonality also encouraged diversification, since farmers growing crops and tending livestock could even out some of the demand for labor.

The other two farming systems represented very different responses to seasonality: plantations and slavery in the South, and specialized farms and migrant workers in the West. Plantations that grew cotton and tobacco needed more seasonal labor than even large farm families could provide. The long growing seasons in the South—six to eight months versus four to six months in the northern states—as well as the fact that it was hard to retain farm workers when there was land in the West—encouraged slavery, which assured plantations a work force. Most plantations had at least twenty slaves and four hundred acres of cotton, the minimum to justify employing a farm manager. The price of slaves, five hundred dollars to a thousand dollars for an adult male, fluctuated in the early 1800s with the prices of tobacco and cotton (Fogel and Engerman, 1974).[3] Slavery spread westward in the southern states, where long-season export crops were grown.

Farm workers lived on the farm family on which they worked, and slaves lived on the plantation. In the western states, farmers were by the 1860s and 1870s planting large acreages of grain and assuming that gangs or crews of harvest workers would show up when they were needed, be paid for their work, and then disappear. This migrant labor system spread after 1869 in California, when the transcontinental railroad lowered transportation costs and interest rates and integrated the western states into the U.S. economy. With the railroad making it easier for aspiring farmers to travel west, and with irrigation systems being constructed and Americans developing a taste for fruit, large farms were expected to be broken up into family-sized units, since this is the only way most leaders thought agriculture could get enough seasonal workers. Restructuring from large to small farms was generally welcomed, so that the western states could develop viable farm communities as in the Midwest.

Large farms in California were not subdivided into family-sized units because enough migrant workers were found. The first large group of migrants were the Chinese who had been imported to build the railroad in the West. After they were laid off, they drifted into cities such as San Francisco and Sacramento, but there they faced discrimination from white workers, many of whom also lost their jobs when the railroad brought manufactured goods from the East. Shut out of city jobs, the Chinese became migrants who were paid only when they worked because they had no other options. Paying seasonal workers only when they worked saved farmers money and raised land prices, and soon land owners argued that, without Chinese migrants, agriculture could not expand or survive in the western states. Furthermore, by working collectively—as they did to construct irrigation systems and to obtain lower transportation rates from railroads—farmers could maximize the pool of seasonal workers available to agriculture, ensuring that workers were available when needed at a "reasonable" cost. Large numbers of migrants put downward pressure on farm wages and reduced the hours of farm work available to a worker in one location. This inherent conflict of interest over the size of the seasonal labor force was often obscured by ethnic and social differences: most farmers were white local residents, while many migrants were minorities far from their usual homes.

California farm labor history is the story of how seasonal farm work emerged as a "last resort" for waves of newcomers with few other U.S. job options. The wages and working conditions that newcomers were willing to accept determined wages and working conditions for all farm workers, which were about half of average manufacturing wages. This wage gap encouraged farm workers and their children to leave the farm work force, causing "farm labor shortages" that led to the arrival of more newcomers.

Missions, *Ranchos*, and Speculation: 1769–1869

California agriculture began with the establishment of twenty-one Spanish missions along El Camino Real (Highway 101) between 1769 and 1833. Indians were employed on the missions, but mission agriculture was not aimed at producing a surplus to sell (Fuller, 1940, 19784–95). Native Americans proved to be unwilling and unreliable farm workers and, at the behest of Franciscan Father Junipero Serra, the Spanish viceroy in Mexico City in 1773 agreed to permit the missions in what is now California to "recruit" workers in what is now the Mexican state of Baja California. The rights of these "first *braceros*" were laid out in a 1773 *reglamento* (Steven Street, 1996–97, 316).

Mexico became independent of Spain in 1821 and the 1833 Secular-ization Act allowed private individuals to own large tracts, five thou-sand to fifty thousand acres in *ranchos*, with the major activity raising cattle. Indian farm workers were often employed to herd cattle, and they were "so cheap that growing crops were protected from cattle by Indian guards rather than fences" (Fuller, 1940, 1976). Farmers complained of too few workers, and many in the 1840s wanted slavery extended to Cal-ifornia to assure a work force. However, the 1848 Gold Rush brought thousands of antislave prospectors to California, and California entered the United States as a no-slave state in 1850. The new state government agreed to recognize the Spanish land grants, but confusion and corrup-tion allowed a few individuals to acquire large tracts of the best Cali-fornia farmland in the 1850s and 1860s.

May 10, 1869, the day the transcontinental railroad was completed at Promontory Summit, north of the Great Salt Lake in Utah, marked a turning point for California agriculture. Transportation costs and inter-est rates fell sharply, and producing crops became far more profitable than grazing cattle. Gold had led to a get-rich-quick or bonanza men-tality, and so-called bonanza wheat farms emerged, planting wheat seed in the fall. If there was rain and high prices, farmers hired "bindle-stiff" migrants to harvest it for high profits. Some 3.5 million acres of wheat were harvested in 1889, when wheat occupied two-thirds of California crop land, and 28 million bushels were exported (Bancroft, 1890).[4] Most farmers' organizations opposed bonanza wheat farms, which left the countryside devoid of people except when migrants arrived for the har-vest. In 1869 the president of the California State Agricultural Society said: "Our lands . . . should be divided up into small farms or parcels, each one of these to become the home or homestead of a family" (Charles Reed, quoted in Daniel, 1981, 20).

Chinese Migrants: 1869–1882

Wheat was the major crop in California until 1900, but there were suc-cessful experiments using irrigation to produce fruits and vegetables. The extension of rail lines into the San Joaquin Valley and southern Cal-ifornia accelerated the shift to fruits, and lower interest rates encour-aged investments in orchards and vineyards. By 1900, fruit accounted for one-third of the state's crop sales, and California was called the orchard for the world. The shift to fruits and vegetables increased the need for farm workers, and the large wheat farmers who owned most California land discussed three options in the 1870s:

- continue large-scale wheat farming and mechanize the harvest, which was relatively easy to do on the flat land in California;
- sell land to family farmers for family-sized fruit farms;
- switch from wheat to fruit and recruit additional farm workers.

The middle option of subdividing and selling land seemed to appeal to most landowners and was widely expected to transform rural California. A governor's report in 1887 noted approvingly that "a great revolution is taking place, whereby the larger land holdings are breaking up, and being sold . . . in small tracts to families that are seeking homes . . . the blanket-carrying tramp is being driven out, and [replaced] by laborers who own the land they till" (quoted in Daniel, 1981, 33).

It was not easy to sell land to aspiring family farmers arriving in California. Many had little money, and no experience using irrigation to produce fruits. Many tried and failed to farm in California. Meanwhile, large farmers who had the capital needed to build irrigation systems, and the resources to wait several years for a first crop, began to switch to fruit. But they worried about getting enough seasonal labor to harvest their fruit crops. State officials urged large farmers to employ workers year round, believing that such a policy would encourage more European immigrants to come to California:

Hitherto the one great objection to an increase of the unskilled white labor population in California has been that . . . those who labor for others work only for three, or at the highest, five or six months during the year. It [seasonal work] was admitted to be an unnatural condition of affairs, and one that should be remedied, but which, under prevailing circumstances, could not be changed. (John Enos, quoted in Fuller, 1967, 433)[5]

Enos continued that he understood why large farmers did not have pay workers year round: "Chinamen in sufficient numbers could be hired during the busiest seasons of the year." Furthermore, he warned employers that they would have to recruit a white work force for their expanding fruit farms, because they "could not expect white laborers to spring out of the ground when the Chinese influx ceased" (John Enos, quoted in Fuller, 1967, 433–34).

Enos, like most state officials, wanted Chinese immigration stopped in order to alter the trajectory of California's farm labor market and economy. Chinese migrants began arriving in "Gold Mountain" during the 1848 gold rush, and twelve thousand were imported to help build the railroad through the Sierra Nevada mountains. The Chinese were laid off by the railroad companies after 1869, and many wound up in California's largest cities, Sacramento and San Francisco, where economies were being restructured by lower-priced goods arriving on the railroad. Factories that had been sheltered by high transport costs closed, and workers arrived on the railroad looking for jobs just as the Chinese moved to cities. The Chinese became the scapegoat for unemployment—fledgling unions organized protests to drive the Chinese out of San Francisco and Sacramento. Farmers did not discriminate, and they hired the Chinese, many of whom had experience with irrigated agriculture. The Chinese organized themselves into crews of twenty to thirty, each with a bilingual crew leader known as "boss man" or "head boy," arranged their own housing and meals while employed on a farm, and left after the work on a particular farm was completed.

The Chinese accounted for 75 percent of seasonal farm workers by the early 1880s, when the anti-Chinese drive reached its peak—total employment on California farms, including farm operators, was about 100,000. California unions and politicians wanted Congress to stop Chinese immigration and prevent Chinese immigrants from becoming U.S. citizens. The Workingmen's party in San Francisco, led by Dennis Kearney, published a manifesto in 1876 that declared "death is preferable to a life on a par with the Chinaman," and the union label was developed to distinguish white- and Chinese-made clothing. In 1879, California voters approved an initiative by a vote of 154,638 to 883 to bar further Chinese immigration, but federal courts held that the initiative was unconstitutional, and California turned to Congress to stop Chinese immigration.

Farmers opposed the effort to bar Chinese immigration. They argued that, without the Chinese, the largest industry in California could not grow and prosper. An editorial in the leading farm publication, for example, argued that agriculture needed to continue importing Chinese migrants because: "California farmers cannot hope to employ Americans or European immigrants because farmers cannot employ them profitably . . . more than 3 or 4 months in the year—a condition of things entirely unsuited to the demands of the European laborer" (*Pacific Rural Press*, quoted in Fuller, 1940, 19813). The Chinese were ideal migrants "because they were not white, did not, indeed could not, have aspirations or expectations comparable to those that white workers" such as becoming family farmers. (quoted in Daniel, 1981, 27). Congress nonetheless approved the Chinese Exclusion (Geary) Act of 1882, which "suspended . . . the coming of Chinese laborers to the United States."

Fruit output increased fiftyfold in the 1880s, the volume of output tripled in the 1890s, and the value of orchard land rose sharply.[6] In 1888, for example, orchards were worth two hundred to three hundred dollars an acre, while land used to produce wheat was worth twenty-five to fifty dollars an acre. Fruit generated more revenue per acre, but also had higher costs, giving fruit farmers an incentive to reduce wages and costs. The Chinese migrants on fruit farms were paid $1.00 to $1.25 per day, while white workers on grain farms were paid $2 to $3 a day (Fuller, 1940, 19816).[7] Without Chinese or similar workers, farm wages would have risen, and land prices would have fallen, or not increased as fast. Large fruit farmers had become accustomed to workers appearing when needed: "With no particular effort on the part of the employer, a farm labor force would emerge when needed, do its work, and then disappear—accepting the terms and conditions offered, without question" (Fuller, 1991, vii). These fruit farmers needed replacements for the now-barred Chinese.

Japanese Migrants: 1885–1908

Chinese migrants facing discrimination in the cities were willing to accept seasonal farm jobs. However, in order to continue expanding, farmers needed another source of migrants, and they found it in Japan, which legalized emigration in 1885. Japanese were encouraged to migrate to Hawaii, California, and other western states to be farm workers, but Japanese immigration peaked between 1901 and 1907, when 130,000 Japanese immigrants arrived in the United States, and half became California farm workers (London and Anderson, 1970, 8; Fuller, 1940, 19829).[8] By 1905, half of California's seasonal farm workers were Japanese, and their availability allowed the amount of irrigated land in California to double from 1.4 to 2.7 million acres between 1899 and 1909, and the value of fruit output to double (Olmstead and Rhode, 1997, 5–6).

Japanese migrants were the only group from which significant numbers climbed the agricultural ladder from worker to farmer, a success based on quickie harvest-time strikes and buying marginal farmland. Like the Chinese, the Japanese organized themselves into crews and agreed to work for the below-normal wages offered to the newest group of farm workers.[9] However, just as the harvest began, they often went on strike for higher wages, and these "quickie strikes" were effective because Japanese crews would not break each other's strikes. Japanese grape workers in 1907 were able to raise wages from $1.75 to $2.50 daily (Fuller, 1940, 19836), and by 1909 Japanese wages of $1.60 daily were equal to those of older Chinese migrants. In another innovation, Japanese workers often harvested the crop in exchange for a share of the crop, giving them experience selling fruits and vegetables and potentially higher wages (Fuller, 1940, 19835).

Quickie strikes dampened the enthusiasm of farmers for the Japanese. With white workers complaining that the Japanese were undermining wages and working conditions, farmers did not object strongly to a 1907 "gentlemen's agreement" that stopped Japanese immigration. Under the terms of this bargain, Japan agreed not to issue passports to citizens seeking to emigrate to the United States if the United States promised to end discrimination against Japanese in the United States. Farmers actively pushed for legislation to prevent Japanese competition after some of the Issei, first-generation Japanese immigrants, were able to buy or lease often marginal land and plant vegetables, which were then sold in competition with white farmers. Farmers persuaded the California legislature in 1913 and 1919 to prohibit non-U.S. citizens from buying farmland, but many of the Japanese who had not naturalized got around this restriction by buying farmland in the names of their U.S.-born and thus U.S.-citizen children, known as Nisei.

South Asians, Europeans, and Mexicans: 1908–1921

In 1900, farm workers and farmers made up about 25 percent of California's total work force, while farm labor was 38 percent of the U.S. work force. The percentage of California workers in agriculture fell to 17 percent in 1920, and to 27 percent in the United States. As California urbanized, farmers worried about where they could get workers to fill the ever-increasing number of seasonal jobs. In addition to the Japanese, Asian immigrants arrived in the western states early in the twentieth century—at least five thousand workers from present day India and Pakistan became California farm workers between 1908 and 1912 (Fuller, 1991, 33). As newcomers, South Asians received lower wages, twenty-five cents to fifty cents per day less than the Japanese. Farmers wanted to import larger numbers of workers from present-day India and Pakistan, under the theory that, as British subjects, they could be admitted despite the general ban on Asian immigrants. However, 75 percent of the first wave of "Hindu" farm workers abandoned farm work, many to become farmers (Fuller, 1991, 34),[10] and farmers dropped the idea of importing South Asians.

The 12 million European immigrants who arrived in the United States between 1900 and 1914 generally avoided California: fewer than 100,000 or less than 1 percent came to the state. California did not get its "fair share" of European immigrants because wages in the major industry, agriculture, were lower than in Midwestern factories. However, after the Panama Canal was completed in 1914, transcontinental railroads lowered prices to travel to California, and some southern European immigrants came to California and became successful farmers, including Italians and Armenians who specialized in grapes and vegetables and Dutch and Portuguese immigrants who began dairies.

The Chinese and Japanese dominated the seasonal farm labor market during the first forty years of fruit and vegetable production in California, but thousands of whites worked, especially on grain farms in the spring, summer, and fall. They then "holed up" in rooming houses in Sacramento and San Francisco during the winter months, so that "white transient workers [Hobos] were an almost permanent part of the rural scene" (Fuller, 1991, 38). Representatives of the Industrial Workers of the World, a radical union that aimed to replace employers with labor coops, tried to educate and organize them to change an economic system that left most poor. Effective IWW leadership, as well as farmers who aroused worker anger by advertising a high wage to recruit workers, and then cut the wage when too many workers appeared, led the first large-scale farm labor action in California: the Wheatland hops riot of 1913, which resulted in the jailing of IWW leaders and an end to "labor troubles" for twenty years (see chapter 3).

World War I drew farm workers into the army and wartime factories, and farm wages rose. Farmers feared labor shortages, and women, school children, and city dwellers were recruited to harvest crops. Farm magazines warned farmers that they would have to treat these workers better: the *Pacific Rural Press* noted in 1917 that Americans were "accustomed to sleeping in beds, (so) it behooves everyone to provide something as cheap and sanitary as possible for American workers" (June 2, 1917, 68). University of California professor Adams warned growers not to overinvest in housing, because they could not count on U.S. workers "to meet the requirements of hard, stoop, hand labor after the war was over" (quoted in Fuller, 1940, 19849; Adams and Kelly, 1918).

The Immigration Act of 1917 restricted immigration by denying admission to "persons . . . who have been induced . . . to migrate to this country by offers or promises of employment"; the act also imposed a head tax of eight dollars per immigrant and literacy test on immigrants—foreigners over sixteen had to read at least forty words in some language. These provisions made it hard for many Mexicans to enter the United States and prompted California farmers and railroads to use the motto, "Food to Win the War," to persuade the U.S. Department of Labor (DOL) "to admit temporarily otherwise inadmissible aliens" to do farm work.[11] Most of these otherwise inadmissible aliens were Mexicans, who were admitted to the United States with contracts that tied them to a particular farm employer and allowed to remain up to one year.[12] This first *bracero* program, from 1917 to 1921, left the Mexican government dissatisfied: many *braceros* experienced discrimination in the United States, and many wound up with few savings because of charges they incurred at farmer-owned stores.

Mexicans and Filipinos: The 1920s

California agriculture did not undergo any major readjustment due to labor shortages during the 1920s, primarily because of immigration from Mexico and the Philippines. The Mexican population in California was 120,000 in 1920, and tripled to 368,000 by 1930—additional Mexican workers came seasonally to California. During the 1920s, Mexican farm worker families traveled around California, introducing the state to children going to school from tents and other temporary farm worker housing. Mexican workers set the tone of the labor market—they determined entry level wages for all seasonal workers. In 1930, Mexicans were 70 to 80 percent of the 72,000 strong seasonal work force (Fuller, 1940, 19871).

Immigration laws in 1921 and 1924 that restricted immigration from Europe did not apply to Mexico and the Western Hemisphere. The U.S. Border Patrol was established in 1924, but did little to impede Mexican migrants. Many Mexicans who arrived intending to return settled in California—at least a third of the million Mexicans who moved north in the 1920s (Garcia y Griego, 1981, 50). Many of those who settled were forced back to Mexico during repatriations in the early 1930s. Between 1930 and 1934, for example, some 300,000 to 400,000 Mexicans, including U.S. citizen children born to Mexican parents, were returned to Mexico to open jobs for Americans (Taylor, 1934). These repatriations discouraged other Mexicans from migrating north during the Depression so that, in 1940, according to the Census, there were fewer Mexican-born U.S. residents, 378,000, than in 1930, 641,000.

During the 1920s, when European immigration was being restricted, there were also calls to restrict Mexican immigration. California farmers made three major arguments in favor of continued Mexican immigration: "normal" workers shunned seasonal farm jobs; farmers could not raise wages because they were price takers in national and international markets; and Mexicans were "homing pigeons" who would not stay in the United States and create social problems. A Chamber of Commerce spokesperson summed up these arguments in testimony to Congress in 1926: "We, gentlemen, are just as anxious as you are not to build the civilization of California or any other western district upon a Mexican foundation. We take him because there is nothing else available. We have gone east, west, north, and south and he is the only man-power available to us" (quoted in Fuller, 1940, 19859). The Farm Bureau asserted that "California's specialized agriculture [requires] a kind of labor able to meet the requirements of hard, stoop, hand labor, and to work under the sometimes less advantageous conditions of heat, sun, dust, winds, and isolation" (quoted in Fuller, 1940, 19840).

Economists noted that farmers were really using continued immigration and the resulting low farm wages to protect the value of their land—land "had been capitalized on the basis of five decades of cheap labor" and high land prices could be maintained only with the "continued availability of Mexican labor" (Fuller, 1940, 19866). Many Californians wanted to end Mexican immigration, arguing that farmers could and should pay higher wages and hire local workers year round. Farmers countered that they could not raise wages, and could only pay workers when they were needed: one said that, if "we should be forced to maintain our [farm] labor when it is idle we would be forced out of business" (Fuller, 1940, 19864).

In addition to Mexicans, some thirty thousand Filipinos arrived in California between 1923 and 1929, and "their immediate employment in California was predominantly in agricultural labor" (Fuller, 1991, 52). The Filipinos were similar to Chinese and Japanese workers, in the sense that most were single men who organized themselves into crews to seek farm jobs, especially in grapes. The combination of Mexicans, Filipinos, and whites provided an ample supply of labor throughout the 1920s. USDA estimated farm labor supply and demand, and concluded that supply exceeded demand by 5 to 20 percent.[13] Farmers during the 1920s formed organizations such as the San Joaquin Labor Bureau to standardize wages in order to prevent what they called the "useless floating around [of workers] in search of a better paying job" (Fuller, 1940, 19861).

The Grapes of Wrath: The 1930s

The 1930s saw an outpouring of books and reports on the plight of California farm workers, but there were no significant changes in the farm labor market, which was marked by crews of newcomers being paid only when they worked. The decade opened with Depression-era wage cuts, followed by a wave of farm worker strikes when the federal government's New Deal programs raised the prices paid to farmers for their crops, but farmers were slow to raise wages for farm workers. White farm families displaced from the Midwestern Dust Bowl arrived in the late 1930s, and their experiences as newcomers in the farm labor market was memorialized in John Steinbeck's novel *The Grapes of Wrath*. The U.S. Senate created a special (La Follette) committee to investigate labor issues, and this committee recommended that workers employed on large farms be protected under nonfarm labor laws; World War II prevented the implementation of the committee's reforms.

Many labor-intensive crops were grown close to California's cities, and the urban unemployed often sought farm jobs during the Depression. Farm prices and wages fell, but in 1933 began to rise after the Agricultural Adjustment Act helped to curtail surpluses of farm commodities. Farm workers also demanded wage increases, and the Communist-dominated Cannery and Agricultural Workers Industrial Union (CAIWU) led a series of strikes that culminated in an October 1933 cotton harvesters strike, one of the largest strikes in California history, involving twelve thousand to eighteen thousand workers. The strike was ended with federal and state mediation, but the leaders of the CAIWU were arrested and jailed a year later.

Dust Bowl Okies and Arkies who lost their land in Oklahoma, Arkansas, and Texas began arriving in California after 1935, driving up to farm houses and asking for work. They expected, based on the hired hand concept, that they would live and work alongside California farmers until they could save enough money to become farmers in their own right. Some farmers did not hire them, saying they were not "tractable" because, "being American citizens, they are going to demand the so-called American standard of living" (Jamieson, 1945, 118).

The Dust Bowl migration was one of the largest desperation migrations in U.S. history. Some 1.3 million people from other states moved to California, and at least 150,000 became farm workers in a farm work force of 200,000. California attempted to block Midwestern migrants from entering the state: the Los Angeles police opened sixteen checkpoints, later found to be unconstitutional, on the California-Arizona border in February-March 1936 to prevent the entry of migrants "with no visible means of support." California also enacted vagrancy laws, allowing police to arrest persons on streets with no money and fine them. Many of those fined could not pay, were sentenced to short terms in jail, and then "lent" to farmers to work off their fines.[14]

Within California, there was a debate over what should be done to help the Dust Bowl migrants. Many lived in tent camps that evolved into "Hoovervilles," and there was concern about a white and English-speaking migrant work force becoming a fertile breeding ground for communism. The so-called "Big-Four" farm labor reformers of the 1930s were economist Paul Taylor, lawyer Carey McWilliams, novelist John Steinbeck, and Senator Robert La Follette, a Republican from Wisconsin. Taylor, who taught at the University of California, Berkeley, grew up on a family farm in the Midwest and wanted a family farming system in California. He argued that migrancy was "an unwitting instrument in the breakdown of the traditional American ideal of the family farm." Migrants "slip through stable and often rich communities, of which [they are] never an accepted part. [Migrancy] offers a breeding ground of social unrest. . . . It lends itself readily to the development of a form of agriculture which is not a way of life, but an industry" (Taylor, 1937). Taylor championed land and water reforms that would lead to the break up of large farms and wanted extension services provided to Midwestern migrants to help them become fruit and vegetable farmers. Taylor hired (and later married) photographer Dorothea Lange to accompany him, and Lange's photographs of migrants, the most famous of which is *Migrant Mother*, helped to persuade the federal government to build a network of migrant labor camps.

Lawyer Carey McWilliams in the mid-1930s wrote a series of articles entitled "Factories in the Fields" that concluded that the structure of California agriculture—large farms, specialization, and migrant labor—was due in part to government benefits such as water subsidies and marketing orders. McWilliams argued that the government should do more for farm workers, and he got a chance to do just that when he was appointed to head California's Division of Immigration and Housing in 1939. McWilliams increased inspections of grower-owned labor camps—he believed on-farm housing made workers more dependent on their employers—and changed the formula that was used to deny relief to migrants who refused to accept farm jobs at prevailing piece rate wages, effectively forcing some growers to increase piece rates. Growers labeled McWilliams "California's number one agricultural pest, worse than the pear blight or boll weevil."

Many journalists began their investigations of farm labor conditions in the sixteen permanent and nine temporary labor camps funded by the federal government's Farm Security Administration (FSA). Camp managers such as Tom Collins in Arvin made their notes available to writers, and John Steinbeck used Collins's notes about the residents of the Arvin camp to develop his characters in the *Grapes of Wrath*.[15] The *Grapes of Wrath*, published in April 1940, prompted President Franklin

Roosevelt to say that "something must be done and done soon" to improve conditions for migrants.

There were two congressional committees with opposing agendas dealing with farm labor issues in the late 1930s, and each held hearings and developed recommendations. The House Committee on Un-American Activities focused on the communists who organized farm-worker protests and called for more restrictions on communists. The Senate's Education and Labor Committee had a subcommittee chaired by Robert La Follette, Jr., that examined the power and antiunion activities of growers and recommended that labor relations and protective labor laws be extended to cover farm workers, or at least those employed on the largest farms. Economist Varden Fuller, whose pioneering history of farm labor showed how low farm wages increased land prices and gave farmers an incentive to keep newcomer migrants arriving to fill farm jobs, testified before the La Follette committee that California agriculture could be profitable with a professional work force paid well enough to keep it committed to farm work (Fuller, 1940, 19882).

The La Follette Committee recommended that farm factories be treated as nonfarm factories, subject to labor and other laws. However, the La Follette Committee recommendations were not implemented, as World War II intervened. Some of the young men who may have become active union organizers in the fields joined the armed forces, while others switched from seasonal farm to factory jobs. The 1930s, a decade of farm labor turmoil, ended in 1942 with the importation of Mexican *bracero* farm workers, not structural reforms.

Braceros: The 1940s and 1950s

The *bracero* program brought rural Mexicans to rural America for over two decades, extending the dependence of California agriculture on a labor force without other U.S. job options and institutionalizing the dependence of many rural Mexicans on the U.S. labor market. In the spring of 1942, California farmers predicted that there would be labor shortages for the fall harvest, and they called for the importation of between 40,000 and 100,000 Mexican farm workers. Reformers complained that there was no shortage of workers, only a repeat of "the age-old obsession of all farmers for a surplus labor supply" (quoted in Craig, 1971, 38–39). The Mexican government, remembering the discrimination and debts of the 1917–21 *bracero* program, insisted that the U.S. government guarantee the contracts that farmers provided to Mexican workers, that farmers pay round-trip transportation from the worker's place of recruitment to the place of work, and that *braceros* receive the same wages as were paid to U.S. farm workers (Craig, 1971, 41).[16] The U.S. government agreed, and five hundred *braceros* arrived in Stockton on September 29, 1942, through another exception to immigration laws for "native-born residents of North America, South America, and Central America, and the islands adjacent thereto, desiring to perform agricultural labor in the United States."

Between 1942 and 1964, some 4.6 million Mexicans were admitted to do farm work; many Mexicans returned year after year, but the 1 to 2 million who participated gained U.S. work experience that would be valuable when the program ended and some decided to continue migrating illegally (Garcia y Griego, 1981). The *bracero* program was small during the war years; admissions peaked at 62,000 in 1944, meaning that less than 2 percent of the 4 million U.S. hired workers were *braceros* (CRS, 1980). Japanese who had been interned under Executive Order 9066 in 1942 were allowed out of camps to be farm workers, and some of the Italian and German prisoners of war were made farm workers.

The wartime *bracero* program ended December 31, 1947. Farmers were still allowed to recruit *braceros* through official channels, but illegal Mexican workers were also available. To avoid paying bribes to get on official emigration lists in Mexico, many Mexicans preferred to emigrate illegally. Once they arrived in the United States, farmers were eager to hire these illegal immigrants to avoid paying transportation costs, as they had to do for officially recruited braceros. Many of these illegal Mexicans were legalized in a process that official U.S. government publications called "drying out the wetbacks" (President's Commission, 1951). "Wetbacks" were Mexicans who entered the United States illegally and found farm jobs. After being discovered by authorities, they were taken to the Mexico-U.S. border, issued documentation, and returned to the farm on which they were found. There were no penalties on farmers for knowingly hiring unauthorized workers, and the number of "wetbacks" soon exceeded the number of legally admitted *braceros*. In 1949, for example, about twenty thousand Mexicans received contracts from U.S. employers, while more than eighty-seven thousand arrived illegally in the United States and then had their status legalized (President's Commission, 1951, 53).

When the Korean War broke out in 1950, farmers argued that the *bracero* program should be expanded in order to avoid labor shortages. The President's Commission on Migratory Labor did not agree—it recommended "no special measures be adopted to increase the number of alien contract workers beyond the number admitted in 1950," which was 67,500 (President's Commission, 1951, 178). To reduce the number of "wetbacks," the commission recommended employer sanctions—fines on employers who knowingly hired illegal workers—and a halt to the practice of legalizing illegal workers after they found U.S. jobs.[17] The Mexican government endorsed the commission's recommendations: "The Mexican government, press, and citizen (sic) . . . contended that the wetback exodus could be stopped only when [U.S.] employers were penalized for hiring them" (quoted in Craig, 1971, 75). However, growers had the upper hand in Congress, which approved PL-78, the Mexican Farm Labor Program, in 1951 (Craig, 1971). In 1952, the Immigration and Nationality Act was enacted. It made harboring illegal aliens a felony punishable by a two-thousand-dollar fine and a prison term of five years, but included the so-called Texas proviso—employing an illegal alien is not harboring, and thus there were no penalties on U.S. employers who even knowingly hired illegal workers.

The PL-78 *bracero* program sowed the seeds for later Mexico-U.S. migration. The availability of *braceros* permitted labor-intensive agriculture to expand to meet a growing demand for fruits and vegetables, creating a demand-pull for Mexican workers in California. Many areas of rural Mexico became dependent on money earned from U.S. jobs, and networks were soon established to link rural Mexican villages with U.S. farm jobs. United States workers who faced *bracero* competition in the fields, but not in nonfarm labor markets, exited for nonfarm jobs, leading to "labor shortages" that brought more *braceros*. The *bracero* share of the work force in citrus, tomatoes, and other major commodities soon exceeded 50 percent, and farm wages as a percent of manufacturing wages fell during the 1950s (Galarza, 1964).

One argument for *braceros* was that, if Mexicans could come legally as guest workers, they would not come illegally as "wetbacks." This argument was proven wrong during the *bracero* program. Between 1942 and 1964, there were 4.6 million *braceros* admitted and 4.9 million Mexicans apprehended in the United States—both numbers double count individuals who entered the United States as a *bracero* several times or were apprehended multiple times. The number of *braceros* and "wetbacks" increased together in the 1950s, and U.S. attorney general Herbert Brownwell toured the border and said he was "shocked" by the lawlessness he saw. Brownwell appointed a ex-general to be Immigration and Naturalization Service (INS) commissioner, and the INS launched "Operation Wetback" in June 1954, which involved the INS and local law enforcement authorities rounding up and returning to Mexico unauthorized migrants (Craig, 1971, 128). During fiscal year 1954, some 1.1 million Mexicans were removed.

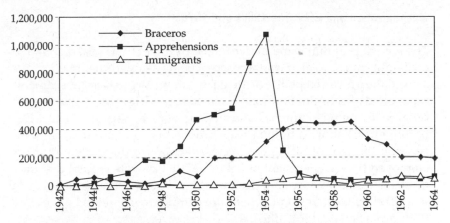

Figure 2.1. Mexican *Braceros*, Apprehensions, and Immigrants

Operation Wetback aimed to have only legal Mexican workers on U.S. farms, and the U.S. Department of Labor (DOL) cooperated to achieve this goal by relaxing regulations on *bracero* housing, wages, and food charges, so that farmers hired legal *braceros* rather than unauthorized Mexicans. Farmers were encouraged to join associations that pledged to hire only "legal *braceros*," and the *bracero*-illegal ratio was soon reversed.[18] The number of legal *bracero* admissions peaked at 445,200 in 1956, and *braceros* spread to new states and crops as DOL accepted farmer assertions that there were labor shortages. Mexican-Americans, unions, and churches opposed the expansion of the *bracero* program, and some farmers continued to complain that *bracero* regulations were too onerous.[19]

During the 1950s, California replaced New Jersey as the garden state of the United States: fruit and nut production rose 15 percent, and vegetable production rose 50 percent. New dams and canals increased the amount of irrigated land, the interstate highway system reduced transportation time to the eastern seaboard. Improved plant varieties and packing technologies made California produce available more months of the year as well as often preferred to local fruits and vegetables in the eastern United States, where most Americans lived. The availability of *braceros* held down wages—average farm worker earnings in California rose 41 percent, from $0.85 an hour in 1950 to $1.20 in 1960, while average factory worker earnings rose 63 percent, from $1.60 in 1950 to $2.60 in 1960. Mexican-Americans, who mostly lived in rural and agricultural areas in 1950, migrated in large numbers to cities such as San Jose and Los Angeles by 1960.

Mechanization and UFW: The 1960s and 1970s

The *bracero* program came under attack in the early 1960s, during the civil rights movement; it was accused of being a government policy that slowed the upward mobility of Mexican Americans, just as government-sanctioned discrimination held back blacks. Criticism of the *bracero* program by unions, churches, and study groups persuaded the U.S. Department of Labor to tighten wage and housing standards, thus increasing the cost of hiring *bracero* workers and reducing the number employed (U.S. Department of Labor, 1959). Growers argued that they needed *braceros* because American workers would not do seasonal farm work and that *braceros* kept agriculture competitive and food prices low (California Senate, 1961, 1963).

President Kennedy was elected in November 1960. The CBS documentary "Harvest of Shame" was aired in November 1960,[20] and the discussion of farm labor that followed convinced Kennedy that *braceros* were "adversely affecting the wages, working conditions, and employment opportunities of our own agricultural workers." Kennedy wanted to end the *bracero* program in 1961, but agreed to a two-year extension of the program because of the "serious impact in Mexico if thousands of workers employed in this country were summarily deprived of this much-needed employment" (Craig, 1971, 172–73). Kennedy encouraged DOL to further tighten *bracero* program regulations in a manner that raised the wages farmers had to pay to U.S. and *bracero* workers, which prompted some farmers to consider mechanization.

Farmers did not want to lose access to *braceros*, and during the summer of 1963, they pressed Congress to extend the program. There were congressional hearings and studies, most of which concluded that, without *braceros*, fruit and vegetable production would shrink and food prices would rise. Farmers received a sympathetic ear from agricultural committees, but far less sympathy from labor committees. On September 17, 1963, thirty-two *braceros* were killed and twenty-seven injured when a bus taking them from the fields to their labor camp collided with a train in Chualar in the Salinas Valley.[21] Their bodies were not claimed immediately, highlighting the lack of accountability that critics said was common in the *bracero* program and setting the stage for a decisive vote in Congress to end the *bracero* program on December 31, 1964—farmers won a final one-year extension. In its last years, the *bracero* program had become a selective labor subsidy to the growers of a few crops.[22]

Many California farmers expected to employ Mexican workers under a different provision of immigration law, the H-2 (changed to H-2A in 1986) program that was used to import Caribbean workers to hand cut sugarcane in Florida and to harvest apples in the Northeast. However, DOL required farmers to pay the higher of three wages to be certified to employ Mexicans as H-2 workers: the minimum, prevailing, or the Adverse Effect Wage Rate (AEWR), and limited the employment of H-2 workers to a maximum 120 days.[23] This was not a problem for the shorter seasons in the East, but California farmers wanted to employ Mexican workers for eleven months a year. Growers were outraged by these DOL actions, and a congressional effort to transfer the authority to certify the need for H-2 workers from the U.S. Department of Labor to the U.S. Department of Agriculture failed in the Senate in 1965 only because Vice President Hubert Humphrey cast the deciding vote against the growers (Congressional Research Service, 1980, 42).

The year 1965 was a "year of transition" in California. The number of U.S. migrants, 465,000, reached a record 15 percent of the 3.1 million U.S. farm workers, as employers recruited workers far and wide, many of whom quit after a few days. Some farmers joined or formed labor associations that acted as "super labor contractors" to recruit and supervise crews of U.S. workers. The associations generally increased labor market efficiency and some were able to reduce or stabilize labor costs and simultaneously increase average worker earnings. The Coastal Growers Association in Ventura County, for example, reduced employment from 8,517 workers in 1965 to 1,292 in 1978 and increased earnings—average hourly earnings rose from $1.77 to $5.63, and average earnings for harvesters rose from $267 (151 hours) to $3,430 (609 hours). Average worker productivity rose from 3.4 boxes an hour in 1965 to 8.4 boxes an hour in 1978 (Mamer and Rosedale, 1980).

A second response to the end of the *bracero* program was labor-saving mechanization. The 1960s was a time of rapid technological change, a celebration of the accomplishments of engineers who were able, in the case of harvesting cannery tomatoes, to work with plant scientists to develop a uniformly ripening tomato and with canneries to handle large volumes of machine-picked tomatoes. The widespread replacement of workers with machines in the fields was expected to continue until there would be only machine operators, not hand harvesters. One study predicted boldly that, if a fruit or vegetable could not be harvested mechanically, it would not be grown in the United States after 1975 (Cargill and Rossmiller, 1969-70).

The third response to the end of the *bracero* program was successful unionization. There had been organizing efforts and strikes during the 1950s and early 1960s, but farmers were usually able to get their crops picked by borrowing *braceros* from their neighbors. In fall 1965, the National Farm Workers Association headed by Cesar Chavez joined a strike called by the Filipino-dominated Agricultural Workers Organizing Committee, a union affiliated with the American Federation of Labor–Congress of Industrial Organizations (AFL-CIO), to protest a decision of California table grape growers to pay lower wages to Filipino grape pickers than had been paid to Mexican *braceros*. The strike failed—table grape growers used labor contractors to get their grapes picked, but Chavez tried a new tactic—he mounted a boycott of the wine and liquor sold by conglomerates that also grew table grapes during the Christmas buying season, and consumers responded.

In the spring of 1966, the reorganized National Farm Workers Association, now called the United Farm Workers Union (UFW), led a three-hundred-mile march from Delano to Sacramento to highlight the grape dispute, and conglomerate Schenley Industries, during the march, became the first table grape grower to sign an agreement with the United Farm Workers. The Schenley-UFW agreement raised wages 40 percent and launched a fifteen-year golden era for California farm workers. Farm workers and their struggles were front page news during the late 1960s and 1970s, as churches, unions, students, and politicians boycotted table grapes, lettuce, and wine in support of the UFW and farm workers. Most growers were not affected directly by union activities, but many were willing to match or exceed "union wages" so their workers would not join the UFW. Competition between the UFW and the Teamsters, the extension of minimum wage and unemployment insurance protections to farm workers, and the hiring of nonfarm personnel managers on many large farms led to predictions that the farm labor market would soon resemble nonfarm labor markets such as construction, which offered higher than average wages to compensate for seasonality. The farm-nonfarm wage gap narrowed: in 1977, farm worker earnings averaged $3.53 an hour, 59 percent of the $6 average in California factories.

Immigration: The 1980s and 1990s

The immigration seeds that would end the golden era for farm workers were planted during the *bracero* program. During the late 1960s, it was very easy for Mexicans to become U.S. immigrants—U.S. farmers simply had to give Mexicans letters offering them jobs. With these letters, Mexicans could obtain immigration visas—the visa was issued on a green card, and many of the Mexicans receiving green cards lived in Mexico and commuted seasonally to U.S. farm jobs, so they were known as green card commuters (Briggs, Fogel, Schmidt, 1977).[24] The UFW, reflecting the position of unions throughout the twentieth century, opposed the presence of green card commuters in the fields, accusing them of working for lower wages because they kept their families in Mexico, where living costs were lower.

Braceros were young men. By the late 1970s, ex-*bracero* green card commuters were getting too old to be farm workers, and some became foremen and contractors. Since they regularly returned to their home villages, they found it easy to recruit their sons and other young Mexicans for U.S. farm jobs. Peso devaluations in the 1970s and 1980s made U.S. jobs more attractive, and the Mexican-U.S. border was porous enough that 70 to 80 percent of those attempting illegal entry succeeded on their first attempt. The presence of unauthorized migrants, who were 20 to 25 percent of California farm workers in the early 1980s (Mines and Martin, 1986), had been obscured by the growth of labor-intensive agriculture in the 1970s, reflecting rising consumer incomes and health consciousness as well as tax laws that encouraged nonfarm investors to buy orchards and vineyards.

The UFW, whose successes at the bargaining table came from threatening consumer boycotts and obtaining favorable labor relations legislation in the state legislature, testified in Congress in support of employer sanctions—fines on employers who knowingly hired illegal workers. Bert Corona, a long-time labor organizer, clashed with Cesar Chavez and the UFW during the 1970s and 1980s over sanctions. According to Corona:

> I did have an important difference with Cesar. This involved his, and the union's position, on the need to apprehend and deport undocumented Mexican immigrants who were being used as scabs by the growers . . . [I] believed that organizing undocumented farm workers was auxiliary to the union's efforts to organize the fields. We supported an open immigration policy, as far as Mexico was concerned. (Quoted in *Rural Migration News*, April 2001)

By the late 1990s, the UFW had come around to Corona's position on immigration.

United Farm Worker activities raised farm wages in the 1970s and helped to increase the efficiency with which farm workers were used so that collective bargaining could be a win-win proposition for farmers and workers. Growers learned that careful management of seasonal workers could raise average worker earnings while keeping harvesting costs stable, and some received favorable publicity as average hourly earnings climbed to six dollars to ten dollars in the early 1980s, and workers drew maximum unemployment insurance benefits in the off season (Lloyd et al., 1988). For the first time, many seasonal workers received fringe benefits such as health care, paid vacations, and pensions. However, strikes for higher wages and benefits opened the door to contractors with crews of unauthorized workers, as growers turned to contractors to get workers to break strikes. Some growers never signed contracts with the UFW, or did not renegotiate first contracts, and contractors steadily increased their share of especially the harvest labor market. The competition between legal and illegal farm workers was often indirect, as nonunion contractors competed with the UFW for the "right" to harvest crops on particular farms (Mines and Martin, 1984).

By the early 1980s, the UFW was losing members and contracts, contractors were expanding rapidly, and labor costs fell with stable farm wages and disappearing fringe benefits. This "downward spiral" in the farm labor market was expected to be reversed by the Immigration Reform and Control Act (IRCA) of 1986, which was to legalize farm workers and stop illegal immigration. In order to retain these newly legalized workers, the theory went, farmers would have to offer higher wages and benefits. The IRCA, strongly supported by the AFL-CIO and most U.S. unions (Briggs, 2001), introduced sanctions on employers who knowingly hired illegal workers and included a Special Agricultural Worker (SAW) legalization program—unauthorized foreigners who did at least ninety days of farm work in 1985–86 could become U.S. immigrants.[25]

The SAW program had very easy legalization requirements because it was assumed that many unauthorized workers were employed by contractors who did not keep records. After an individual asserted that he did at least ninety days of qualifying farm work, the burden of proof shifted to the INS to disprove the worker's claim. The INS was not prepared for the large volume of applications—1.3 million instead of the 400,000 expected—or the significant fraud—at least half of the applicants did not do the qualifying farm work they claimed. However, since the INS could not disprove the claimed work histories of SAW applicants, 1.2 million foreigners became legal immigrants, including 1 million Mexicans, with no obligation to continue to work in agriculture.[26]

The SAW program legalized too many farm workers, and sanctions did not stop illegal immigration. The result, according to a federal commission, was that "rather than a stabilization of the labor supply, there is a general oversupply of farm labor nationwide . . . [which has] generally interfered with workers' ability to organize. With fraudulent documents easily available, employer sanctions have been largely ineffective" (CAW, 1992 xxii). Special Agricultural Workers who were legitimate farm workers found themselves in a position similar to Mexican Americans in the 1950s—if they stayed in the fields, they faced wages that were depressed by the continued arrival of newcomers from Mexico. Many left for the nonfarm labor market, where there was less wage-depressing competition from new arrivals—the percentage of SAWs dropped from 38 to 15 percent in the 1990s.

During the 1990s, the percentage of "fraudulently documented" farm workers rose and topped 50 percent by the late 1990s. Some farmers worried that, with over half of their workers illegal, INS enforcement could lead to labor shortages. Farmers knew they could obtain legal workers through the H-2A program, but few had the free housing that was required for H-2A workers, and many feared that applying for DOL certification would lead to government, union, and legal services "harassment" (GAO, 1988). To avoid the H-2A program, farmers sought congressional approval of a new guest worker program, one in which "free agent" foreign workers would "float" from farm to farm seeking jobs, legalizing the status quo, since the new guest workers would not be tied to any particular farm, so the farmers who employed them would not be responsible for their housing or transportation.

The UFW, churches, and a new pressure group, Latino advocates, strongly opposed a new guest worker program, and they persuaded President Clinton to issue a statement June 23, 1995, that said: "I oppose efforts in this Congress to institute a new guestworker or '*Bracero*' program that seeks to bring thousands of foreign workers into the United States to provide temporary farm labor." Clinton's opposition led to the rejection in Congress of guest worker proposals in 1996 and 1997, but in 1998 the U.S. Senate approved a free-agent guest worker program. A veto threat stopped its consideration in the House.

Farmers did not give up their quest for an alternative guest worker program. After Vincente Fox was elected president of Mexico, and George Bush was elected president of the United States, there was an expectation that the United States and Mexico would soon negotiate a new guest worker program, which both Fox and Bush endorsed. However, U.S. Latino advocates urged Fox to demand legalization, not guest workers (the "whole enchilada"), and Bush was reluctant to anger conservatives in Congress by embracing the expansive legalization Mexico wanted. As a result, negotiations bogged down in summer 2001, and then were stopped by the terrorist attacks of September 11. In 2002, a new compromise is being discussed: "earned legalization," a type of guest worker program under which unauthorized workers would first get a temporary work permit, and if they continued to work, in agriculture or elsewhere for four to six years, they would earn a immigrant visa or green card. If earned legalization is approved, California agriculture will likely continue to rely on workers who are born and grow up outside the United States in the twenty-first century.

3

Farm Worker Unions

As long as we, Mexican farm workers, keep our place and do our work, we are tolerated, but if the Mexican worker joins a union . . . and if he dares to strike, then all the local institutions feel duty bound to defend . . . their ideal of the American way of life. These communities, then, do not know what to do with us, and they don't know what to do without us.

Cesar Chavez, from U.S. Senate hearings, 1979

Farm workers seem to be an attractive target for unions: there are millions of them, wages are low, and workers are receptive to promises of higher wages and better working conditions. But organized farmers had the upper hand over unorganized farm workers throughout the twentieth century, largely because most farm workers found exiting the farm labor market a surer path to upward mobility than joining or forming a farm labor union to voice demands for higher wages and benefits. As a result, there have been few persisting union-management agreements in agriculture. The longest collective bargaining relationship in California agriculture is between the Teamsters and Bud Antle (now part of Dole Food Company), which began in 1961. By contrast, U.S. unions such as the United Auto Workers and the United Steel Workers have had continuous relationships with major employers in their target industries since the mid-1930s.

The scarcity and short duration of most union-management agreements reflects the ease with which farm employers were able to unify rural residents and local law enforcement agencies against many farm worker organizers, who were portrayed as "outside agitators" with radical agendas determined to transform the economy. Federal and state governments were slow to extend labor relations rights to farm workers because of the agrarian ideology that most farm workers were family members or hired hands on family farms, making factory labor laws "inappropriate" and organizing and bargaining difficult. Many farm workers have little education, are not U.S. citizens, and are scattered across thousands of workplaces, making it hard to bring farm workers together in an effective union to press demands on employers.

In this chapter, I highlight several periods of farm worker union activity in California and summarize the activities of radical unions before World War I and in 1933, the efforts of traditional unions to organize farm workers in the 1950s, and the UFW's boycott strategy since 1965. One theme running through these periods is that workers were often inspired to take action by "unfair" employer decisions, such as advertising for workers at a high wage, and then cutting the wage when too many workers appeared. While there has been continuity in the sources of worker frustration, there is no link between farm worker unions—the unions of 1915 played no role in the strikes of 1933, those of 1933 were absent from organizing activities in the 1940s and 1950s, and the UFW achieved its first successes outside the "House of Labor," the AFL-CIO.

Union Activity from World War I to 1965

Pre–World War I Wobblies

The American Federation of Labor (AFL) began as a national organization of craft unions in 1886—member unions, such as carpenters or bricklayers, organized workers into unions according to their craft or occupation, so there were separate carpenters and bricklayers unions. The AFL in 1903 announced plans to organize farm workers, but its member unions never seemed committed to a farm worker union, in part for fear that organizing drives would upset farmers, who could use their power in Congress and state legislatures to restrict all union activities.

The Industrial Workers of the World (IWW), also known as the "Wobblies," was a revolutionary union founded in 1905 by Eugene Debs and other radical labor leaders who felt betrayed by conventional unions. Their goal was to replace what the IWW called a "wage-slave system" with worker-run cooperatives. The IWW wanted to organize all workers into "one big union," skilled as well as unskilled, and include minorities such as the Chinese and Japanese, who were excluded from most AFL unions, under the slogan "An injury to one is an injury to all" (Brissenden, 1920).

The IWW successfully organized many of the wheat harvesters in the Midwestern states. During the peak months, 250,000 mostly white workers migrated from Texas to Canada harvesting wheat and other grains between 1900 and 1925. Most traveled by riding freight trains, and migrants without an IWW "red card" were sometimes prevented from riding the rails.[1] A typical IWW "plan of action" sent an IWW organizer or "job delegate" to get a job where workers were dissatisfied, and then to lead a strike that brought IWW leaders to the farm. Some employers tried to harvest crops with strikebreakers, which led to picket line violence as young single men attracted to the IWW often tried to prevent strikebreakers from replacing them.

In California, IWW organizers also concentrated on migrants who harvested grain, so-called "harvest stiffs or bindle stiffs" (Steven Street, 1998). Wobblie organizers, who were often superb orators, mingled with farm workers during the winter months when they "holed up" in cities and explained from soapboxes why migrants needed to support radical change in the U.S. economic system to improve wages and living conditions. Local authorities often used unconstitutional means to restrict the activities of IWW organizers, which helped the IWW publicize itself. For example, Fresno in 1910 denied IWW organizers the right to make speeches and distribute literature, but publicity about this unconstitutional interference with free speech helped raise awareness of and membership in the IWW. The IWW claimed ten thousand to twelve thousand members in northern California in 1912 (Jamieson, 1945, 60).

The Wheatland hops riots of 1913 illustrate the clash of extremes in farm fields that led to violence and ultimately the demise of the IWW in California (Jamieson, 1945, 60–63; Daniel, 1981, 89–91). Wheatland is a small community thirty miles northeast of Sacramento in Yuba County, and the hops used to make beer was a major crop.[2] Chinese and Japanese workers dominated the fruit, sugar beet, and vegetable work forces, but many hops harvesters were migratory white men. Employer Durst advertised for twenty-seven hundred workers to harvest hops in August 1913, offering a higher-than-usual piece rate wage of a dollar a hundred pounds, even though Durst could employ only about thirteen hundred workers because of the limited capacity of his drying kilns and available housing. However, when twenty-eight hundred workers traveled to Wheatland, Durst cut the piece rate to ninety cents. The workers protested, the IWW helped them to form a protest committee and present a list of demands to Durst, including the one-dollar wage promised. Durst agreed to a few of the workers' demands, but called the local sheriff on August 3, 1913, saying that the IWW-led workers were trying to take over his ranch. When the sheriff tried to arrest a strike leader, violence broke out, and a district attorney, deputy sheriff, and two workers were killed. Most of the workers left before the National Guard arrived to restore order, and no contract was signed between Durst and the IWW. Replacement workers picked Durst's hops.

Wobblie leaders were convicted of inciting a riot and sentenced to prison. Governor Hiram Johnson appointed a Commission on Immigration and Housing in 1913 to examine "the first California labor cause célèbre," and economist Carleton Parker concluded that the Wheatland riot "embodied the state's great migratory labor problem" (Parker, 1920, 172). Farm workers had legitimate grievances, and the "real cause" of the trouble was the "inadequate housing and the unsanitary conditions under which the hop pickers were compelled to live" (quoted in Daniel, 1981, 91). Parker and the commission urged growers, despite the "general superabundance" of farm workers, to honor the wage promises they made in handbills and urged the state to enact and enforce housing and sanitation standards in farm labor camps.[3] The commission hired inspectors to check on the nine hundred farm labor camps in the state and praised the attempts of a few growers to diversify crops in order to employ fewer workers for longer periods.[4]

The 1920s: FLCS as the Enemy

During the 1920s, there were few strikes in rural California, even though many of the large farms hired hundreds of workers. California had 30 percent of the large-scale cotton and specialty crop farms in the United States in the 1920s, and 60 percent of the large scale fruit and vegetable farms, and most of these "industrialized farms" or "factories-in-the-fields" grew only one or two crops and hired and laid off "gangs of laborers as needed" (U.S. Senate, 1942, part 47, 17217).[5] In many cases, farmers formed associations to standardize marketing practices, negotiate freight rates with railroads, and establish "standard wages" for farm workers and thus minimize "the useless floating of labor" in search of higher wages.[6]

Nonfarm businesses attempted to stave off unionization in the 1920s by treating workers better. Many developed formal grievance mechanisms to handle worker complaints and to regulate the activities of the first-line supervisors who dealt with workers. The U.S. government curtailed immigration from the Eastern Hemisphere in 1921 and again in 1924, which put upward pressure on wages and further encouraged employers to switch from the stick to the carrot to motivate workers. Many nonfarm firms tried to get workers to identify with the employer, to think of themselves as "Ford men" or a "Chrysler men." California farmers' associations, by contrast, encouraged farm workers to identify with a commodity or area, but not a particular grower. Farm workers could be peach or cotton pickers, but not Tejon Ranch Company employees.[7] The combination of linking workers to crops, and then using independent contractors to get crews of workers, widened the gap between farmers and workers.

The farmer-worker gap was widened even further by the preference of many growers for contractors who could supply Mexican workers. A Whittier lemon grower said: "Mexicans as a rule work quietly and uncomplainingly and are well satisfied with wages and conditions. When a troublemaker appears, he is discharged at once" (quoted in Jamieson, 1945, 73). Many farmers hired workers only through contractors, and the contractors, often settled Mexicans who knew some English, often had incentives that were different from those of workers. For example, a citrus grower could give a contractor seven cents for a fifty-pound box of oranges, and the contractor might then offer workers six cents a box. However, the contractor could make more money by requiring workers to ride to and from the grove with him for twenty-five cents a day; many workers needed rides. If the contractor had a crew of forty, they might be done in three hours, but the contractor made ten dollars in transportation fees. A crew of twenty, by contrast, could work six hours, but they would generate only five dollars in transportation fees (Fisher, 1953, 34).

Many workers knew they were being cheated by contractors, and worker protests about contractors prompted Mexican cantaloupe harvesters in the Imperial Valley to strike in 1928 to demand direct hiring, not hiring via contractors. The Confederation of Mexican Labor Unions claimed a membership of two thousand in California, and it wanted a union hiring hall to match farm workers with seasonal jobs. Although no contract was signed, the Imperial growers agreed to end the practice of withholding 25 percent of each worker's wages until the harvest was completed, and growers rather than contractors became responsible for assuring that workers received their full wages (Jamieson, 1945, 77).

Communists in 1933

The peak year for farm worker strikes was 1933, and the reason for the wave of strikes was that the prices received by farmers were rising, but wages were not. Farmers' prices fell between 1929 and 1932, as U.S. gross domestic product (GDP) fell by one-third, the unemployment rate reached 24 percent, and the farm work force was swelled by urban unemployment. Farmers cut wages—from thirty-five to fifty cents an hour in 1929–1930 to fifteen to sixteen cents in 1933. The major union active in California fields was the Communist-dominated Cannery and Agricultural Workers Industrial Union (CAWIU), and it followed the IWW pattern of taking over the leadership of spontaneous worker protests and strikes and helping workers to present demands to employers.[8] CAWIU-led strikes were often violent, in part because growers and their foremen worked closely with local law enforcement authorities; in many cases, growers and their foremen were deputy sheriffs.

There were thirty-seven strikes involving forty-eight thousand farm workers in fourteen crops in California in 1933, culminating in an October cotton harvesters strike. Harvest-time strikes during the spring and summer of 1933 usually resulted in wage increases, so that by fall, workers were prepared to strike again to get a wage increase for picking cotton, the crop that employed the most workers. Cotton farmers met in September as usual to set a standard piece rate wage and agreed to pay 60 cents per one hundred pounds of cotton picked, up from 40 cents in 1932, but well below the $1.50 of 1929. Cotton harvesters were expecting wages to rise to at least $1, and the CAWIU called a strike on October 4, 1933, to support its demand for $1 per one hundred pounds. Growers evicted the ten thousand to twenty thousand strikers and their families from on-farm labor camps, and most moved into CAWIU-run tent camps, which paradoxically reinforced the strike's effectiveness.

The strike was condemned by farmers, and they were supported by local leaders. A Tulare newspaper editorialized that "the strike would vanish into thin air overnight if the outside agitators were rounded up and escorted out of the county, as they should be" (Jamieson, 1945, 103). An undersheriff expressed common feelings in rural areas: "We protect our farmers here in Kern County. They are our best people. They are always with us. They keep the country going. They put us in here and they can put us out again, so we serve them. But the Mexicans are trash. They have no standard of living. We herd them like pigs" (quoted in Jamieson, 1945, 103). Farmers, who were often deputized during emergencies, tried to break up striker rallies, and in the town of Pixley, they killed two Mexican workers. State officials, who rushed to investigate, urged local authorities to disarm the growers, but they issued more gun permits. Reporters and photographers arrived to cover the strike, and they reported that growers, not strikers, were at fault for not raising wages or agreeing to mediation—growers opposed mediation on the grounds that it would further Communist subversion by strengthening the CAWIU.

The strike continued, and it appeared that the cotton crop would be lost. To avoid crop losses, UC professors were sent on fact-finding missions, and they eventually recommended a seventy-five-cent piece rate to a state commission set up to resolve the dispute. Banks persuaded farmers to pay seventy-five cents by threatening to withhold financing for the 1934 cotton crop if they did not, and the government announced that workers who did not go to work by October 16, 1933, would be denied federal relief in the winter months. The seventy-five-cent wage appeared to be at least a partial victory for the CAIWU, and it prompted farmers to form a new organization, the Associated Farmers of California, which persuaded most rural counties to enact antipicketing ordinances, which could be used to prosecute CAWIU organizers.

The Associated Farmers, which described itself as an organization of farmers, was financed largely by nonfarm banks, railroads, canneries, public utilities, and the Industrial Association of San Francisco. The Associated Farmers found a reason to go after CAWIU leaders in the summer 1934, when Harry Bridges and his International Longshoremen's Association (ILA) organized a general strike in San Francisco in support of its demand for a union-run hiring hall to allocate work on the docks. San Francisco newspapers—allegedly at the behest of the Associated Farmers—reported that CAWIU leaders lead a farm worker strike in support of the ILA. In July 1934, fourteen CAWIU leaders were arrested and convicted of instigating violence and sent to prison. The CAWIU showed that workers would strike to protest a refusal of farmers to raise wages, but CAWIU's policy of not signing contracts, and the opposition that was aroused by its communist orientation, persuaded growers to organize themselves into what proved to be effective antiunion associations.

The 1935 the National Labor Relations Act (NLRA, also known as the Wagner Act) granted organizing and collective bargaining rights to most nonfarm workers. As originally introduced, the NRLA included farm workers, but they were removed "for administrative reasons" before enactment. Most observers concluded that "political realities" were responsible for the exclusion. Farm groups argued that most farm workers were hired hands who had a master-apprentice relationship, not an employer-worker relationship, and that unions of farm workers would be too powerful because they could call harvest-time strikes. Thus, Senator Robert Wagner, a Democrat from New York, the main author of the NLRA, "recognized that the inclusion of agriculture might create widespread opposition from the farm labor lobby and thereby jeopardize passage of the NLRA" (Schauer and Tyler, 1970, 4).

Farm workers were also excluded from the Social Security Act of 1935 (and thus from Unemployment Insurance) and the Fair Labor Standards Act of 1938, which established minimum wages.[9] Unions affiliated with the American Federation of Labor (AFL) nonetheless launched several "march inland" campaigns to organize farm workers, as the Teamsters and Longshoremen's unions, well established in San Francisco, thought they could persuade farmers to recognize them as representatives of farm workers by threatening to refuse to transport or load farm commodities. Thus, the organizing strategy was to go straight to the grower, ignoring farm workers. Most growers often responded truthfully that their workers did not want to be represented by these unions.

The AFL's rival confederation of unions, the Congress of Industrial Organizations (CIO), included unions that had left the AFL in a dispute over how to organize. The CIO organized workers by industry, including all workers in an auto plant in the United Auto Workers. A CIO union, the United Cannery Workers (UCW), used its own version of the march-inland strategy to organize field workers in the late 1930s and 1940s. The UCW represented workers in packingsheds and canneries, many of whom were the wives of field workers, and it too went to growers and demanded recognition as the bargaining representative for field workers. The Associated Farmers were able to use the rivalry between AFL- and CIO-affiliated unions to successfully discourage unionization among field workers, especially among Midwestern Okies and Arkies who had been antiunion small farmers in the Midwest.[10]

The violence of 1930s farm labor disputes led some reformers to paint worker-employer struggles in black and white terms, in which workers were the noble victims of greedy farm employers in a very flawed farming system. The La Follette Subcommittee of the U.S. Senate's Labor Committee concluded that

> the economic and social plight of California's agricultural labor is miserable beyond belief. Average annual earnings for agricultural laborers are far below the minimum standard necessary even for the maintenance of . . . proper levels of health and decency. Agricultural laborers are ill-fed, ill-clothed, poorly housed, and almost completely lacking in many other things commonly considered necessary for civilized life. They have no job security, and except in rare instances no job preference or seniority.
>
> The California agricultural laborer is under-employed and frequently meets the unfair competition of child and relief labor. He has no control over wage rates and no voice in fixing them. He must be housed for the most part in private labor camps dominated by the employer. He lacks adequate medical attention. His children are unable to secure satisfactory continuous education. He has no adequate protection from industrial accidents and no workmen's compensation. State minimum-wage and maximum-hour laws do not give him any protection. Residence requirements often bar him from relief. Organized protests on his part have been met with the blacklist, the denial of free speech and assemblage through the application of illegal ordinances of various kinds and through acts of outright vigilantism. His right to organize and bargain collectively is unprotected. (U.S. Senate, 1942, 37–38)

The committee concluded that only federal intervention could help farm workers to level the playing field with large farmers:

The business interests dominant in the agricultural department of the State Chamber of Commerce were the great corporate employers long dependent upon a docile oversupply of farm labor. They could conceive but one objective: the suppression by all available means of the unrest among agricultural employees. The most effective weapons for such a campaign of suppression were obviously the agencies of State and local law enforcement. The agricultural interests therefore envisaged a campaign to bend these [law enforcement] agencies to their purposes, a "red" hunt and a "red" scare to prejudice public opinion against protests lodged by the workers or their leaders, a chain of citizens' committees to influence local law-enforcement officers and support them in their activities, and a centralized direction to coordinate activities throughout the State and to track down the radical union organizer wherever he might go. (U.S. Senate, 1942, 41)

The 1940s and 1950s: *Braceros*, Not Unions

The La Follette report led to proposals for farm labor reform legislation, but World War II broke out, and farm workers were not included under labor laws. Farm worker and other strikes ended, since union activities that caused production losses were considered unpatriotic, and many farm workers entered the armed forces or went to work in wartime factories.

Instead of farm labor reforms, farmers used fears of labor shortages that might reduce the U.S. food supply to gain access to legal Mexican workers, *braceros* (strong arms). The U.S. government negotiated a bilateral agreement with Mexico to permit the admission of Mexican farm workers after farmers convinced the U.S. government that they tried and failed to find U.S. workers. Few farmers sought *braceros* during World War II; the maximum number of *braceros* in California during the war was 37,000, or less than 20 percent of seasonal farm workers (California Senate, 1961, 72). Most temporary worker programs last longer and get larger than expected, and the *bracero* program was no exception. California had about 200,000 seasonal workers in the 1950s, and there were 20,000 *braceros* in 1951 and to 51,000 in 1957, when *braceros* were 80 percent of the lemon harvesters, 75 percent of the tomato harvesters, and 61 percent of the lettuce harvesters.

Unions tried to organize non-*bracero* farm workers in the 1950s, but failed. The AFL chartered a National Farm Labor Union (changed to the National Agricultural Workers Union or NAWU in 1956). Its leader, Ernesto Galarza,[11] testified frequently that *braceros* were used illegally to break NAWU-called strikes for higher wages. During most strikes, farmers evicted U.S. workers from their on-farm housing and then "borrowed" *braceros* from neighbors to harvest their crops. The NAWU would protest to the U.S. Department of Labor—*braceros* were not to be employed as strikebreakers—but, by the time DOL agreed with the

NAWU, the harvest had been completed. Galarza testified that "union-ization was futile while the *bracero* Program remained."[12]

The rival AFL and CIO federations of unions merged into the AFL-CIO in 1955, and in 1959 the AFL-CIO chartered the Agricultural Workers Organizing Committee (AWOC), which established a headquarters in Stockton and announced that its goal was 2 million members, which would have made it the largest union in the United States. The AWOC had successful organizers from nonfarm unions, and they thought that the fastest way to get members was approach the contractors who hired hundreds of thousands of workers in daily "shape-ups" in the skid-row areas of cities in agricultural areas. This strategy was not popular with workers. The contractors deducted union dues from their pay, but the workers did not feel that the union did anything for them.

There were farm worker protests and strikes in California agriculture between World War I and 1960, but none led to stable unions or collective bargaining agreements with farmers. The Industrial Workers of the World appealed to workers with grievances about broken wage promises, and the Cannery and Agricultural Workers Industrial Union called strikes to demand that wages be raised as farm prices rose, but these radical unions were suppressed by farmers and their rural allies. Mainstream unions attempted to organize farm workers, especially in the 1940s and 1950s, but they failed. The main reasons for this failure were a surplus of workers, which made the traditional union weapon of withholding work (strikes) ineffective; inappropriate leadership and tactics, such as organizing workers via employers or contractors; and confusion among workers as to the source of their low wages—was it the contractor, farmer, or employer association? There were two legacies from the pre-1960s organizing: the Agricultural Workers Organizing Committee became a Filipino-dominated worker organization that merged with the United Farm Workers union (UFW) in 1967, and Bud Antle, a Salinas lettuce grower whose nonfarm workers were represented by the Teamsters,[13] signed a contract covering field workers in 1961 in exchange for a $1 million Teamsters loan, which Antle used to develop the vacuum-cooling process that revolutionized the lettuce business.[14]

The Rise of the UFW

Cesar Estrada Chavez (1927–1993) has been the best-known Mexican-American since the late 1960s: more U.S. schools, streets, and libraries are named for Chavez than any other Hispanic. Chavez was born in Arizona, and his family lost its farm and became migrant farm workers in the 1930s. Chavez got out of farm work and into social activism, and left a job registering voters in the *Sal Si Puedes* (Get out if you can) barrio of San Jose, California, in 1962 when the Community Serivce Organization headed by Saul Alinksy refused to help farm workers organize a union. Chavez moved to the Tulare County city of Delano and, with the help of school teacher Dolores Huerta, launched the Farm Workers Association (FWA) to help farm workers complete government paperwork in exchange for $3.50 monthly dues, and to show them that an organization could improve their lives. In 1964, the FWA was renamed the National Farm Workers Association (NFWA), and in 1965 the NFWA conducted a successful rent strike against the public housing authority in Tulare County.[15]

1965–1974: Grapes, *La Causa*, Teamsters

In the summer of 1965, the Filipino-dominated AWOC called a strike against Coachella Valley table grape growers to protest the wage disparity between Mexican and U.S. Filipino grape pickers—$1.40 an hour versus $1.25 an hour. The growers did not recognize the AWOC as the representative of their workers, but raised wages to $1.40 an hour, which ended the action and sent workers went back to work. Several months later, when the grape harvest began in Delano, growers again announced a $1.25 an hour wage, plus a piece rate of 15 cents a box. The AWOC called a strike on September 8, 1965, demanding $1.40 an hour plus 25 cents a box, and asked Chavez's NFWA to help them. The AWOC and the NFWA joined forces, established picket lines, and solicited donations to provide benefits to strikers. Growers harvested their grapes with FLC-supplied workers, and did not recognize the AWOC-NFWA.[16]

Chavez quickly assumed leadership of the strike and urged a consumer boycott, convinced that, "with the help of the public, [farm workers] can develop the economic power to counter that of growers" (Daniel, 1987, 367). Chavez urged workers to be nonviolent, so that the struggle in the fields would be portrayed as a case of powerless farm workers against powerful agribusiness.[17] Chavez's major innovation was to apply pressure to growers when there were no crops to be harvested, and to enlist unions, churches,[18] students, and politicians to picket liquor stores before Christmas 1965, urging Americans not to buy the liquor products of Schenley, a conglomerate with 3,350 acres of vineyards near Delano. The boycott was successful: Schenley liquor sales fell, and Chavez kept the boycott in the news with a succession of high-profile visitors to Delano. For example, in March 1966, the U.S. Senate

Subcommittee on Migratory Labor held a hearing in Delano, and Senator Robert Kennedy had a televised argument with the Kern County sheriff over the constitutional rights of Americans. The sheriff said he arrested UFW supporters because he knew they were about to break the law, and Kennedy countered that Chavez and the farm workers had the right to boycott and picket and not be arrested until after they broke laws.[19] On March 17, 1966, the NFWA began to march from Delano to Sacramento and attracted a great deal of media attention (Dunne, 1967). As the marchers neared Sacramento for their final rally on Easter Sunday, Schenley agreed to raise wages by 40 percent, from $1.25 to $1.75 hourly, plus 25 cents per box, or about twice the minimum wage.[20]

Chavez then began organizing against another large grape grower, DiGiorgio Fruit Corporation, a target of unions since the 1940s.[21] DiGiorgio responded that its farm workers were already represented by the Teamsters union. Chavez protested, emphasizing that there had not been an election to determine the preferences of the farm workers— since farm workers were not covered by federal or state labor laws, there was no need for an election to determine if workers wanted to be represented by the UFW or Teamsters. Politicians, churches, and nonfarm unions pushed for an election at DiGiorgio supervised by the American Arbitration Association. DiGiorgio reluctantly agreed, and in the August 1966 election, the UFW got 530 votes and the Teamsters 331. DiGiorgio negotiated an agreement in April 1967 but went out of business in 1968.[22]

The UFW often used the same tactic as the Teamsters had used at DiGiorgio to be recognized and negotiate contracts. The UFW collected signatures from workers that authorized the UFW to represent them, announced to the farmer that it represented their farm workers, and asked the farmer to sign the union's standard contract or begin negotiations. If the farmer refused, the UFW threatened to launch a consumer boycott of their products. This strategy led to contracts covering the workers employed by vineyards such as Almaden, Christian Brothers, and Paul Masson in 1967.[23]

The UFW used this we-represent-your-workers approach in January 1968, when it sent letters to the state's table grape growers requesting that they recognize the UFW. The growers did not respond, and the UFW launched a nationwide boycott of grapes, *La Causa*, that made the UFW and Cesar Chavez household names. The grape boycott is considered one of the most successful consumer boycotts in U.S. history. According to a September 1975 Harris poll, 12 percent of Americans avoided grapes in the late 1960s and early 1970s.[24] Per capita grape consumption fell 24 percent, from 3.4 pounds per person in 1968 to 2.2

Table 3.1. California Table Grapes: 1965–75

	Table Grapes Pounds (000)	Value ($000)	Average Price/Pound	Per Capita Consumption Pounds/ Person/Year
1965	779,261	108,342	0.14	
1966	780,050	123,195	0.16	
1967	513,923	150,913	0.29	
1968	713,922	200,121	0.28	3.4
1969	661,436	131,858	0.20	2.8
1970	414,237	100,847	0.24	2.2
1971	351,987	101,864	0.29	2.2
1972	376,346	125,117	0.33	2.1
1973	457,084	133,145	0.29	2.5
1974	476,134	175,337	0.37	2.6
1975	550,275	199,744	0.36	2.7

Source: Alston et al., "The California Table Grape Commission Promotion Program: An Evaluation," (1997), 96–97.
Per capita consumption data is for the United States and Canada.

pounds per person in 1970–71 (Alston et al., 1997). Grape growers formed the California Table Grape Commission in 1968 to promote grapes. Chavez was hailed as the Latino Martin Luther King and was featured on the cover of *Time* magazine July 4, 1969, under the headline, "The Grapes of Wrath: Mexican-Americans on the March."[25]

The activities of Chavez and the UFW attracted national attention. The U.S. Senate's Subcommittee on Migratory Labor held hearings throughout the United States—in 1969–70 on migrant and seasonal worker powerlessness and in 1971–72 on farm workers in rural America. Some growers alleged that Chavez and the UFW were being supported by communists, and the FBI investigated Chavez, sending agents to UFW rallies and compiling what became a 1,434–page dossier. However, a leading farm labor historian who reviewed the FBI's report concluded that the FBI "found nothing on Chavez": no communist leanings, no marital infidelities, only "a man with a single-minded devotion to farmworkers" (Steven Street, 1996, 349).

On April 10, 1970, grape grower Lionel Steinberg's David Freedman company signed a contract with the UFW, ending *La Causa*. Other grape growers followed, recognizing the UFW and signing contracts that offered harvesters a $1.75 hourly wage plus a piece rate of 25 cents per box of grapes picked. In July 1970, twenty-three Delano growers signed UFW contracts, giving the UFW a total of 150 contracts covering twenty thousand workers (Majka and Majka, 1995, 12). These contracts required farmers to hire workers through a UFW-run hiring hall, and growers made contributions to UFW-administered health and pension plans. The contracts also included clauses restricting mechanization and pesticide usage and were to be administered with local ranch committees comprised of workers. The UFW aimed to follow in the footsteps of construction and longshoremen unions by being the organizing institution in what had been a casual labor market, with the UFW's hiring hall allocating work according to each worker's seniority with the UFW.

The UFW had a rival in the field, the Teamsters union, which represented truck drivers as well as many of the workers employed in canneries and processing sheds. When the UFW sent its "we-represent-your-workers" letter to lettuce growers in 1970, most responded that they could not negotiate with the UFW because their field workers were already represented by the Teamsters under five-year agreements. The UFW attacked the Teamsters and the growers in the media, emphasizing that many workers did not know the Teamsters represented them, and that the "secret contracts" were signed so that the lettuce growers would not have to deal with the UFW. There was conflict between the UFW and the Teamsters, as rival pickets faced each other on rural roads, and the Teamsters were accused of "union busting" in their efforts to keep the UFW from representing lettuce workers. The UFW mounted a boycott of lettuce, but it largely failed—the Teamsters wound up representing 70 percent of California lettuce workers and the UFW 15 percent.[26]

Despite the setback in lettuce, the UFW negotiated agreements with farmers around the state and reached a high water mark in March 1973 when it claimed sixty-seven thousand members and 180 contracts covering forty thousand farm jobs; in some cases, UFW members were employed only a few weeks under UFW contracts. But the summer and fall of 1973 proved disastrous for the UFW: the UFW ended 1973 with 12 contracts, while the Teamsters had 305.[27] As their UFW contracts expired, most table grape growers switched to the Teamsters, complaining that the UFW had been unable to operate its hiring hall and administer the 1970–73 contracts effectively; E & J Gallo, the world's largest winery, joined them in switching to the Teamsters in August 1973. Many growers preferred the "business union" approach of the Teamsters, whose contracts had a minimum wage of $2.30 hourly (the federal minimum wage was $1.60 an hour in 1973 and $2 in 1974), but they did not include a union-run hiring halls, mechanization, and pesticide clauses.

The UFW and the Teamsters made an agreement that left field workers to the UFW in 1966, but after their expulsion from the AFL-CIO in 1967, the Teamsters considered the agreement void (the Teamsters, the largest U.S. union, was accused of having ties to organized crime). The Teamsters did not want another union to call a harvest strike that might put Teamster truck drivers and packingshed workers out of work, and they may have wanted farm worker dues of eight dollars a month (two hours pay a month after 1976). However, the most important reason for Teamster-UFW rivalry in the early 1970s was probably the fear that the UFW, which had arisen to state and national prominence very quickly, might expand from the fields to the packinghouses and canneries, where the work force was becoming increasingly Hispanic (Sosnick, 1978).

The UFW called strikes and established picket lines to protest these Teamster-grower contracts. Many growers asked local judges to issue injunctions to prevent the UFW from picketing their operations because, they argued, their workers were already represented by a union. The judges complied, and thirty-two hundred UFW picketers were arrested in 1973 for violating these injunctions. When UFW picket lines encouraged workers to leave the fields, growers turned to contractors to get workers, and the UFW established a "wet line" patrol along the Mexico-U.S. border to discourage Mexicans from entering the United States to break their strikes. Even as the UFW was losing contracts with growers, it remained very successful in the media and politics, attracting a procession of leaders including Democratic senator Edward Kennedy of Massachusetts to its first constitutional convention in Delano in September 1973.

1975–1982: ALRA, Elections, Contracts, Strikes

In 1974, when battles in the fields between UFW and Teamster supporters began again, some growers started to agree with many Californians that a law was needed to resolve whether farm workers wanted to be represented by a union, and which one. The UFW was portrayed in the media as "the farm worker union," but the Teamsters represented far more farm workers. However, the UFW was an early supporter of the Democratic candidate for governor, Jerry Brown, and after he won the November 1974 election, Brown made the enactment of a farm labor relations law his top priority. Farm labor relations laws had been proposed regularly in the early 1970s in the legislature, but farmers, who had an ally in Governor Ronald Reagan, did not want a simple extension of the NLRA to farm workers—they wanted a ban on harvest time strikes and other provisions for the "unique agricultural industry"

(Daniel, 1987; H. Levy, 1975, Sosnick, 1978, 374–75). Farmers tried to enact one version of their proposal as an initiative in 1972, but Proposition 22 lost 42 to 58 percent.

The UFW originally asked that farm workers have the same labor relations rights as nonfarm workers, that they be included under the NLRA, or that California enact a state-level NLRA covering farm workers.[28] However, after the success of the grape boycott, the UFW agreed with farmers that a farm labor relations law should not be a state NLRA. The UFW, over the objections of the AFL-CIO, asserted that it needed the right to call secondary consumer boycotts and to operate member-only hiring halls (Sosnick, 1978, 371).

The compromise, which gave farm worker unions more boycott rights than they would have had under the NLRA, was the Agricultural Labor Relations Act (ALRA). It was eventually supported by the UFW, growers, and the Teamsters. The ALRA was signed into law June 5, 1975, so that the first elections could be held during the peak harvest period, and on September 5, 1975, the fifteen artichoke workers employed by Molera Agricultural Group near Castroville made history by casting votes in the first ALRB-supervised election. The UFW and the Teamsters competed vigorously in these first ALRA elections, since elections were allowed on farms in the middle of multiyear Teamster and UFW contracts that had been signed without elections. There were 5 to 6 elections a day in the fall of 1975, a total of 418 in the first five months the ALRA was in effect and, of the 361 elections in which a winner was certified, the UFW won 198 or 55 percent and the Teamsters 115 or 32 percent (Taylor, 1976, 66).

Many observers predicted that California agriculture would become a heavily unionized industry, and that both farm workers and the farm labor market would change as a result of unionization. A typical prediction went as follows: given the "continued competition" between the Teamsters and the UFW, "this presages more organizing battles and attempts to outdo one another at the bargaining table . . . higher wage settlements . . . will push the farmers to cut labor costs, most likely by mechanizing field jobs" (*Business Week*, October 13, 1975). Unionization was expected to close nonfarm-farm wage gaps, implying a doubling of farm wages (Taylor, 1976, 67). The UFW was widely considered the best vehicle for upward mobility for Mexican Americans, and an October 1976 poll found that 46 percent of respondents had a favorable view of the UFW; only 20 percent an unfavorable view.[29] However, more experienced observers were more skeptical: Fuller and Mason asserted that unionization will "continue to be more exceptional than dominant" (1977, 79), adding that farm worker unions representing a small share of farm workers could nonetheless "become politically influential in respect to laws and programs affecting all farm workers" (1977, 80).

The UFW, Teamsters, and growers focused their attention on the ALRB, and it quickly became a controversial state agency. The ALRB faced an enormous challenge; it had to hire staff, develop regulations to implement the ALRA, and supervise hundreds of elections and deal with charges that unfair labor practices (ULPs) were committed from its first day of operation. The agency was under a microscope, and unions and growers complained regularly about ALRB actions, as, for example, when the Teamsters and farm employers complained that ALRB staff were pro-UFW because some took UFW organizers with them in state cars to farms for elections and to investigate allegations that the ALRA had been violated. The regulations issued by the five-member board were even more controversial, including an emergency 1975 regulation that gave union organizers automatic access to enter grower property and talk to farm workers. This "access rule" prompted growers to block supplemental funds for the ALRB in February 1976; ALRB activities did not resume until July 1, 1976. The UFW, still a powerful player in state politics, fought the growers who had blocked funding for the ALRB with Proposition 14, which would have amended the state constitution to require funding for the ALRB, preventing another hiatus. Growers relaxed their opposition to funding the ALRB and organized to defeat Proposition 14. With the ALRB back in action, and many legal scholars saying Proposition 14 set a bad precedent, Proposition 14 was rejected by voters in November 1976, but farm labor had been a major statewide issue in three successive years—1974, 1975, and 1976.

By 1977–78, most Californians thought the farm labor issue was "resolved," and that pickets would be a thing of the past and farm workers would begin to be paid like other workers. Many events supported this view. The UFW signed another pact with the Teamsters leaving field workers to the UFW and reported progress in organizing and bargaining—ninety contracts covering thirty thousand farm workers (*Business Week*, January 30, 1978). State laws were changing to treat farm workers like other workers. The short-handled hoe was banned in 1975, and unemployment insurance benefits were extended to almost all California farm workers in 1978.[30]

However, rising farm wages and the introduction of fringe benefits were pushing up farm labor costs, and the mechanization predicted in the 1960s began to show up in the form of prototype machines to harvest lettuce, grapes, and olives. Many of the harvesting machines were developed by University of California researchers. In 1978, the UFW joined the California Rural Legal Assistance organization in charging that the University of California was using tax monies to develop machines that displaced farm workers and small farmers, and reduced the UFW's bargaining power. Stopping mechanization research became the UFW's "No. 1 legislative priority" (*Business Week,* January 30, 1978).

In 1979, acting as a traditional union, the UFW won a Pyrrhic victory from which it never recovered. In the Imperial Valley next to the Mexican border, the UFW had contracts with twenty-six lettuce and vegetable growers—some operated only in Imperial, while others operated mostly in the high-wage Salinas Valley, and moved to the Imperial Valley so that they could supply fresh vegetables year round. Most of these contracts had been negotiated in 1975–76, and they raised wages from $3.11 an hour to $3.70 an hour by 1978 (the federal minimum wage was $2.10 in 1975, and $2.65 in 1978). The UFW demanded a 42 percent wage increase for entry-level workers, which would have raised entry-level wages from $3.70 to $5.25 hourly.[31] Employers estimated that, if they agreed to the UFW's wage and fringe benefit demands, their labor costs would increase from 123 to 190 percent, and they countered with an offer of a wage increase of 21 percent over 3 years (11 + 3 + 7). In response to the growers offer, the union called strikes in mid-January 1979, and the UFW as well as employers placed ads in Mexicali newspapers (most workers lived in Mexico and commuted daily to U.S. farm jobs) explaining the demands and offers.

The strike, which involved some forty-three hundred workers for three months, affected some of the largest U.S. vegetable growers, such as Bruce Church and Sun Harvest, a subsidiary of United Brands (Chiquita bananas). To get around the strike, these growers hired replacement workers. Cesar Chavez complained that many of these replacement workers were unauthorized Mexicans: "Employers go to Mexico and have unlimited, unrestricted use of illegal alien strikebreakers to break the strike" (U.S. Senate, 1979, 5). There were daily battles on the picket lines, and a UFW striker was killed. The strike as well as disease reduced the supply of winter lettuce by one-third but, in a surprise to the UFW, lettuce prices tripled, and winter lettuce revenues in 1979 were twice what they were in 1978 (Carter et al., 1981).[32] Many sympathetic observers questioned the UFW's demands and strategy. One article noted that "although Chavez claims the union is striking to win wage parity with industrial workers, most observers say he purposely brought on the strike in an attempt to rally the union" (*Business Week,* March 5, 1979).

The UFW strike was losing momentum by the summer of 1979, when Salinas Valley's Meyer Tomato on August 12, 1979, agreed to raise wages

43 percent over three years, to $5.29 by 1982. Lettuce grower West Coast Farms agreed to raise wages to $5.71 in 1982 (the federal minimum wage was $3.35 in 1982), and the wage leader, Sun-Harvest, agreed to a $5.25 minimum wage, plus a doubling of the employers' pension contribution to $0.38 per hour. Newspapers hailed the "record contracts" won by the UFW for farm workers. Back in the Imperial Valley, the UFW charged that the lettuce growers in February 1979 did not bargain in good faith when they broke off negotiations, raised wages, and began to hire replacement workers. The ALRB agreed with the UFW, and in a 3-1 decision, the ALRB ordered the Imperial Valley growers to pay tens of millions of dollars to farm workers, including those who went on strike.[33]

"Record contracts" for farm workers seemed to prove the predictions that unions could dramatically raise wages and transform the farm labor market. However, Sun Harvest and several of the other conglomerate growers that were most vulnerable to consumer boycotts of their nonfarm products went out of business, reducing the power of the UFW's favorite weapon.[34] Second, the UFW became more distant from field workers. In 1971 it had moved its headquarters from Delano to a former sanitarium southeast of Bakersfield named La Paz,[35] and in the early 1980s UFW leaders spent more time there than in the fields. Some farm workers were not satisfied with Chavez's leadership, and nine elected union representatives led a walkout at the UFW's September 1981 constitutional convention to protest the slowness of payments from the UFW's medical plan.[36] When Chavez rejected advice to have a paid and professional staff, many non-Hispanics left or were pushed out of the UFW.

Third, the UFW seemed to squander its significant political action committee (PAC) funds—the UFW's PAC contributions to statewide candidates in 1982 were second only to the doctors' PAC—as the UFW got deeply embroiled in legislative leadership struggles and supported losing candidates. In 1982, over the bitter opposition of the UFW, Republican George Deukmejian was elected governor, and he appointed ex-Republican legislator David Stirling to be the ALRB's general counsel, the gatekeeper office that receives, investigates, and decides whether ULPs were committed.[37] As Deukmejian changed the leadership of the ALRB, the UFW argued that the agency was transformed into an arm of the growers to hurt rather than help farm workers and sought to have the ALRB defunded. The ALRB can award makewhole wages to workers if an employer refuses to bargain in good faith with the union. The UFW complained that Stirling reduced by 90 percent the makewhole award that his Democratic-appointed predecesor recommended for one group farm workers, and traveled to the settlement hearing in the employer's plane (cited in Fogel, 1985, 135–36).

Fourth, the UFW suffered major reversals in the California courts.[38] The ALRB decision ordering Imperial Valley growers to pay tens of millions of dollars in makewhole wages for refusing to bargain in good faith in 1979 was overturned: a California Court of Appeals in 1984 concluded that the growers were engaged in lawful hard bargaining, not unlawful bad-faith bargaining. The UFW position was further weakened by another Court of Appeals decision in 1987 in which the court ruled that, even if employers do bargain in bad faith, if they can show that even good faith bargaining would not have led to higher wages they cannot be ordered to pay makewhole wages.

One lettuce grower proved to be particularly troublesome. The UFW was certified as bargaining agent for Bruce Church (later BCI) farm workers in 1977. In January 1979, BCI was one of the Imperial Valley growers against whom the UFW called a strike, and the UFW urged consumers to boycott Lucky (now Albertson's) grocery stores and McDonald's restaurants because they bought BCI lettuce. BCI, which grew about 60 percent of its lettuce in California and 40 percent in Arizona, sued the UFW in Arizona for engaging in illegal secondary boycott activities—secondary boycotts are lawful under the ALRA in California, but unlawful under Arizona farm labor law. BCI twice won multimillion dollar judgments against the UFW, but they were reversed on appeal. Even though the UFW ultimately did not have to pay any money to BCI, the suits occupied much of the time of union leaders; Chavez was in Arizona to testify in a BCI suit when he died in 1993.

1984–1993: Wrath of Grapes

UFW membership fell from thirty thousand in the early 1980s to six thousand in 1984–85, and the media, which had been very supportive of Chavez and the farm workers, began to carry critical articles.[39] A typical article opened with the plight of the farm worker, an acknowledgment of the accomplishments of the UFW to get the ALRA and other legislation, and then recited the UFW's failures, including its controversial forays into legislative politics, Chavez's placement of relatives in UFW leadership positions, and his embrace of controversial movements such as Synanon. Chavez rejected the advice of friendly union leaders to hire professional lawyers and organizers and relied instead on volunteers. Thus, one reporter described the UFW as "not primarily a farm worker organization. It was a fund-raising operation, run . . . far from the fields of famous Delano, staffed by members of Cesar's extended family and using as its political capital Cesar's legend and the warm memories of aging boycotters" (Bardake, 1993, F1).

To regain its old momentum, Chavez on July 12, 1984, launched a Wrath-of-Grapes boycott in an attempt to pressure grape growers to stop using what it called five dangerous pesticides.[40] The UFW said it was returning to its 1960s tactic because the ALRB was not protecting farm workers. Chavez complained that "in four years we have won elections covering 18,000 farm workers and we haven't got one damn contract to show for it" (*BNA Daily Labor Report*, June 18, 1985).[41] Chavez said he hoped to "once again bring together liberals, church groups, workers, and others to support us until the full meaning of the California labor law is restored and provides protections workers must have." However, instead of noisy pickets in front of grocery stores, the UFW under Wrath of Grapes sent 20 million to 30 million letters to consumers in zip codes believed to include UFW sympathizers, asking them to boycott stores that sold grapes. The UFW's hoped that 5 to 10 percent of a store's customers would boycott, and that the low profit margins of grocery stores would get them involved on the side of the UFW, as they pressured grape growers to deal with the UFW.

During the summer of 1988, Chavez called attention to the Wrath-of-Grapes boycott with a thirty-six-day "fast for life," and sympathetic religious, union, and political allies agreed to "pass the boycott cross" from one to another to maintain publicity. However, table grape consumption rose, to over 7 pounds in 1992–93, up from 6 pounds in 1984–85.[42] Some cities and counties passed resolutions that prohibited the use of public funds to buy California table grapes for schools, jails, and other facilities, but even sympathetic observers urged the UFW to redirect its energies from the grape boycott and return to organizing farm workers in the fields.[43] The UFW, it was alleged in a major series of newspaper articles entitled "Fields of Pain" and "Fields of Betrayal?" went into the fields only to block other unions seeking to represent farm workers, preserving its monopoly in the media as the representative of farm workers (*Sacramento Bee*, December 8–11, 1991, A1 and February 23, 1992, A1).

The UFW had no table grape contracts when Cesar Chavez died on April 23, 1993. There was an outpouring of praise for Chavez, as flags flew at half staff and thirty thousand people attended a funeral procession in Delano. President Clinton, who awarded Chavez a posthumous Medal of Freedom in 1994 said:

All Americans have lost a great leader . . . An inspiring fighter for the cause to which he dedicated his life. Cesar Chavez was an authentic hero to millions of people throughout the world. We can be proud of his enormous accomplishments and in the dignity and comfort he brought to the lives of so many of our country's least powerful and most dispossessed workers. He had a profound impact upon the people of the United States.

Many of the eulogies described Chavez as a man who "epitomized the spiritual and political goals of [Latino] people" and who helped "an entire race of people find its place in America" (*Los Angeles Times*, April 24, 1993, A1). Mexican president Salinas said: "Those of us in Mexico have a great admiration for Cesar Chavez and his struggle. He was a fighter for . . . Mexican workers . . . we remember him with gratitude" (*San Diego Union-Tribune*, April 24, 1993, A1). In 1999, Chavez was inducted into the Labor Hall of Fame by the AFL-CIO, and several states, including California, made Chavez's March 31 birthday a holiday (http://www.chavezday.ca.gov/). Chavez said that he wanted to be remembered for "attack[ing] that historical source of shame and infamy that our people in this country lived with: the humiliation brought upon generations of dark-skinned farmworkers by corporate agribusiness."

After 1994: A New UFW?

Arturo Rodriguez, Chavez's son-in-law, became the new UFW president and announced that the UFW would return to its roots by resuming its organizing activities and allowing nonfarm workers to "join" the UFW for a twenty-dollar annual fee.[44] In April 1994, the UFW repeated the path of the 1966 march from Delano to Sacramento and announced that it had secured five thousand signatures from farm workers in its "Every Worker Is an Organizer" campaign (*Sacramento Bee*, August 23, 1993, B13). As the UFW requested and won elections, newspaper headlines read "The UFW Is Back" or "The New UFW."

One of the most significant UFW victories under Rodriguez was at Bear Creek Production Company (Jackson & Perkins Roses) in December 1994, involving fourteen hundred peak and four hundred year-round workers. Bear Creek is the UFW's largest contract, and the UFW sought to make the contract a model of cooperation, with workers providing suggestions to management on how to improve efficiency and reaping rewards in the form of higher wages and better benefits. Bear Creek, in turn, developed a Cesar Chavez rose, and the UFW helped to market it to Hispanics. The UFW settled its long-running dispute with lettuce grower BCI in May 1996, signing a five-year collective bargaining agreement covering 450 lettuce harvesters in a Salinas library named for Chavez. The agreement raised the wages of BCI workers to at least

$6.62 in 1996, and $7.23 in 2001, but BCI restructured during the agreement, reducing the number of covered workers.[45]

Most UFW contracts in 2000 were with producers of commodities such as flowers and mushrooms, companies that tend to hire workers for long seasons. Most mushroom workers, for example, pick mushrooms year-round under contracts that guarantee pickers seven dollars an hour and establish piece rates that enable pickers to earn eight to ten dollars an hour. The UFW struggled unsuccessfully for a contract at Pictsweet Mushrooms in Ventura, California, setting the stage for the UFW's major fight in 2002, the push for binding arbitration when a contract cannot be negotiated. The UFW won an election in 1975, but there has been no contract at Pictsweet since 1987, when the plant was sold to its current owners. The UFW began negotiations for a contract in January 2000, but was unable to reach an agreement. Workers who did not want UFW representation tried three times to have the UFW decertified, but there has been no vote because Pictsweet was found to have unlawfully supported the decertification effort.

To prevent negotiations from dragging on, as at Pictsweet, the UFW persuaded the California legislature to pass a law that would require a certified union and an employer who cannot agree on a contract within ninety days to request that the ALRB appoint an arbitrator to resolve their differences. The arbitrator's decision would be binding on the employer and the union. The UFW says binding arbitration is needed because, between 1975 and 2001, workers on 428 California farms voted in ALRB-supervised elections for UFW representation, but only 185 contracts were signed between the UFW and growers, an election-to-contract rate of 45 percent. Farm employers oppose the UFW bill, arguing that the ALRA already includes a makewhole remedy for bad-faith bargaining, and noting that binding arbitration is generally used only in disputes where workers cannot strike, as for police officers and firefighters. Mandatory mediation was approved, ad went into effect January 1, 2003.

In 1994, workers at Oceanview Produce voted to have the UFW represent them, and in 1995, strawberry pickers at VCNM Farms also voted for UFW representation. Oceanview, a Dole subsidiary, stopped growing strawberries, displacing several hundred workers, and VCNM destroyed its strawberries and went out of business. These votes convinced the UFW that the state's twenty thousand to twenty-five thousand strawberry pickers could be organized, but that high-level pressure must be brought on strawberry growers and packers. The UFW launched a "Five Cents for Fairness" campaign, calling attention to the fact that most pickers received a piece rate wage of about 5 cents a pint box, and that their wages could be doubled if consumers were willing to pay an additional 5 cents. AFL-CIO president John Sweeny agreed to support the strawberry campaign with about ninety thousand dollars a month, and the UFW soon had a hundred full-time organizers at work.

The UFW targeted the largest employer of strawberry pickers in the United States, Garguilo, a Monsanto subsidiary. With encouragement from leading Democratic politicians, Monsanto agreed to sell Garguilo to prounion investors, who renamed it Coastal Berry. Coastal paid some of the highest farm worker wages in California and offered a range of health and other benefits, but not all Coastal workers wanted to be represented by the UFW. In a surprise development, the Coastal Berry Farmworkers Committee (CBFWC), a group of Coastal workers opposed to UFW representation, won a July 1998 election by a vote of 523–410.[46]

The UFW challenged the election, and a new election was held in May 1999, which the CBFWC again won, 646–577. A third election was held in June 1999, which the committee won 688–598. The UFW asked the ALRB to create two bargaining units at Coastal Berry, one in southern California, where the UFW had won a majority, and another in the northern California, where the committee won. The ALRB agreed, and in May 2000, the CBFWC was certified to represent eight hundred Coastal Berry workers in Watsonville, and the UFW to represent seven hundred Coastal workers in Oxnard. The UFW-Coastal agreement provides for a minimum hourly wage of $6.25 in 2001 ($6.25 is California's minimum wage), $6.75 in 2002 (the minimum wage in 2002 is $6.75), and $7.00 in 2003.

Time will tell if the change of leadership at the UFW, and the election of a Democratic governor in 1998, will add members and contracts in the twenty-first century. Optimists point to 1990s UFW election victories and new contracts, as well as the prominence of UFW president Rodriguez in politics and labor circles—Rodriguez is one of forty-three AFL-CIO vice presidents. Pessimists emphasize that contractors continue to increase their share of especially the harvest labor market, and that continuing illegal immigration prevents unions from negotiating higher wages and more benefits. The UFW remains a major player in Democratic party politics in California and was very active in the campaigns against Propositions 187 (1994), 209 (1996), and 227 (1994); all were nonetheless approved by California voters.[47] Perhaps the UFW will switch to organizing nonfarm workers. The UFW changed its constitution to permit organizing nonfarm workers, and in November 2000 won its first NLRB-supervised election at furniture maker Guy Chaddock & Co in Bakersfield, California.

Union Members and Wage Trends

The ALRB has certified ten unions to represent farm workers in California agriculture since 1975. There have been over 1,600 elections supervised by the ALRB, and 775, or almost half, resulted in a union being certified to represent farm workers. Two-thirds of all California farm worker elections were held between 1975 and 1978, and a union was typically certified as the bargaining representative for farm workers in this first wave of elections. However, after 1981, there were as many elections held to decertify an existing union as to decide whether workers wanted to be represented by a union.

The UFW claims 27,000 members and fifty contracts, but reported only 5,945 members at the end of 2000 to DOL; the UFW says that the 27,000 figure reflects the total number of workers employed sometime under UFW contracts in California, Florida, and Washington during the year.[48] The UFW reported an annual income of $7.2 million in 2000, including $1.8 million or 24 percent from dues[49] and $4 million in contributions.[50] Expenditures were $6.8 million, in part because UFW officers and volunteers receive low wages; Cesar Chavez was paid less than six thousand dollars annually when he was UFW president. The UFW has a National Farm Workers Service Center (NFWSC), led by Chavez's son, that owns the six-station Radio Campesina network and builds and rehabilitates housing—the NFWSC has built six hundred single-family homes and purchased or developed twenty-six hundred rental housing units in the Central Valley.

The largest and longest continuous contract in California agriculture is that between the Teamsters Local 890 and the Bud of California subsidiary of Dole Fresh Vegetables.[51] Their 1997–2003 agreement covers thirty-five hundred lettuce and other vegetable workers in California and Arizona, and raised wages from at least $7.40 an hour in 1997 to $8.20 an hour by 2003; minimum wages under this contract were $7.25 an hour for most of the 1990s. Teamsters 890 has twelve thousand members in California and southwestern Arizona, including four thousand farm workers.[52] Much of the Teamster-UFW conflict in the 1960s and 1970s involved Teamsters Local 1973, formed in 1973 and also headquartered in Salinas.

Other farm worker unions in California include the Christian Labor Association (CLA), which has two hundred contracts that each cover the one to ten workers employed in dairies and poultry farms; the CLA had 360 dairy members and 90 poultry members in the mid-1990s. Several unions were begun by ex-UFW leaders, including the Fresh Fruit and Vegetable Workers (FFVW), affiliated with the United Food and Com-

Table 3.2. U.S. and California Farm and Manufacturing Earnings, 1962–2001

	1962	1965	1968	1971	1974	1977	1980	1983	1986	1989	1992	1995	1998	2001
U.S. Manufacturing	2.39	2.61	3.01	3.57	4.42	5.68	7.27	8.83	9.73	10.48	11.46	12.37	13.49	14.84
U.S. Farm Earnings	1.01	1.14	1.44	1.73	2.25	2.87	3.66	4.11	4.70	5.36	5.82	6.21	7.47	8.44
Ratio US Farm to Mfg	42%	44%	48%	48%	51%	51%	50%	47%	48%	51%	51%	50%	55%	57%
U.S. Minimum Wage	1.15	1.25	1.60	1.60	2.00	2.30	3.10	3.35	3.35	3.35	4.25	4.25	5.15	5.15
CA Manufacturing	2.54	3.09	3.57	4.26	4.98	6.01	7.71	9.52	10.37	11.24	12.27	12.55	13.66	14.72
CA Farm Earnings	1.27	1.42	1.67	1.97	2.78	3.53	4.51	4.85	5.64	6.39	6.43	6.63	7.71	8.67
Ratio CA Farm to Mfg	50%	46%	47%	46%	56%	59%	58%	51%	54%	57%	52%	53%	56%	59%
CA Minimum Wage	1.00	1.30	1.65	1.65	2.00	2.50	3.10	3.35	3.35	4.25	4.25	4.25	5.75	6.25
	1962	1965	1968	1971	1974	1977	1980	1983	1986	1989	1992	1995	1998	2001
Ratio U.S. Farm to Mfg	42%	44%	48%	48%	51%	51%	50%	47%	48%	51%	51%	50%	55%	57%
Ratio CA Farm to Mfg	50%	46%	47%	46%	56%	59%	58%	51%	54%	57%	52%	53%	56%	59%

Sources: Economic Report of the President, http://w3.access.gpo.gov/eo.
USDA, NASS, Farm Labor; http://usda.mannlib.cornell.edu/data-sets/inputs/91005/ and http://usda.mannlib.cornell.edu/reports/nassr/other/pfl-bb/
"Farm Earnings" are annual averages for all hired workers.

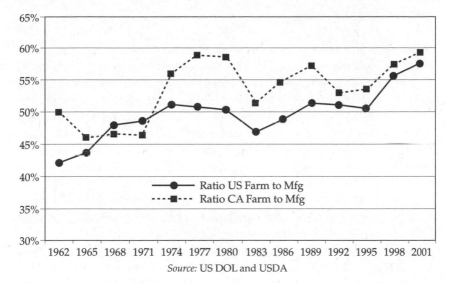

Figure 3.1. U. S. and California Farm and Manufacturing Earnings, 1962–2001

mercial Workers union.[53] Other unions are associations of farm workers that win one or two contacts, such as the civic committees formed by Mixtec and Zapotec Indians from the southern Mexican state of Oaxaca; one of these won an election in 1991 at a San Diego packinghouse.

A quarter century of union activities have not been able to close the nonfarm-farm wage gap. In California, the ratio of average farm worker earnings to manufacturing earnings climbed from 46 percent in 1965 to 59 percent in 1977, and then slipped back to 51 percent in 1983, and 52–53 percent in the early 1990s. There was a similar pattern throughout U.S. agriculture, where the ratio of farm to manufacturing wages rose from 44 percent in 1965 to 51 percent in 1974 and 1977, fell to 47–48 percent in the 1980s, and then climbed in 1998 and 2001. In the late 1970s, UFW contracts often called for minimum or entry level wages that were twice the minimum wage, but in the 1990s, several UFW contracts had minimum wages equal to California's minimum wage, and some called for entry-level wages below those negotiated in early 1980s levels, in nominal dollars. The ratio of farm to manufacturing earnings may understate the gap in the 1990s for two reasons: fewer farm than factory workers receive fringe benefits, the cost of health insurance rose sharply in the 1990s, and more farm workers were hired through contractors in the 1990s—their lower hourly earnings are not included in the farm earnings.[54]

Unions Outside California

States with large FVH sectors include Florida, Washington, North Carolina, and Michigan. The UFW also has contracts in Florida and Washington but the "bright spots" for farm worker activity are in states such as Hawaii and Ohio.[55] Five large landholding companies controlled the Hawaiian economy for most of the past two centuries, and they imported waves of immigrants to work on sugar and pineapple plantations. After the International Longshore and Warehouse Union organized dockworkers, it marched inland to organize field workers, most of whom lived in company housing on plantations.[56] After strikes in 1946 and 1947, most Hawaii field workers were represented by the ILWU. The seventy-five hundred hired farm workers in Hawaii—many of whom are Filipinos—earned an average eleven dollars an hour in 2002.

The Ohio-based Farm Labor Organizing Committee (FLOC) was founded in 1967 by Baldemar Velasquez and became a union in 1979.[57] Velasquez refined the UFW's boycott strategy: FLOC threatened consumer boycotts of the pickle and tomato products processed and sold by food companies Campbell's and Heinz unless they persuaded the farmers who grew pickles and tomatoes, and hired workers to pick them, to recognize FLOC as the farm workers' bargaining representative. In 1985, after a march from Ohio to Campbell headquarters near Philadelphia, FLOC reached three-way agreements with Campbell's Vlasic subsidiary and Vlasic's tomato and pickle growers in Ohio and Michigan.[58] Farmers who grow tomatoes and cucumbers under contract with Campbell's recognized FLOC as the union for about eight hundred farm workers, and Campbell's raised the prices it paid to farmers to cover higher wage and benefit costs.[59] Since farm workers were excluded from the NLRA, there did not need to be elections to determine worker preferences, and there were none (Edid, 1994). FLOC reached similar contracts with Heinz, Green Bay, and Aunt Jane's.

FLOC has offices in Florida, where many of the cucumber pickers live when they are not in Ohio, and in North Carolina, where FLOC has been trying to organize pickle harvesters employed by growers who deliver cucumbers to Mount Olive Pickle since 1998. Mount Olive refused to enter into three-way contracts with FLOC as Campbell's-Vlasic did, arguing that farmers are the workers' employers. FLOC claimed 4,000 members in the early 1990s, reported 5,350 members on its LM-2 reports (reports that unions must file with the U.S. Department of Labor providing information on members and union finances) in the mid-1990s, and 7,000 members in 2000.

In New Jersey, the Supreme Court found in the 1950s that the state's constitution permitted workers not covered by the NLRA to organize and bargain with employers without retaliation. New Jersey farmers have long relied on seasonal Puerto Rican workers, and these workers formed or joined organizations to protect their interests and lobbied the New Jersey legislature to raise the minimum wage for farm workers. The largest organization, CATA (Comite de Apoyo a los Trabajadores Agricolas), was founded in 1979 and had several hundred members in New Jersey and southeastern Pennsylvania in 2000, but no contracts. CATA aims to empower and educate farm workers through leadership development; CATA cofounded the Farmworker Health and Safety Institute to educate farm workers about the dangers of pesticides. In February 2000, workers at three Pennsylvania mushroom farms, under guidance from CATA, voted to have the Unión de Trabajadores Agrícolas y del Hongo (United Mushroom and Agricultural Workers Union) represent them.

Florida and Texas have both farm worker unions and self-help organizations, but few contracts (Edid, 1994). The Farmworker Association of Florida provides credit and related services for three thousand members, but has no contracts with Florida growers. The Coalition of Immokalee Workers has been trying for several years to persuade tomato growers to raise the piece rate they pay for picking thirty-five-pound buckets of mature green tomatoes between December and April. Most growers pay forty to forty-five cents a bucket; the coalition is calling for a seventy-five-cent piece rate. In 2001–2002, the coalition called for a boycott of Taco Bell, which buys tomatoes from southwest Florida growers. Taco Bell has refused to deal with the Coalition and says the dispute is between pickers and growers.

The Border Agricultural Workers Project (BAWP), based in El Paso, organized workers who pick chili peppers in southern New Mexico and persuaded one New Mexico grower to sign a one-year contract with the union to avoid a lawsuit against the grower for violating minimum wage laws (*Daily Labor Report*, November 16, 1992); this contract was not renewed. The BAWP and other farm worker assistance organizations provide temporary housing for chili pickers, who are often bussed for two or three hours each way to chili fields in New Mexico.

Arizona in 1972 enacted an Agricultural Employment Relations Act administered by a seven-member Agricultural Employment Relations Board (AERB) that includes two growers, two workers, and three public members, plus two alternates.[60] Unlike the California ALRA, the purpose of the AERA is not to bring peace and justice to the fields; it is to prevent obstacles to the free flow of agricultural products that might arise from labor strife.[61] The AELA prohibited unions from going onto farm property to organize workers and allows criminal penalties for violations. At the behest of the UFW, a three-judge federal panel in Phoenix declared the Arizona AERA unconstitutional in April 1978, but the U.S. Supreme Court reversed this decision, holding that the constitutionality of specific provisions of the AERA such as the no-secondary boycott provision must be tested on a case-by-case basis. There has been relatively little union activity in Arizona agriculture. In its most active year, 1986–87, six election petitions were submitted, and one election was held. Between 1981 and 1991, there were ninety-one ULP cases filed and eighteen complaints were issued by the AERB general counsel, who is part of the Attorney General's office (AERB, 1991, 7).

In the late 1970s and early 1980s, there was hope that Lupe Sanchez, founder of the Arizona Farm Workers Union (AFWU), would become the Cesar Chavez of Arizona. Sanchez helped some three hundred illegal alien farm workers near Phoenix to negotiate an agreement with the successor to citrus farm Goldmar (owned by the Goldwater family) in 1979. Under the agreement, twenty cents for each hour worked went into a Farmworker Economic Development Corporation fund that aimed to create jobs in Guanajuato, where most of the migrants originated. Grower Art Martori, who negotiated with the AFWU, agreed to admit the three hundred workers as legal H-2 workers, which required him to build housing for them. Sanchez was praised for drawing a salary of only $3,600 per year and for attracting $100,000 of Martori's money for investment in Mexico, plus another $1.5 million from U.S. foundations and churches. The project later fizzled, allegedly because of financial mismanagement.

In Oregon, the Northwest Treeplanters and Farm Workers United (PCUN in Spanish) began to assist farm workers in 1985, and called a strike of 120 workers against one of the largest growers in the Willamette Valley in 1991; the strike resulted in a wage increase, but no contract. PCUN had four contracts covering 50 workers in 2000, and claimed 4,500 members in Oregon, including half who reside year-round in the state. Since the early 1990s, PCUN has been boycotting cooperative NORPAC, owned by 240 farmers, that supplies fruits and vegetables to institutions such as schools. In 2002, PCUN called off the boycott after 21 NORPAC grower-members agreed to allow PCUN to organize workers on their farms. The Oregon legislature approved a farm labor relations bill in March 2002 that farmers favored but PCUN opposed because it outlawed secondary boycotts. It was vetoed by the governor, who said it deserved more scrutiny.

In Washington, the UFW fought for a state farm labor relations law modeled on the ALRA and against proposals to allow growers of cherries and other short-season crops to house seasonal workers in tents. In 1995, the UFW won an election at the state's largest winery, Chateau Ste. Michelle (a unit of UST in Connecticut), after threatening a boycott and signed an agreement covering about two hundred workers.[62] The contract raised wages 6 to 7 percent, to ten dollars an hour. In the late 1990s, the UFW cooperated with its old nemesis, the Teamsters to organize forty thousand apple harvesters (UFW) and fifteen thousand packing house workers (Teamsters). However, packinghouse workers, who are covered by the NLRA, voted against Teamster representation in 1998, and no contracts covering harvesters were signed.

In New York, a Cornell University Task Force in 1991 recommended that the state enact a law giving farm workers the right to organize and bargain with farm employers. Backed by the AFL-CIO, worker-friendly New York State legislators introduced a farm labor relations bill in 1994 (Edid, 1994). However, no bill was passed; the assembly approved a farm labor relations bill in 2000, but the senate did not act, so New York farm workers do not have collective bargaining rights.

Collective bargaining aims to enable farm workers to help themselves to increase wages and working conditions. During the twentieth century, farm worker union activities have been "much ado about nothing" because diverse farm workers often share only one goal—to find a better nonfarm job as soon as possible. Farmers have been well-organized to resist farm worker unions, and the government has often put obstacles in the way of farm worker unions. At the dawn of the twenty-first century, there is more agreement on trends affecting farm workers and the farm labor market than on what these trends mean for unions and collective bargaining. The major trends likely to influence the relative strength of unions and farm employers include the rapid growth of the Hispanic population, presumed to be sympathetic to farm worker unions and thus to increase support for boycotts; continued immigration from Mexico that will make it hard for unions to use traditional weapons such as strikes to push up wages; and changes in the food sector, such as the consolidation of grocery stores that tends to put downward pressure on farm prices. Farm worker unions believe that an amnesty for currently unauthorized farm workers would embolden them to join unions and press for wage increases. Farm employers prefer guest workers, who may be harder to organize.

The realization by farm worker unions and farm employers that their struggles are being played out on a larger stage has broadened the interest of unions in pesticides, water, and other issues. The UFW, for example, remains a major player in Democratic party politics in California and has begun to influence largely Latino lawmakers on diverse rural issues. The union has lobbied against legislation that would allow farmers to sell their water to cities, a business that benefits the farmers but reduces jobs for farm workers. Other priorities are the use of state funds to promote farm commodities and development of tighter regulations on pesticides.

Box 3.1. UFW Chronology: 1962–2002

- 1962: NFWA/UFW established by Cesar Chavez and Dolores Huerta as a farm worker assistance organization in Delano
- 1965: NFWA/UFW joins a strike called by Filipino table grape harvesters; boycotts liquor products of Schenley, which also grew grapes; FBI begins to compile what became a 1,434-page dossier on Chavez.
- 1966: Chavez leads Delano to Sacramento march; Schenley agrees to raise wages by 40 percent, from $1.25 to $1.75 an hour
- 1968: UFW informs grape growers it represents their workers and launches a consumer boycott of California table grapes, *La Causa*
- 1969: Chavez featured on the cover of *Time* magazine July 4, under the title, "The Grapes of Wrath: Mexican-Americans on the March"
- 1970: Table grape growers to recognize the UFW and 150 sign contracts covering twenty thousand workers, but most lettuce growers sign Teamster contracts.
- 1973: UFW claims 180 contracts and sixty-seven thousand members in March, which were reduced by December to 12 contracts and a handful of members
- 1975: ALRA enacted in California; UFW wins 55 percent of the first 361 elections, and the Teamsters 32 percent
- 1976: ALRB ran out of money and closes for five months; UFW's Proposition 14—to require funding for the ALRB—is not approved by voters
- 1978: California extends unemployment insurance to almost all farm workers; UFW joins suit accusing the University of California of developing labor-saving machines to displace farm workers
- 1979: UFW calls strikes in support of a demand for a 40 percent wage increase; wages rise from $3.75 to $5.25 hourly, but some firms go out of business
- 1981: UFW testifies in favor of employer sanctions to discourage illegal immigration; internal dissent leads to exit of non-Chavez relatives from UFW
- 1982–84: Republican governor elected and makes ALRB appointments; courts reverse awards of makewhole wages to workers in 1979 strikes.
- 1984: UFW launches letter-based "wrath of grapes" boycott

- 1988: Chavez fast brings publicity to the grape boycott effort
- 1993: Chavez dies on April 23; lauded by U.S. president Clinton and Mexican president Salinas
- 1994: Arturo Rodriguez, Chavez's son-in-law, named UFW president, and Rodriguez repeats the 1966 Delano to Sacramento march.
- 1995: UFW claims twenty-four thousand members; wins an election at strawberry grower VCNM, which goes out of business
- 1996: Rodriguez appointed to the forty-three-member AFL-CIO Executive Council, and UFW launches strawberry organizing campaign. UFW claims twenty-six thousand members and settles dispute with vegetable grower Bruce Church, Inc that began in 1978
- 1997–2000: Strawberry campaign attracts national interest and support, and the UFW sends 150 organizers into the fields. Local Coastal Berry Farmworkers Committee (CBFWC) wins July 1998, May 1999, and June 1999 elections at Coastal Berry; CBFWC represents workers in northern California, UFW in southern California; UFW wins its first NLRB supervised election in November 2000.
- 2001–02: UFW boycotts Pictsweet Mushrooms, where there has been no contract since 1987; ALRA is amended to provide for mandatory mediation if employer and union cannot negotiate agreements.

Source: Rural Migration News, http://migration.ucdavis.edu

II UNIONS AND COLLECTIVE BARGAINING

The people of the state of California seek to ensure peace in the
agricultural fields by guaranteeing justice for all agricultural workers and
stability in labor relations."
                        California Agricultural Labor Relations Board, 1978

Industrialization moved workers from farms to factories, where conflict
and cooperation defined labor relations. Employers and workers rarely
agreed on a fair wage or effort, and Congress and state legislatures enacted labor relations laws to channel inevitable conflicts over fair wages
and adequate effort into contracts that could facilitate the labor-management cooperation on which profits and wages depend. Labor relations laws grant workers the right to organize themselves into unions
and establish rules under which unions and employers negotiate agreements that determine wages for two or three years. The collective bargaining process has been likened to playing sports, with labor law
analogous to rules of the game and the government agency that administers the law analogous to umpires or referees. Each team's abilities
are analogous to the bargaining strength of the employer and the union.

Farm workers were excluded from 1930s federal labor laws because
it was assumed that most farm workers were hired hands on family
farms who were not interested in labor laws meant to protect factory
workers. Since then, the federal government has included farm workers
under most basic labor laws, such as social security, but often at different levels than nonfarm workers, as with minimum wage and unem-

ployment insurance laws. States may extend full labor law protections to farm workers and California pioneered the extension of many labor laws to farm workers. A major extension came in 1975, with the enactment of the Agricultural Labor Relations Act (ALRA), which granted California farm workers the right to form or join unions and defined employer and union interference with these worker rights as unfair labor practices (ULPs).

In this part of the book, I explain how the state of California's implemented the ALRA. In chapter 4, I explain the structure and operation of the Agricultural Labor Relations Board (ALRB), the state agency that administers the ALRA, and review election procedures that determine whether workers want to be represented by a union. In chapter 5, I examine the unfair labor practices of employers and unions that interfere with the worker rights granted by the ALRA. In chapter 6, I analyze the most visible aspect of union activities—strikes and boycotts called to put pressure on employers to agree to the union's demands—and the remedies for violations of the ALRA.

4

The ALRA, ALRB, and Elections

It is hereby stated to be the policy of the State of California to encourage and protect the right of agricultural employees . . . to negotiate the terms and conditions of their employment.

California Labor Code 1140.2

The ALRA grants four major rights to workers: "Employees shall have the right to self-organization, to form, join or assist labor organizations, to bargain collectively through representatives of their own choosing, and to engage in other concerted activities for the purpose of collective bargaining or other mutual aid or protection, and shall also have the right to refrain from any or all such activities" (ALRA Section 1152). The ALRA prohibits employers and unions from interfering with these four worker rights and establishes the ALRB to supervise elections and to remedy ULPs, charges that there has been interference with worker rights.[1]

Like the National Labor Relations Board (NLRB), the federal agency on which it was modeled, the ALRB is an agency with two distinct parts: a general counsel (GC) and a five-member board. The GC acts as a prosecutor, receiving written charges that the ALRA has been violated, investigating them, and issuing a formal legal complaint if it appears that there was a violation of worker rights. The GC complaint spells out what happened (e.g., employer Brown fired union activist Jose) and which section of the ALRA was violated by this action (ALRA Section 1153c makes it unlawful to discriminate against a worker for engaging in union activities), and then the GC becomes the lawyer for the party that filed the charge in a hearing before the judicial or board side of the ALRB. An employee of the board, an administrative law judge (ALJ), travels to the area where the alleged violation occurred and hears testimony from workers, union representatives, and employers about the incident. During this hearing, the charging party or plaintiff is represented by the GC, and the respondent or defendant by his own attorney. The ALJ writes a four-part decision that summarizes what happened (the facts), the law or that section of the ALRA that deals with such situations, an application of the law to the facts in this situation, and orders a remedy, such as an order to dismiss the charge or an order to the employer to reinstate a fired worker with back pay. ALJ decisions may be appealed to the five-member board in Sacramento, and then to the California courts. The ALRB is required to follow NLRB decisions "where applicable." The ALRA and the NLRA differ "in 11 major areas" (Eagle, 1998), but four are most contentious: access to employees and elections, secondary activities, remedies, and decertification.

Elections and ULPs

Unions can be recognized as bargaining representatives for workers only after they are certified by the ALRB as the bargaining agent for workers on a farm, which can occur only if they win an ALRB-supervised secret ballot election. After certification, the employer must bargain with the union in good faith to reach agreement on all matters pertaining to wages, benefits, and working conditions—the parties do not have to agree, but they must bargain with the intent to reach agreement. Thus, unions set the collective bargaining process in motion by asking the ALRB to supervise an election. Between 1975 and 2001, the ALRB has supervised elections on 1,250 California farms, and unions were certified as bargaining representatives in 1,000, or 84 percent, of these elections (ALRB, Annual Reports). More than 130,000 votes were cast in these elections, but the number of farm workers affected by union votes is far larger because elections can be held when 50 percent of a farm's peak work force is employed and some eligible workers do not vote.[2]

The ALRB certifies the results of each election after resolving any election objections filed by unions, employers, or workers and then determining which union, if any, won the vote. Some elections are set aside or not certified—objections are raised to about half of the ALRB-supervised elections. Table 4.1 shows that two-thirds of the elections were held in the first five years the ALRA was in effect, between 1975 and 1979. During the first few months after the ALRA went into effect, the ALRB was deluged with petitions from unions to hold elections—there were 544 petitions for elections between September and December 1975,

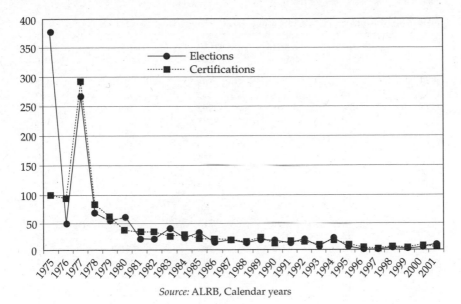

Source: ALRB, Calendar years

Figure 4.1. ALRB Elections and Union Certifications, 1975–2001

or about 34 a week, and the ALRB held 24 elections a week (Segur and Fuller, 1976, 26–27).[3] After elections had been held on most of the farms that were involved in pre-ALRA union activities, the number of elections fell to 125 in the first half of the 1980s, an average of 25 a year, and then fell even further to 116 in the late 1980s, to 23 a year. Election activity almost ground to a halt in the 1990s. There were only 21 elections held in the late 1990s, less than were held during a typical week in fall 1975. During the 1990s, many of the elections that were held were requested by workers seeking to decertify the union that represented them.

If workers, unions, or employers believe that the ALRA has been violated, they file unfair labor practice charges with a local office of the ALRB and, if the regional director/general counsel believes there was a violation, a complaint is issued. Between 1975 and 2001, some 14,500 charges were filed with the ALRB, and 4,000, or 28 percent, have gone to complaint—many charges are withdrawn or dismissed, and others are consolidated for the complaint hearing before an ALJ.[4] Charges and complaints have been more spread out than elections, but it is perhaps noteworthy that half of the charges, and 60 percent of the charges that went to complaint, occurred when the ALRB was led by persons appointed by Democratic governor Jerry Brown. During the next fifteen years, when ALRB leaders were appointed by Republican governors,

Table 4.1. ALRB Elections, Certifications, ULP Charges, Board Decisions 1975–2001

	Elections Held	Certifi- cations	ULP Charges	ULP Complaints	Board Decisions
1975	379	100	503	181	27
1976	48	96	447	107	63
1977	270	295	992	506	94
1978	70	84	521	281	108
1979	57	61	1,280	458	73
1980	61	39	900	338	64
1981	26	38	780	350	49
1982	28	37	933	255	105
1983	43	31	1,025	166	76
1984	28	32	569	147	52
1985	33	25	658	101	39
1986	19	24	315	52	32
1987	23	22	275	53	27
1988	18	18	199	38	20
1989	23	26	282	34	21
1990	20	16	403	130	19
1991	17	20	324	38	21
1992	20	17	334	75	16
1993	7	11	207	56	20
1994	22	17	429	88	20
1995	8	11	230	37	14
1996	3	4	441	59	15
1997	1	1	175	33	10
1998	5	3	308	31	7
1999	4	2	298	17	7
2000	7	9	588	153	5
2001	7	5	1,114	276	5
July-02					6
Total	1,247	1,044 84%	14,530	4,060 28%	1,009

Source: ALRB, data are for calendar years

5-year period data					
1975–79	824	636	3,743	1,533	365
1980–84	125	138	3,307	918	282
1985–89	116	115	1,729	278	139
1990–94	86	81	1,697	387	96
1995–99	21	21	1,452	177	53
2000–01	14	14	1,702	429	10

Percent by 5-year period					
1975–79	66%	61%	26%	38%	36%
1980–84	10%	13%	23%	23%	28%
1985–89	9%	11%	12%	7%	14%
1990–94	7%	8%	12%	10%	10%
1995–99	2%	2%	10%	4%	5%
2000–01	1%	1%	12%	11%	1%

the agency received a third of the total charges and issued a fifth of the complaints. There was a sharp increase in charges and complaints in 2000–01. Between 1975 and 2001, the board issued about 1,000 decisions, but these involved only four hundred farms—more than twenty ALRB decisions concerned one farm alone. Many of the complaints that turn into ALJ decisions are appealed to the board, and the pattern of board decisions tracks the pattern of complaints, with a noticeable lag.

Access, Elections, and Successorship

Unions must organize workers, win elections, and be certified as the bargaining representative for workers before they can bargain with the employer, and unions have an incentive to complete this process as soon as possible, since they collect dues of 2 or 3 percent of worker pay only after a contract is signed. The ALRA regulates labor relations in one industry in one state and was enacted to resolve a decade of conflict between parties who did not trust each other, so the ALRA lays out election procedures in considerable detail. In the nonfarm sector, by contrast, the NLRB has flexibility to determine if workers want to be represented by a union. There are five major differences between farm and nonfarm election procedures (see table 4.2):

- Farm worker unions can request an election only after they obtain authorization cards from a majority of currently employed workers, and an election can be held only if employment is at least 50 percent of peak (50–50 rule); the NLRA requires a 30 percent showing of interest among workers, and has no peak employment requirement.
- Farm worker unions can be certified to represent workers only after winning a majority vote in an ALRB-supervised secret-ballot election; a farm employer may not voluntarily recognize the union.[5]
- Once a union submits a valid petition requesting an election, the ALRB must act quickly, holding an election within seven days (or two days if a strike is in progress); disputes are resolved after the election, when migrants may have moved on. The NLRB, by contrast, has no fixed time table between petition and election, although most nonfarm elections are held within thirty days.
- Unions seek to represent workers who share a "community of interest." All of the farm workers on a farm are normally in one wall-to-wall bargaining unit, while the NLRB has discretion to permit one or several bargaining units, especially if the employer has several operations.
- To vote in an ALRB-supervised election, workers must be on the payroll during the payroll period before the union files its election

Table 4.2. ALRB and NLRB Election Procedures

Procedure	ALRB	NLRB
Petition may be filled by:	Employee Group of employees Labor organization	Employee Group of employees Labor organization Employer
Showing of interest required (for petitioner):	50 percent	30 percent
Time allotted for investigation of petition:	7 days	Unlimited, generally within 30 days.
Hearing on election issues:	Postelection	Preelection and postelection.
Who can collectively bargain with employer:	Labor organization certified after a secret ballot election.	Labor organization can be (1) certified after a secret ballot election or (2) recognized as bargaining agent by employer without an election.
Bargaining unit:	All agricultural employees; workers employed on several farms generally in same unit.	NLRB determines appropriate unit; can be employer unit, craft unit, plant unit, or a subdivision.
Contract bar:	Up to 3 years, except that a petition for election can be filed during the last year of a contract.	Up to 3 years except that a petition for an election can be filed not more than 90 days but at least 60 days before the contract expires.
Holding an election:	By board order only.	By board order or by agreement between the parties.
Eligibility period for voting:	Pay period preceding filing of the petition.	Voters must be employed during eligibility period set by the Board and on the date of the election.

petition, but they do not have to be employed on election day to vote. In an NLRB-election, workers must be on the payroll when the union files its petition and on election day.

Most of these differences reflect "unique agricultural circumstances." Farmers who spent decades arguing that agriculture was different, and thus needed exemptions from labor and immigration laws, found it hard to argue against ALRA provisions and ALRB regulations designed to deal with the unique features of agriculture (Hayes, 1984). For example, to avoid having year-round mechanics and seasonal workers in different bargaining units, the ALRA generally requires all employees on a farm to be in one wall-to-wall bargaining unit. This avoids separate units of white mechanics and Hispanic field workers and requires that the union, not the employer, must balance the desires of year-round workers for better pension benefits against seasonal worker demands for higher piece-rate wages (Grodin, 1976). The 50–50 rule prevents the election from being held when only year-round workers are employed.

Resolving election-related disputes after the election means that, if a union asks for an election, asserts that employment is at least 50 percent of peak, and the union assertion appears to be true (e.g., the union files the petition in September), the ALRB will normally hold the election—even if the employer objects that employment is not 50 percent of peak—so that seasonal workers can vote before their jobs end. After the election, the employer may file a technical objection and present evidence to convince the ALRB that employment was not 50 percent of peak. The ALRB must then resolve the peak employment issue before it certifies the election results.

Access: From Organizing to Elections

Unions initiate most organizing campaigns, but often in response to employer actions, which explains the adage: "employers organize their workers into unions" when they fail to deal with employee dissatisfaction. Workers turn to unions for many reasons, including favoritism in hiring or work assignments, substandard wages or benefits, or when an employer is nonresponsive to worker concerns. In most instances, union organizing begins with a handful of aggrieved workers who voice their complaints to other employees. If they find dissatisfaction among fellow employees, they may contact the union, and are more likely to do so if the union has organizers who regularly visit workers. When a union formally attempts to organize workers, it leaves a paper trail at the ALRB. Farm worker unions file a notice of intent to obtain access (NA) with the employer and the ALRB so that nonemployee union organizers have the right to come onto the farm and talk to workers about the benefits of the union.

A major issue in California agriculture is the right of union organizers to go onto farms and talk to workers—should union organizers have the right to enter farmers' private property to talk to workers? Nonfarm employers persuaded the U.S. Supreme Court during the 1940s that union organizers should not be allowed to enter their private property to organize workers, with the caveat that (1) employers may not restrict the right of employees to organize fellow employees and (2) union organizers must be permitted to talk to workers on employer property if the union has no reasonable alternative means of communicating with workers. Nonfarm unions petition the NLRB to get access to workers on employer property, such as to visit workers on ships, isolated resort hotels, and logging camps.[6]

The ALRB in one of its first regulations presumed that farm worker unions would ask for access to workers on farms and, given the "realities of the farm labor market," the ALRB would normally grant them access. The ALRB's access rule gives union organizers automatic but limited access to workers on farms because many farm workers live and work on employer property; farm workers who live off the farm enter and leave a farm at different points, so that there is no single public place for organizers to talk to workers; and farm worker characteristics, such as little education and lack of English, limit the ability of organizers to effectively communicate with them through printed literature, radio, or other media. After much litigation, the ALRB access rule was upheld by the California and U.S. Supreme Courts.[7]

The access rule limits union organizers by number, time, and manner: two organizers may take access to the first thirty workers on a farm, and there can be one additional organizer for each additional fifteen workers; union organizers can have access for up to three hours per day—one hour before work, one hour during lunch, and one hour after work. While taking access to workers, union organizers may not disrupt agricultural operations or abuse their access privileges by, for example, remaining too long or talking to workers who are working. Union organizers are entitled to access for up to four thirty-day periods per year if there are no bars to access. As soon as the union has obtained authorization signatures from at least 10 percent of the employees in the bargaining unit, the union may file a Notice of Intent to Organize (NO) with the ALRB, and then the employer must provide the ALRB with a complete list of worker names, street addresses, and job classifications within five days. The ALRB gives this employee list to the union, so that organizers can visit workers at their homes.

Access disputes are resolved in three types of cases: election objections, unfair labor practices, and motions to deny access. A union or employer can object to an election outcome when an employer or union violates the access rule, such as an employer denying access to union organizers; the ALRB can set aside elections in such cases. The ALRB can order an employer to cease and desist from denying union organizers access to workers, and the ALRB can deny access to a union organizer who abuses access privileges. Employers who deny access to union organizers may prevent a free election and commit unfair labor practices. In Western Tomato Growers & Shippers, Inc, Ernest Perry, a labor camp operator, organized a *posse comitatus*[8] of ten to twenty men to keep union organizers from taking access to tomato pickers.[9] The posse brandished guns to deter union organizers from entering fields to talk to pickers and assaulted a union organizer next to a field, so that pickers witnessed the assault. The UFW filed a ULP charge, and the ALRB found that Perry's conduct denied union organizers the access to which they were entitled, and reasoned that, since workers saw Perry assaulting union organizers, the assault might have encouraged them to refrain from union activities to avoid similar treatment at the hands of Perry and the posse. Perry denied the union organizers access in September 1975, and the ALRB in 1977 ordered Perry to give the UFW unlimited access to tomato pickers for the rest of 1977.[10]

Some farmers house workers in labor camps on their farms. The ALRB originally ruled that union organizers must have full access to workers in employer-owned labor camps, that is, the number, time, and manner restrictions on access did not apply to labor camps. After 350 union sympathizers came at night to the Sam Andrews Lakeview labor camp that housed 240 workers during a summer 1981 melon strike, honking their car horns and flashing lights, Andrews banned UFW organizers from his labor camps. The UFW filed charges against Andrews, and the ALRB agreed that Andrew's limits on organizer access to its camps were unlawful. The ALRB ordered Andrews, a cotton and vegetable farmer, to pay the UFW attorneys' fees and to give UFW organizers one hour of extra access. The California Supreme Court, in a 5–2 decision in 1988, reversed the ALRB and held that growers can establish reasonable access to on-farm labor camps, so that "employees residing in the communal bedroom [do] not to suffer visits by unrestricted numbers of union representatives at any and all hours of the day and night and [so that the grower can] insure peace and quiet for the employees during normal sleeping hours."[11] If a union complains, the ALRB can review the growers' rules.[12]

What happens when union organizers abuse access privileges by staying more than one hour or disrupting farming operations? In Ranch No. 1, Inc., the ALRB concluded that a UFW organizer intentionally disregarded the access rule when he remained in a field one and one-half to two hours and talked to workers on break as well as those who continued to harvest onions, thus disrupting agricultural operations.[13]

Ranch No. 1, an onion and grape operation, was harvesting onions for piece rate wages in August 1977; the usual work day was 5:30 a.m. to 1:30 p.m., although there was no standard lunch hour. A UFW organizer stayed in the onion fields and defended his actions by saying that there was no established lunch hour for onion workers. The ALRB certified the UFW as the bargaining representative for Ranch No. 1 workers despite employer objections, but the organizer who abused access was banned from taking access in the Fresno area for sixty days.

The access rule remains the ALRB's most controversial regulation. In 1996, the chair of the board attempted to revise the access rules, and the ALRB held several hearings, during which growers advocated a change to the NLRB's practice of requiring unions to prove, on a case-by-case basis, that they needed to get access to workers in the workplace. However, the board in May 1998 decided not to change the access rule. The access debate illustrates how farm employers would like to be treated as nonfarm employers in some situations, such as access, but in others, such as for immigration or overtime laws, farmers argue that agriculture is unique.

Technical Objections to an Election

Unions set the ALRB's election machinery into motion by filing an election petition with the ALRB that asserts that the farm named in the petition is the appropriate bargaining unit; current employment satisfies the 50–50 rule; and there is no election bar, such as another union certified to represent workers or a valid election held during the previous twelve months. The union petition must be signed by a majority of the workers on the employer's payroll or be accompanied by copies of union authorization cards from a majority of the current employees. The ALRB's regional director checks the union petition and schedules an election within two (if there is a strike) or seven days. Workers line up to vote; their names are checked off at a table outside the voting booth staffed by the ALRB, representatives of the employer, and the union(s); and ballots are normally counted as soon as the election is over. If no choice gets a majority vote, there a run-off election between the two top-vote getters within seven days.

After an election is held, the employer or union may file written objections, asking the ALRB to set aside the election or pretend it never happened. There are two major types of election objections:

- technical objections, as when the employer asserts that the union named the wrong bargaining unit in its petition; these are normally

filed by employers, since unions assert that the election satisfies ALRB regulations in their petitions.
- improper preelection conduct objections, which assert that workers were prevented by employers or unions from exercising their free choice; these are most often filed by unions

There are four major technical objections after ALRB-supervised elections. They deal with: (1) who is the employer; (2) was employment at least 50 percent of peak when the election was held; (3) what is the appropriate bargaining unit; and (4) exactly who is eligible to vote. In the 1990s, a fifth objection involving the definition of agriculture—is the employer a farmer—has arisen.

Who Is the Employer?

The ALRA's defines an agricultural employer as "any person acting directly or indirectly in the interest of an employer in relation to an agricultural employee" (Section 1140.4), including land owners, farm operators, custom harvesters, and farm management companies. The major exclusion is farm labor contractors (FLCs),[14] who were excluded at the behest of the UFW, which argued that unions could not establish stable bargaining relationships with contractors because farmers set wages and working conditions for workers that contractors bring to farms.[15] This means that a contractor's crew of thirty or forty workers might be employees of ten different farm operators during one season and could potentially vote in ten union elections—one on each farm where the crew worked. However, contractors who bring workers to farms, and also bring equipment and make managerial decisions on how and where to pick, can be considered custom harvesters and thus employers under the ALRA.

Suppose a union petitions for an election when there is a contractor crew and workers who were hired directly by the farm operator on the farm. After an election, an employer may raise a technical objection, arguing that the contractor crew should not have voted, since they were employed by a custom harvester, that is, the employer is arguing there should be two bargaining units and two elections. In Kotchevar Brothers,[16] the UFW won the October 7, 1975, election among thirty-nine workers hired directly by Kotchevar, but Kotchevar objected, arguing that the employees of grape harvester Walker who were due to arrive in mid-October should have been included in the bargaining unit. The question was whether Walker was a contractor or a custom harvester. Walker provided harvest labor and harvesting equipment, and decided where and how to harvest Kotchevar's wine grapes. Kotchevar hired one year-round worker and thirty to sixty seasonal workers to prune in

December–January, and a crew of thirty-nine seasonal workers in September 1975 to harvest table grapes. Thus peak employment numbered sixty among directly hired workers during the winter pruning season, and permitted an election when thirty or more workers were employed, in other words, in December–January and August–September. The wine grape harvest involved an additional sixty to eighty workers brought to the farm by Walker, bringing total employment to more than one hundred. The ALRB dismissed Kotchevar's objections and concluded that Walker was a custom harvester whose workers should be in a separate bargaining unit—Walker brought workers and equipment to the Kotchevar ranch and made decisions about where and how to harvest independently.

The ALRB looks at several factors to decide whether an intermediary who brings workers to a farm is a contractor or a custom harvester.[17] In the citrus industry, many contractors became custom harvesters by buying forklifts and trucks and thus supplying both harvest workers and equipment to pick and transport oranges, lemons, and avocados to packing houses, and making harvesting decisions in consultation with the packing house rather than the farm operator.

Is Employment 50 Percent of Peak?

In California agriculture, employment peaks in September and reaches a low in January. Since all workers on a farm are normally in one wall-to-wall bargaining unit, when an election is held determines who votes. The ALRA permits elections to be held only when the number of workers on an employer's payroll is at least 50 percent of the farm's peak employment for the current calendar year, which limits elections to three to six months on many crop farms.[18] On a dairy or livestock operation, the ALRB simply checks the current payroll (say, 100 employees) against the peak payroll (say, 120) to ensure that the 50 percent rule is satisfied. Seasonality introduces complexity. If there are ten year-round workers, thirty seasonal workers in July, and ten seasonal workers in August, then an election can be held only in July and August, when employment is twenty or more (twenty is 50 percent of July's peak employment of forty).

What if there is high worker turnover—should workers or job slots be used to determine peak employment?[19] Suppose the employer has sixty names on the payroll, but there were never more than thirty workers employed on any one day because of high worker turnover. The ALRB concluded that average employment—job slots—should determine peak employment in high turnover situations. The UFW petitioned for an election at Saikhon on November 17, 1975, when there were 120 workers employed, but Saikhon said peak employment was 360.[20] The ALRB resolved the issue by counting job slots in the payroll period before the union's election petition is filed. For example, suppose 283 employees were at work on Monday, 185 on Tuesday, 189 on Wednesday, 168 on Thursday, 151 on Friday, and 74 on Saturday—this means there were 1,050 man-days worked during the week (this was one week of employment in Gallo's Sonoma vineyards in September 1993). Average daily employment is 175 (from 1,050 divided by 6 days), and a union could petition for an election when there were at least 88 workers employed, that is, one-half of 175.

The Appropriate Bargaining Unit

A third technical objection is that the union wants to represent the wrong bargaining unit, meaning that it is improperly including or excluding workers who have a "community of interest." The ALRB generally requires wall-to-wall bargaining units to avoid fragmentation of bargaining units by ethnicity (white year-round workers in one union and Hispanic field workers in another) and to ensure that most farm employers normally deal with only one farm worker union.[21]

The ALRB creates separate bargaining units only if a farm has two or more noncontiguous operations. If an employer with two separate farms objects to the election, that is, asks that the employees on physically separate farms be in different units, the ALRB looks at the management structure, the extent of common supervisory practices such as work rules and employee handbooks, and any bargaining history to determine whether to have one or two bargaining units (the employer in such situations, knowing the outcome of the vote on the separate farms, may want to have a union at only one farm).[22] In Holtville Farms, Inc., the ALRB found that common ownership, joint financial management, shared facilities, and centralized control of labor relations made two farms owned by one family a single employer.[23]

Even when no workers are exchanged between farms, because of fears that exchanging workers may spread disease, the ALRB found that two poultry farms ninety miles apart were one bargaining unit because they shared centralized management and similar personnel policies. In Prohoroff Poultry Farms,[24] an election was held March 11, 1983, on two poultry farms in San Diego County, with the UFW winning at the main farm 68–5, and losing at the second farm 2–14. The main ranch in San Marcos produced eggs, and the second ranch in Potrero grew chicks until they were ready to be transported to the main ranch for egg production.[25] Employees did not move between ranches to prevent the spread of disease, but the board found that a single bargaining unit was appropriate because the entire business was operated from the main ranch, the employees at the two farms received the same fringe benefits, no union had won during a previous election, and the employer did not object.[26]

In 2000, the ALRB board said there was no "legislative preference for comprehensive bargaining units" when it decided that Coastal Berry's Watsonville and Oxnard operations should be separate bargaining units (see chapter 3).[27] The UFW lost three elections at the 1,500 employee Coastal Berry (formerly Gargiulo) in 1998–99, including the last election in June 1999. However, Coastal had physically separate operations in northern and southern California, and the ballots were counted separately. The board agreed with the UFW that there should be separate bargaining units, concluding that the ALRA provided discretion to fashion appropriate bargaining units when farms were physically separate. This decision paved the way for the Coastal Berry Farm Worker Committee to be certified to represent eight hundred Coastal Berry workers in Watsonville, and the UFW to represent seven hundred Coastal Berry workers in Oxnard.

Who Can Vote?

The fourth technical objection concerns who can vote. The ALRA stipulates that all agricultural employees who worked during the payroll period preceding the filing of the election petition are eligible to vote, including employees on strike, paid sick leave, and on paid vacation. There are no age or legal requirements that must be satisfied to vote in ALRB elections. If the employer violates labor laws by employing children, or violates immigration laws by employing illegal aliens, these workers can vote in ALRB elections. In most elections, three weeks are involved in determining voting eligibility, since most payrolls are weekly. Week 1 is the prepetition payroll period—persons on this payroll list are eligible to vote. The union files the election petition with the ALRB during week 2, and the election is held seven days later during week 3. This means that some workers who are no longer working on the farm when the election is held can vote, because they were employed two weeks ago, while some workers who are employed on election day cannot vote, because they were hired within the past two weeks.

Supervisory and managerial employees, guards, and close family relatives of the employer are not eligible to vote. Some farms also have nonfarm subsidiaries, such as a commercial packing shed or transportation company, and the nonfarm employees employed by a farm's nonfarm subsidiaries cannot vote in ALRA elections. More complex are cases of "mixed work"—persons employed in both the farm and non-farm operations of an employer. The ALRB has ruled that if packing shed workers also regularly do farm work, they must be considered "farm workers,"[28] but clerical employees are farm workers only if the "bulk" of their work involves the farm operation.[29]

The issue of mixed-work employees has led to a new technical objection—employers asserting that their workers are nonfarm workers, and thus not covered by the ALRA. The NLRA excludes "any individual employed as an agricultural laborer." Agriculture, in turn, has a primary and a secondary definition:

[Primary] farming in all its branches . . . [including] the cultivation and tillage of the soil, dairying, the production, cultivation, growing and harvesting of any agricultural or horticultural commodities, the raising of livestock, bees, fur-bearing animals, or poultry, and [Secondary] any practices . . . performed by a farmer or on a farm as an incident to or in conjunction with such farming operations, including preparation for market and delivery to storage or to market or to carriers for transportation to market.

The gray areas arise when farm employers grow and process or prepare their commodities for market. Until the 1990s, the NLRB held that workers employed in on-farm packing and processing facilities were considered nonfarm workers if at least 20 percent of the broccoli or melons they packed came from other farmers.[30] If less than 10 percent of the produce came from other farmers, the packer or processor was considered to be an extension of the farming operation, and the packing or processing workers were farm workers. Situations with 10 to 20 percent off-farm produce were handled on a case-by-case basis.

In 1990, an NLRB regional director ruled that if *any* commodities are bought regularly from other farmers, the packing and processing workers involved in handling the mix of farm-produced and purchased commodities were nonfarm employees.[31] In Camsco Produce, a California mushroom farm produced 375,000 to 400,000 pounds of mushrooms a week, and bought 100 pounds of exotic mushrooms from other farmers to have a full line of mushrooms for its grocery store customers; these bought mushrooms made Camsco's truck drivers nonfarm workers. In a second case, the UFW petitioned the ALRB to hold an election at Produce Magic, a Salinas-based custom harvester (not a farm operator) of lettuce and other vegetables. Produce Magic owned no land, but hired one hundred workers to cut and pack heads of lettuce into cartons in the fields, and asked the NLRB to define the lettuce workers as nonfarm, which would block the ALRB election. The NLRB in 1995 agreed with Produce Magic that its field workers who packed heads of cut lettuce and put them into boxes were nonfarm workers, and that only the workers who cut heads of lettuce were clearly farm workers.[32]

These NLRB decisions suggest that employers may be able to choose whether they want workers covered by the ALRA, NLRA, or both. Teamsters Local 890 won an NLRB election in April 1999 to represent the employees of Associated-Tagline, a Salinas-based fertilizer company that hired workers to mix fertilizers in an off-farm location, and then drive to fields and spread the fertilizer.[33] The Teamsters filed a petition with the ALRB for an election to represent Tagline employees when they were spreading fertilizer on fields, and the ALRB agreed that there could be an election to determine if Tagline employees wanted to be represented by the Teamsters for the farm work part of their work day. This decision emphasized that the nature of the work employees do, not whether their employer is a farmer (Tagline was not a farmer), determines whether individuals are farm workers.

Preelection Conduct

After an election, either the union or the employer can object by alleging that the other party campaigned unlawfully or improperly, thereby preventing workers from making a free choice. There is a major difference between ALRB and NLRB evaluations of improper preelection conduct. The NLRB has established a "laboratory condition" standard against which to judge campaign conduct, in the sense that an election is viewed as "a laboratory in which an experiment may be conducted, under conditions as nearly ideal as possible, to determine the uninhibited desires of the employees."[34] In evaluating allegations of improper conduct, NLRB focuses on "the substance, materiality, and timing of preelection campaign statements, evaluating threats, promises, or the like, which interfere with employee free choice,"[35] and sets aside elections that violates laboratory standards.

The ALRB adopted a lower "outcome determinative test," so that the party objecting to an election must show that improper preelection activities affected the outcome of the election. This higher hurdle for the complaining party was justified by the ALRB on farm-nonfarm differences: "NLRB elections can be easily rerun where statements or conduct preceding the election fall short of laboratory conditions, whereas in the agricultural setting, rerun elections, in most cases, must be postponed until a subsequent period of peak employment."[36] This means that, if a union organizer threatens three workers who would not sign authorization cards, the ALRB might not overturn the election if the other fifty employees did not learn of the threat before the election, and the union won by a large margin. However, if an employer grants a wage increase just before an election, his activities may well have affected the outcome, forcing a new election.

Other outcome-changing activities include employer threats or interrogations of workers about their union activities, promises of benefits for voting against the union, or employers engaging in surveillance and other activities that create an atmosphere of fear. These four types of unlawful preelection conduct have been summarized as TIPS (*Threats*, *Interrogations*, *Promises*, *Surveillance*). Most TIPS charges are filed by unions against employers, and the ALRB must evaluate the conduct the union complains about to determine if it affected the outcome of the election. Most TIPS objections are also unfair labor practices and are covered in that discussion.

In evaluating employer conduct, there is an asymmetry between what employers and unions can say before an election. The ALRB scrutinizes employer statements more carefully because of the economic reality that the employer writes checks to workers. If the employer promises to raise wages a dollar an hour if the workers vote for no union, workers may believe him, because they know that the employer can implement the decision. A union that promises a dollar-an-hour wage increase, by contrast, only wins the right to bargain for the wage increase. Because of "the economic dependence of the employees on their employers," the U.S. Supreme Court ruled that employer campaign statements cannot contain "a threat of reprisal or force or promise of benefit."[37] The ALRB has interpreted this Supreme Court decision to mean that "an employer may not promise or grant a wage increase during an organizing campaign unless it is a regularly scheduled increase."[38]

Hansen Farms offers a case in which employer threats and promises forced a union-certification election to be redone.[39] The UFW lost two elections in September 1975, the second by a vote of 300 to 247, and complained that thirty preelection TIPS committed by Hansen affected the outcome of the election. These TIPS included threats and promises made to ten to twelve crews of twenty-five to thirty workers each by Hansen in "captive audiences," meetings that Hansen's employees were required to attend. Hansen's defense was that he read in English a letter drafted in consultation with his attorney that included no promises or threats. Hansen's speech was translated into Spanish by one of his foremen for the workers. However, some of the workers testified that Hansen deviated from the letter and promised better wages if no union won the election. Others testified that a Hansen foreman told them, away from the captive audience speeches that, if the UFW won the election, Hansen might plant mechanically harvested alfalfa instead of labor-intensive lettuce, implying there would be fewer jobs if the union won.

In Anderson Farms, the ALRB concluded that the "election must be set aside in light of employer's pervasive ULP's, including unlawful promise of benefits, numerous discriminatory discharges, threats of loss of employment, and interference with communication between employees and organizers in company fields and labor camps."[40] Anderson Farms, or Andco, was a 35,000-acre, Davis-based farm with 8,700 acres of tomatoes in 1975 and peak employment of 900. The UFW launched an organizing drive at Andco in June 1975, and an election was held September 24–25, 1975, with no union receiving 370 votes and the UFW 290. The UFW asked that the election be set aside because of, inter alia, Anderson's preelection promises of benefits in exchange for a no-union vote. Anderson hired a Sacramento-area translator, Gutierrez, and he went from one tomato sorting machine to another just before the election to "explain Andco benefits to workers," including a health care plan that Andco implemented in June 1975, but workers first learned about the new benefits from Gutierrez just before the election. The ALRB agreed with the UFW that Gutierrez's activities were promises designed to produce a no-union vote and set the election aside. Gutierrez's activities, plus Andco's blocking of access to workers in its labor camps and laying off workers soon after they accepted union authorization cards, were found to be part of a pattern that led the ALRB to refuse to certify the no-union vote.

After the UFW lost an election September 26, 1977, at Giumarra Vineyards by a vote of 673 to 900, the UFW filed more than forty objections, asking the ALRB not to certify the no-union outcome because of Giumarra threats.[41] The ALRB reviewed the UFW's allegations, agreed that Giumarra TIPS had affected the outcome, and refused to certify the "no union" result, thus permitting the UFW to request another election when 50–50 conditions were satisfied.[42] Giumarra said during the preelection campaign that he did not want the UFW to represent Giumarra workers, and distributed a letter to workers that read, "Our company does not want or need a union." Giumarra also distributed several leaflets to employees, including one that outlined current wages and benefits. These letters and leaflets were not ULPs, since it is lawful for an employer to express his views about unions and to provide factual information to employees.

However, one of the leaflets contained a veiled threat that could have affected the outcome of the election. It read: "If you are not a citizen and engage in a strike, you could be immediately deported by the INS. Even if you have a green card, the law says they *must* deport you!" (emphasis in original). Many Giumarra employees were immigrants, and the ALRB concluded that these immigrant employees could interpret the leaflet as follows: unions mean strikes, and strikes mean deportation, so a no-union vote means less chance of deportation. The ALRB considered the leaflet an unlawful threat to encourage a no-union vote because it is not correct—illegal workers can be deported whether they strike or do not strike and legal immigrants or green card holders cannot be deported for striking. The ALRB's majority concluded that the false statements in this leaflet, as well as other Giumarra activities, unlawfully affected the outcome of the election.

Farm Employer Successorship

Farms are sold more often than factories—in many cases, especially in fresh vegetables, farmland is leased and not owned, so "selling the farm" can mean not renewing a lease. If farm workers elect a union to represent them, what happens to their union representation if the farm is sold? If there is a contract in effect, it usually includes a successorship clause that requires the buyer to honor the contract, and thus may affect the value of the farm, much as leases can affect the value of an apartment building. If there is no contract, successorship rules determine the union obligations of the new employer, as might occur if a farm is sold after the union won an election, but before a first contract is negotiated.

Under NLRB rules, the labor obligations of the buyer are determined on a case-by-case basis, with critical factors being continuity of the business and continuity of the work force. For example, if an auto assembly plant is sold, the new owner must normally negotiate in good faith with the union if the same workers are used to produce autos, that is, the new owner has work force and business continuity.[43] The ALRB presumed that agriculture was different because of seasonality and focused on business continuity, not work force continuity, to determine the union obligations of buyers or successor employers. This means that the buyer of a farm normally inherits the union obligations of the seller if he/she grows the same crops, even if the farm is sold at a time of the year when there are few workers employed.

At Highland Ranch in San Diego County, the UFW won an election July 28, 1977, and was certified as bargaining representative November 29, 1977.[44] On November 29, 1977, Highland's lease to grow vegetables on the Camp Pendleton Marine Base was sold to San Clemente Ranch, along with Highland's equipment. The UFW filed a ULP charge against

Highland for going out of business without bargaining, and against San Clemente, which also refused to bargain. Highland-San Clemente argued that, because there was only one employee at the time of the sale, there was no work force continuity and no obligation to bargain. The ALRB announced its business continuity rule and held that San Clemente was a successor employer to Highland because it grew the same crops with the same equipment on the same land with the same supervisors and some of the same employees.

When a business closes, its labor obligations normally cease, unless the reason the business closed was to avoid union obligations. One business cannot close, for example, and reopen under a different name just to avoid the union. In agriculture, many farms are owned by families, and one family tried to shuffle ownership from some members to others to avoid union obligations. Certified Egg Farms, which had a contract with the Teamsters, sold its stock to Olson Farms, Inc., and went out of business.[45] The ALRB found that the sale of Certified's stock to Olson, so that Certified ceased to exist, did not end Certified's obligations to the Teamsters because there was continuity in the business: the same workers gathered and processed eggs in the same operation owned by the same Olson family. Olson's defense was that, since the agreement was between Certified and the Teamsters, and Certified no longer existed, there was no need for Olson to bargain with the Teamsters or to deduct and forward dues to the Teamsters as the Certified-Teamsters agreement required. The ALRB disagreed and found Olson to be a successor employer to Certified; all that changed was that the Olson family shuffled shares among themselves.[46]

Gourmet Harvesting-Gourmet Farms is a similar case.[47] Gourmet Farms was organized in 1973 to grow vegetables and field crops on owned and leased land in the Imperial Valley. Gourmet Harvesting was organized in 1974 to provide labor services for Gourmet Farms, as well as other growers. On March 22, 1977, there was an election at Gourmet Harvesting, and the UFW was certified as the bargaining representative for Harvesting's farm workers. The first contract expired and, on January 19, 1979, the UFW called a strike against Gourmet and many other Imperial Valley vegetable growers in support of its demand for a wage increase. Gourmet Harvesting and Gourmet Farms lost money during the strike, and in July 1979, Gourmet Harvesting went out of business, and Gourmet Farms took over Harvesting's buses and equipment, and hired workers through ex-Harvesting's foremen—without informing the UFW. Over a year later, in October 1980, Harvesting—now out of business—resumed negotiations with the UFW, and two years later, the UFW alleged that Gourmet Harvesting/Farms failed to negotiate over the decision to go out of business. The ALRB concluded that Gourmet Farms was a successor employer to Gourmet Harvesting, and that Farms inherited Harvesting's bargaining obligations. However, the board found that Farms did bargain with the UFW, since negotiations continued sporadically after the takeover, and dismissed the UFW's charge of failure to bargain.

Union Decertification

A union can be decertified after it is certified if workers vote to end union representation or vote to switch from one union to another, that is, a union certified to represent the workers on a farm loses its status only after the ALRB decertifies it or certifies another union. There are often pro- and antiunion workers. If the vote for union representation was close, and the union that was certified is slow to negotiate a contract that raises wages, workers may become dissatisfied and seek its decertification. In high-turnover situations, the new workers hired may seek to decertify the union that previous workers elected. Farm workers may ask the ALRB to conduct a decertification election under a 30–50 rule, which means that dissatisfied workers may file a decertification election petition if it is signed by at least 30 percent of the employees and is submitted during the last year of the contract when 50 percent of the peak work force is employed.[48] However, the ALRB may refuse to allow a decertification election if there are unresolved ULP charges and complaints against an employer.[49]

The rules governing employer and union conduct during decertification elections are the same as for elections; in particular, employers may not make threats or promises and may not assist dissatisfied workers in a manner that interferes with employee free choice. After unions "lose" a decertification vote, they often charge that the employer unlawfully helped dissatisfied workers, so the ALRB must review the union's allegations to determine if the employer activities complained about were "outcome determinative." The UFW won an election at Abatti Farms on January 28, 1976, and even though a contract was signed, some workers refused to join the UFW. Abatti refused to fire them as the contract required.[50] Near the end of this contract, two dissatisfied workers took a leave of absence to circulate a decertification petition full-time among Abatti employees, and the vote in the decertification election was 149 for no union, 125 to retain the UFW, and 121 challenged ballots. Abatti asserted that this vote proved that workers no longer wanted to be represented by the UFW and stopped bargaining.

When Abatti refused to bargain, saying the UFW no longer represented Abatti workers, the UFW charged Abatti with bad faith bargaining, alleging that the decertification election was not valid because Abatti unlawfully assisted in the decertification effort. The UFW cited as an example a foreman who drove the dissatisfied workers to the ALRB office to get the correct petition, and Abatti allowing the decertification petition to circulate at a company-hosted Christmas party. The ALRB agreed with the UFW, concluding that Abatti's activities were "outcome determinative," meaning there would have been no decertification election without Abatti's involvement. Thus, Abatti's refusal to bargain was a per se, or obvious, ULP, and Abatti owed makewhole wages and benefits to its workers, originally estimated to be $18 million, but settled in 1994 for $1.6 million.[51]

A similar case of unlawful employer assistance occurred in Solomon-Cattle Valley Farms.[52] Farmer Solomon in September 1981 requested that his attorney help dissatisfied workers who wanted to decertify the UFW. Solomon's attorney said that his personal involvement in the decertification effort would be unlawful employer interference, but he arranged for the dissatisfied employees to receive free legal counsel from the Western Growers Association (WGA), and Solomon conveyed this message to the dissatisfied employees, who circulated a decertification petition. A decertification election was held, "no union" won a majority of the votes cast, and Solomon considered the UFW contract void. He subsequently refused to meet with the union. The UFW charged Solomon with refusing to bargain and asked that the decertification election be set aside because Solomon's activities were "outcome determinative." The ALRB agreed, noting that Solomon could have lawfully distributed ALRB decertification forms, but Solomon could not be the causal agent whose actions led to the decertification effort.

5

Employer and Union Unfair Labor Practices

It shall be an unfair labor practice for an agricultural employer [or labor organization] to interfere with, restrain, or coerce agricultural employees in the exercise of [their right] . . . to form, join, or assist labor organizations, to bargain collectively through representatives of their own choosing, and to engage in other concerted activities.

ALRA Section 1153–4(a); 1152

The ALRB protects worker rights by determining whether the charges filed by workers, unions, and employers alleging that unfair labor practices committed by employers or unions interfered with the rights of workers guaranteed in the ALRA. Law is inductive, not deductive, so the ALRA does not include lists of employer or union activities that are ULPs. Instead, the ALRA lays out broad principles, such as prohibiting unions and employers from interfering with workers who are exercising their ALRA rights, and the ALRB reviews written charges or allegations that assert, for example, that an employer fired a worker in retaliation for union activities.

ALRA Section 1153 includes six types of employer ULPs, for example, an 1153(a) employer ULP is employer interference with agricultural employees who are exercising their 1152 rights, and covers situations that range from supervisors threatening union organizers in front of workers to firing workers who refuse to work because it is too hot. In such cases, the employer may commit an interference ULP by discouraging farm workers who observe the threat from engaging in union activities for fear that they too may suffer from violence at the hands of the employer or his agents if they engage in union activities, or by discouraging workers from going on strike for higher wages when they think that they deserve additional pay. Almost all charges filed against employers allege an 1153(a) interference violation. The other two most frequently charged employer ULPs are Section 1153(c) violations, which occur when employers discriminate against farm workers because they engaged in union activities, and 1153(e) violations, which occur when an employer does not bargain with a certified union representative "in good faith."

ALRA Section 1154 lists eight union ULPs, but the most common are 1154(a), union threats; 1154(b), union discrimination; and 1154(c), bad-faith bargaining. The National Labor Relations Act of 1935 included only employer unfair labor practices, but the Labor-Management Relations Act of 1947 (Taft-Hartley) amended the NLRA to guarantee workers the right not to engage in union activities and defined union ULPs. After congressional hearings in the 1950s highlighting the lack of democracy in some unions, the Labor Management Reporting and Disclosure Act (LMRDA) of 1959 (Landrum-Griffen Act) spelled out the rights of union members vis-à-vis their unions. The ALRA includes the union unfair labor practices in the amended NLRA, but permits farm worker unions more power to decide who among their members are "in good standing." The NLRA defines good standing as the payment of dues and fees, while the ALRA permits unions to define good standing as the payment of dues and fees as well any other lawful requirements adopted democratically by the union during its convention.

Section 1153(a): Employer Interference TIPS

ALRA Section 1153(a) makes it an employer ULP to interfere with, restrain, or coerce agricultural employees who are exercising their 1152 rights to form or join a union or to engage in other protected concerted activities (PCA). There are two major types of employer interference that lead to 1153(a) ULPs: interference when workers are engaged in union activities, and interference when workers spontaneously engage in protected concerted activities, such as refusing to work on a hot day. Employers may replace but not fire workers for engaging in protected concerted activities. The most common employer interference are TIPS: threats or violence directed against employees or union organizers; interrogations of workers about their union activities; promises of benefits to persuade workers to vote in a certain way; surveillance or observing workers who are engaged in union activities. Many TIPS are ULPs that result in remedies such as requiring employers to rehire fired workers with back pay.

Employer threats against union organizers that are witnessed by workers may discourage them from engaging in lawful union activities, and thus are ULPs. If there is a dispute about exactly what happened, and whether it was a threat, the version of events provided by the party with the most credibility is accepted. For example, in Bruce Church, Inc., workers Jimenez and Ramirez campaigned for the UFW in their own crew and in other crews.[1] The foremen of these other crews threatened and eventually fired the two pro-UFW workers for insubordination and swearing at supervisors. The two workers denied that they had interrupted the work of the nearby crews (they argued that they did their campaigning during crew breaks), and that they had not sworn at the foremen. The ALJ discredited the BCI foremen's testimony and credited the workers version of events. The foremen said they were not concerned about UFW activities, even though Bruce Church was campaigning for a no union vote. Other workers reinforced the fired workers' version of events, not the foremen's. Since the workers' version of events was deemed most credible, Bruce Church was found to have committed 1153(a) threat and 1153(c) discrimination ULP's by discharging the two pro-UFW workers and was ordered to reinstate them with back pay.

Interrogation or questioning employees about their union views, sympathies, or activities can interfere with an employee's rights. Employer Steve Arnaudo asked employee Vincente Hernandez where he was when he missed work, and Hernandez lied and said he had been in Tijuana.[2] Arnaudo responded that he knew Hernandez had been at the UFW convention in Fresno, evidence of both interrogation and surveillance. Before the union election September 30, 1975, Arnaudo told some of the fifty workers he did not want any Chavistas and threatened to switch from growing tomatoes to nonlabor intensive alfalfa if the UFW won the election. In October 1975, as the season was winding down, but not yet over, Arnaudo laid off several pro-UFW workers with five to ten years experience. The laid-off workers, including Hernandez, filed a ULP charge, and the ALRB concluded that Arnaudo's interrogation of Hernandez was an 1153(a) ULP, and that the timing of the October 1975 layoffs was motivated by a desire to retaliate against prounion workers.

Many California farmers hire labor consultants to encourage a nounion vote when they learn that a union is attempting to organize their workers. In Oasis Ranch Management,[3] the ALRB held that the activities of two labor consultants hired by Oasis to discourage the eighteen to twenty-five workers employed on a thousand-acre date palm ranch from supporting the Union de Trabajdores Agricolas Fronterizos (UTAF) constituted unlawful interrogation. Oasis asked the labor consultants to interview its workers to determine if they had any problems with Oasis. The consultants misrepresented themselves to workers, saying they were from the state and wanted to know about the workers' problems. After several workers were laid off and not recalled, or recalled but not to their old jobs, they filed a ULP charge. The ALRB agreed that the activities of the consultants were unlawful interrogations designed to determine which workers supported the union. However, when Oasis ranch manager Dennis Maroney held a meeting with eighteen year-round workers to solicit their grievances and promised to increase their wages at the end of the discussion, he promptly rescinded the wage increase after being informed that no wage increases could be granted during an organizing drive. Maroney's action was not considered a ULP, since it was promptly rescinded.

Surveillance of employee union activities or giving the impression of surveillance is considered an infringement of workers' rights. If employers or their agents watch workers, the workers may not exercise their union rights for fear of retaliation. The ALRB has found that employers committed ULPs when they monitored and photographed union organizers at the workplace and at workers' homes. Surveillance can also be more subtle, as when a ranch manager sat in his pickup truck holding paper and pencil while watching a union organizer talk to workers; even if he wrote nothing down, he gave the impression of surveillance.[4] However, in 1997, the ALRB decided that two supervisors of tomato harvesters did not engage in surveillance when they observed workers holding a rally in a public park. The supervisors met at an apartment complex across from the park every day during the harvest to review and plan for the next day, and they sometimes gestured to workers who were on their way to UFW's rallies. The ALJ found that such gestures were unlawful surveillance, but the ALRB overruled her decision and said that they were innocent supervisor-worker communication.[5]

Section 1153(a): Employer Interference-PCA

Employers can also commit 1153(a) violations of worker rights when they interfere with the protected concerted activities of two or more workers even when no union is involved. Spontaneous strikes or protests are protected concerted activities, and the workers involved cannot be fired or disciplined in retaliation for engaging in such activities. Strikers can be replaced, meaning the employer can hire a new worker to fill the job left vacant by the striking worker—but workers cannot be fired for striking. The difference between firing and replacing workers becomes clear when a striking worker returns to work—if the job vacated by the striking worker is not filled by a replacement worker, the employer must rehire the returning striker.[6]

Protected concerted activities (PCA) often involve spontaneous strikes, as when workers refuse to work to protest wages or working conditions. The case that established the principle that concerted activities are protected, even if they violate company rules, was *NLRB v. Washington Aluminum Co.*[7] In this case, seven employees in a Baltimore machine shop left work—they went on strike—just as the work day started because the furnace was not working and the outside temperature was below 22 degrees; that is, they refused to work because it was too cold. The U.S. Supreme Court upheld the NLRB's conclusion that these workers were engaged in PCA to protest the company's failure to supply adequate heat and could not be fired for walking off the job without making a specific demand, in this case, for a 60-degree workplace. Having no bargaining representative, they took direct action to let the company know they wanted adequate heat, even though the company had a rule that forbade employees from leaving work without permission. The U.S. Supreme Court acknowledged that an employer may discharge employees for "cause," but an employer may not retaliate against an employee for engaging in peaceful and one-time protected concerted activities. The seven workers were thus entitled to reinstatement with back pay.[8]

In California agriculture, workers are more likely to engage in spontaneous strikes to protest heat rather than cold. The ALRB found that an employer unlawfully discharged a crew of workers who refused to work because it was very hot (103 degrees).[9] Pappas was a cantaloupe grower in the San Joaquin Valley who hired Sam Bernal (Chato) to supervise the harvest, and Chato used Benny Zamudio to provide half of the harvest workers; both Chato and Zamudio had the authority to hire and fire workers. Worker Esteban and ten other crew members lived in Zamudio's labor camp while harvesting cantaloupes on the Pappas farm.[10] On July 19, 1978, Esteban complained on behalf of the crew that the drinking water was not cold. On July 20, the crew began harvesting at 5:30 a.m., and by 2:30 p.m., the crew again complained of hot drinking water. When Zamudio ordered the crew to repick a field they had picked a few days earlier, they refused, citing the heat and the hot drinking water as well as the probable few ripe melons. Zamudio drove the striking workers to the labor camp, paid their wages in cash, and told them to leave. The workers filed a ULP charge, alleging that they were fired for engaging in a protected concerted activity, refusing to work for a low wage in the heat. The ALJ/ALRB agreed, and ordered Pappas to rehire the crew with back pay. Workers who strike weekly can be fired for insubordination, but a single concerted refusal to work is a protected activity, provided it is not violent, unlawful, in breach of contract,[11] or "indefensibly disloyal."

Anthony Harvesting illustrates the difference between firing and replacing workers who engage in protected concerted activities.[12] Anthony Farms grew vegetables in the Salinas Valley, and Anthony Harvesting harvested them. On November 21, 1990, the thirteen-member broccoli harvesting crew showed up at 6:30 a.m. to pick broccoli, but it was too icy to begin work, and some of the workers left for coffee or to run errands. At 7:30 a.m. work began, and at 4:30 p.m., the workers demanded overtime pay, arguing that they had been working since 6:30 a.m., and that California law requires time and a half overtime pay for farm workers after ten hours of work in one day. The supervisor reminded the nonunion crew that, since they did not begin to work until 7:30 a.m., they were not entitled to overtime pay until after 10 hours or work, that is, until after 5:30 p.m. As a result of the dispute, no more broccoli was cut on November 21, 1990. When the crew returned the next work day, a replacement crew was already harvesting broccoli. Anthony ignored the returning workers, and told them to leave. They assumed they had been fired in retaliation for demanding overtime pay. The ALRB agreed the crew was unlawfully fired, and ordered Anthony to put the crew on a preferential rehire list and provide them with $58,700 in back pay.[13] The lawful procedure would have been for Anthony to: (1) tell the returning workers they had been replaced, and (2) offer to put the returning strikers on a recall list and rehired them as vacancies appeared.

Employers do not escape liability for retaliation against workers engaged in PCA by waiting until the next year to retaliate. Stamoules Produce harvested crops, including melons, near Mendota.[14] Because of low melon prices, Stamoules reduced its melon acreage by one-third between 1985 and 1986, from 3,300 acres to 2,200 acres, and reduced the number of thirteen-member harvesting crews from twenty to ten. In 1985, worker dissatisfaction with conditions in the Stamoules labor camp and unpaid travel time from the camp to the fields—up to four hours daily—led to a UFW organizing drive. There was an election on August 10, 1985, and no union won. Two of the harvesting crews were not rehired in 1986, and they filed a ULP, alleging that Stamoules's refusal to rehire them was retaliation for their organizing efforts to a year earlier.[15] The two crews were told that they were not needed. Stamoules had no seniority system for rehiring crews, but crews that had been working for ten or more years—as the complaining crews had—expected to be the first to be rehired and usually were. Stamoules' arguments about which crews were rehired in 1986 were inconsistent—the clear pattern was that crews engaged in union activities were not rehired. Stamoules was ordered in 1990 to offer seasonal melon harvesting jobs to the workers who were not rehired in July 1986 and to offer these workers back pay for the earnings they lost because they were not rehired between 1986 and 1990.[16]

Workers are protected even if, for example, they leave the workplace and break company rules, as the workers in the Baltimore machine shop did. In Springfield Mushrooms, Inc., the ALRB concluded that three workers were unlawfully fired for refusing to clean up on June 15, 1985.[17] After picking mushrooms for piece-rate wages, the foreman told the three that they had to clean up the mushroom beds for a lower hourly wage. The three workers protested that cleanup work was voluntary and left, even though the foreman warned them that cleanup was mandatory. When they returned to work, they were told that they had been fired for insubordination; however, the three were rehired one month later. Regardless of whether cleanup was mandatory or voluntary, the workers were engaged in PCA—refusing to work for the lower wage paid for unpopular cleanup work. Springfield could have replaced the three by saying: you refused to clean up, your jobs are vacant, and workers will be hired to fill them on a first-come, first-served basis. In this case, Springfield did not have consistent reasons for refusing to rehire immediately the three workers and was ordered to provide them with back pay for the time they were not working.[18]

Section 1153(b): Company Domination of a Union

Section 1153(b) of the ALRA prohibits an employer from dominating, interfering with, or giving financial or other support to a labor organization. The most common 1153(b) ULP charges involve allegations that the employer favored one union over another during preelection campaigns. In Jack G. Zaninovich, one union complained that it was not given access to workers while another union was, and employer favoritism toward one union was also the charge in Royal Packing Co.[19] In E. & J. Gallo Winery, the UFW complained that Gallo gave the Teamsters access to workers without interference, but followed and photographed UFW organizers.[20]

Both the ALRA and the NLRA prohibit company unions, which were often created by employers during the 1920s under the so-called American Plan to forestall "real unions." Company unions are prohibited under U.S. labor law for fear that they might compete with independent unions for the loyalty of workers, leading to more and not less workplace conflict.[21] In the nonfarm economy, most company union cases involve employee-created committees that serve as a forum for workers and employers to meet and discuss workplace issues, such as employee suggestion committees or committees of elected workers that meet regularly with supervisors. Some of these employee-participation-in-management efforts are called quality-of-working-life (QWL) or total quality management (TQM) programs, and some are modeled on plant-level European works councils, which are nonunion bodies with elected worker representatives that meet regularly with employers to discuss workplace issues.

The legal status of employer-created workplace organizations is cloudy. A 1959 U.S. Supreme Court decision concluded that employee committees that discussed problems of mutual interest to workers and employers and handled grievances at nonunion plants were unlawful because of the prohibition against employer assistance of unions. In the cases considered by the Supreme Court, the employer retained the power to review or overrule committee decisions.[22] However, a unanimous NLRB ruling in 1977 approved a job enrichment program at General Foods in which employees were divided up into small teams, and the teams by consensus divided up their work.

In 1992 the NLRB found five committees staffed by employees who were selected by supervisors to be unlawful. Each committee at Electromation, a maker of electrical components in Indiana, had responsibility for discussing pay, smoking, and other work-related issues. The NLRB ordered its employee committees disbanded, as well as similar committees in sixteen other firms (in most of these cases the committees were established during union organizing drives).[23] The NLRB's Electromation decision was upheld by a U.S. Court of Appeals in 1994, which prompted Republicans in Congress to introduce the Teamwork for Employees and Management Act (TEAM) to explicitly make such employees committees lawful. TEAM has not been approved by Congress; it has been blocked by those who argue that virtually all large U.S. employers already have some form of lawful employee-management cooperation, and that TEAM would simply legalize committees established to head off union organizing drives.

There are few employer-created workers' committees in California agriculture. One exception is the UFW-Bear Creek partnership, which is not like Electromation because Bear Creek has a contract with the UFW.

According to the UFW, supervisors and union representatives at Bear Creek meet regularly to resolve disputes before they escalate into grievances, and workers are encouraged to make suggestions for faster and better work in exchange for job security and higher earnings.

Section 1153(c): Employer Discrimination

ALRA Section 1153(c) prohibits an employer from discrimination in hiring or firing, or any other condition of employment, in order to encourage or discourage membership in a labor organization. Workers who file ULP charges alleging that an employer committed a 1153(c) ULP must be able to answer yes to four questions:

- Was there a discriminatory act by the employer against one or more employees?
- Were the employees who were discriminated against engaged in union activities?
- Did the employer know of these union activities?
- Was one reason for the employer's discrimination an antiunion reason?

After the employee provides yes answers to these questions, the burden shifts to the employer, who must show that, even without the worker's union activities, the employer would have taken the same discriminatory act, such as firing or disciplining the worker.

A straightforward case of 1153(c) discrimination occurred in Andco Farms.[24] The Terrazas, a family of three, were tomato sorters who accepted authorization cards from a UFW organizer while an Andco foreman watched. That night the foreman visited the Terrazas at their home and told them were being laid off because there was not enough work. However, Andco hired four new tomato sorters the next day. When the Terrazas filed an 1153(c) ULP, they could answer yes to the four questions: discriminatory act (layoff), union activity, employer knowledge of this union activity, and an antiunion motivation for the layoff, since Andco was opposing the UFW's organizing drive. By laying off the Terrazas and hiring four new workers, Andco's defense was discredited, and Andco was ordered to rehire the Terrazas with back pay.

Most employers defend themselves against 1153(c) ULP charges by arguing that they took the discriminatory action for legitimate business reasons, such as firing the worker because he was too slow. In such "dual motive" cases, if the worker files a ULP charge, the ALJ/ALRB must decide whether the discrimination (say, a firing) was motivated by a lawful reason (the union activist was drinking on the job) or the unlawful reason (his union activities). After the worker who files the ULP charge answers yes to the four questions, the burden of proof shifts to the employer to show, in the words of the U.S. Supreme Court, that the employer "would have acted in the same manner for wholly legitimate reasons."[25] The key to an employer's defense when charged with an 1153(c) ULP is consistency in personnel policies, for example, the employer never hires unauthorized workers or always fires workers who drink on the job.

Inconsistent personnel policies often discredit an employer defense that the discrimination was motivated by "wholly legitimate reasons." Nursery owner Nishi, for example, refused to rehire employees Bernal and Batres after they were detained by the Immigration and Naturalization Service (INS) in January 1980.[26] When they returned to Nishi one week later, Nishi said that he could not rehire them because they were illegal aliens. Bernal and Batres filed an 1153(c) ULP, alleging that they were not rehired because of their involvement in a UFW organizing campaign during the summer of 1979. They were able to answer yes to the four questions: discriminatory act (Nishi's refusal to rehire them), union activities (talking to fellow workers about the UFW); employer knowledge (Nishi knew), and antiunion motivation (Nishi responded to the union campaign with a no-talking rule and a larger than normal wage increase). The burden of proof then shifted to Nishi to prove that, even without union activities, Bernal and Batres would not have been rehired for legitimate business reasons. Nishi said the major reason for refusing to rehire was that he feared fines for rehiring workers he knew were unauthorized. Federal fines for hiring unauthorized workers were introduced only in 1987–88, and Nishi could not prove he never rehired illegal aliens—five of the ten employees working in January 1980 had been detained by the INS. Nishi said he instituted the "no unauthorized workers" rule in September 1979, three months before the refusal to rehire, but he did not tell anyone about the new rule or write it down. Since Nishi failed to provide a wholly legitimate reason for refusing to rehire the workers, he was ordered to rehire them with back pay.

A discriminatory act violates section 1153(c) only if the employer's motivation is to encourage or discourage protected union activities. Since an employer rarely says "I am firing you for your union activities," the ALJ/ALRB must infer the employer's true motivation. An employer who argues that the discrimination was motivated by lawful reasons often has this defense discredited by contradictory evidence. For example, an employer may say that union-activist workers had to be laid off for business reasons, but then turn around and hire new employees. The ALJ/ALRB may infer that, since the employer's stated reason for discrimination was untrue, the underlying motive was an unlawful one.

Section 1153(d): Discrimination for ALRB Activities

Section 1153(d) of the ALRA prohibits agricultural employers from discharging or otherwise discriminating against farm workers for filing charges under or testifying before the ALRB. As under 1153(c), workers alleging an 1153(d) ULP must answer yes to the four questions, and then the burden of proof shifts to the employer to prove that the same discriminatory action would have been taken without the worker's participation in ALRB activities.

Bacchus Farms was a twenty-six-hundred-acre vineyard in Madera County that reassigned three workers after they attended an ALRB hearing. There was an election on September 16, 1975, the UFW won, and Bacchus filed a technical objection, alleging that employment was not 50 percent of peak. Three Bacchus workers attended the December 18, 1975, hearing called to deal with election objections, and at least one testified. The next day, the three were transferred to new and less desirable jobs. They filed an 1153(d) ULP charge, and the ALRB agreed that their reassignments were retaliation for their participation in the ALRB election hearing. Bacchus was ordered to restore the three workers to their old jobs and provide them with the difference between what they would have earned in their old jobs and what they actually earned.

Section 1153(e): Bad Faith Bargaining

After a union is certified, the employer must bargain with the union in good faith, which means the employer and union must bargain "with the intent to reach agreement" on a written contract that sets out wages, fringe benefits, and workplace rules for two or three years. The U.S. Supreme Court has defined good-faith bargaining as "a desire to reach ultimate agreement . . . a serious intent to adjust differences and to reach an acceptable common ground."[27] The collective aspect of bargaining emphasizes that workers are collaborating through their union to determine, for example, the balance between higher wages and more benefits, while the bargaining aspect emphasizes that unions and employers may have different perspectives on how much labor costs should rise.

ALRA Section 1155.2(a) describes good faith bargaining as having three concrete elements: (1) meet at reasonable times; (2) "confer in good faith with respect to wages, hours, and other terms and conditions of employment," and (3) sign a written contract if an agreement is reached. Good-faith bargaining does not require agreement—only the intent to reach agreement. The chairman of the U.S. Senate Labor Committee in 1935 described the process: the NLRA "escorts them [union bargainers] to the door of their employer and says 'here they are, the legal representatives of your employees.' What happens behind those doors is up to the parties themselves." This means that the content of the agreement is of secondary concern—unions can lawfully ask members to go on strike to put pressure on an employer for an agreement that will put the employer out of business.[28]

Unions consider bad-faith bargaining as the most serious employer ULP because it affects all workers in the bargaining unit, not just the subset who are discriminated against for their protected concerted or union activities, and it can undermine support for the union. Consider a typical scenario. The union campaigns to represent workers, promising to negotiate higher wages. The union wins the election and is certified as bargaining agent, but the employer unlawfully delays bargaining and thus the wage increase, which may cause the workers to lose faith in their union, weakening it so much that the union cannot call an effective strike. In such cases, the employer has benefited economically by bargaining in bad faith. To prevent employers from benefiting economically when they engage in bad-faith bargaining, the ALRA includes a unique "makewhole" remedy—employers may be required to make the employees whole for the wage and benefit losses they suffered during bad-faith bargaining. The Labor Law Reform Act of 1977, which was being discussed when the ALRA was drafted, but did not become law, would have allowed the NLRB to require employers to pay makewhole if they failed to bargain in good faith for a first contract.

An employer bargaining in bad faith rarely says: "I'll never sign a contract with a union." Thus, if a union charges an employer with bad faith bargaining, the ALRB must review the union's charges for evidence of bad faith, the employer's defense, and then decide whether the employer was bargaining in good or bad faith. The ALRB looks for one or more of three major indicators of bad-faith bargaining: dilatory or delaying tactics and surface bargaining, such as going through the motions of bargaining, but never reaching an agreement; per se violations, such as unilateral changes in wages; and bargaining table misconduct, such as refusing to bargain over mandatory bargaining subjects.

Dilatory Tactics and Surface Bargaining

Unions provide a service to their members—higher wages and work rules. Employers may try to delay bargaining in order to delay wage and benefit increases, or go through the motions of bargaining but not reach an agreement, especially in negotiating a first contract. Between 1986 and 1993, for example, about one-third of the bargaining units for which unions were certified to represent workers in the nonfarm economy did not obtain a first agreement within one year, a result in some cases of employer bad-faith bargaining (Commission on the Future of Worker-Management Relations, 1995, 74).

Dilatory or delay tactics include delaying the scheduling of meetings, canceling meetings or showing up late, or attaching preconditions to negotiations. An employer may try to slow bargaining by sending a negotiator who has no authority to bind the employer to any agreement reached, or switch negotiators frequently, forcing the new negotiator to review previous discussions. Refusal or delay in submitting proposals and counterproposals can also delay bargaining unlawfully.

O. P. Murphy delayed negotiating sessions, sent negotiators who did not know much about Murphy's tomato-growing operations, and failed to respond to the UFW's request for wage and employee data.[29] Murphy hired five crews of forty workers each to pick "mature green" fresh tomatoes into buckets between August and October. The UFW was certified as the bargaining agent for Murphy's workers on March 17, 1977, and several weeks later, sent a letter to Murphy with a proposed contract, asking Murphy to sign it or schedule negotiations. Murphy did not respond, a second letter was sent, and the first negotiating session was not held until almost three months later, on June 29, 1977. There were twelve bargaining sessions before the tomato harvest was completed in October 1977, but there was little progress toward an agreement in these sessions—Murphy provided a partial response to the UFW's proposed contract only on August 24, 1977. The UFW accused Murphy of unlawfully delaying bargaining, and Murphy countered that the UFW did not plan to bargain seriously until harvest workers returned, and some could be included on the bargaining team. Furthermore, Murphy argued that slow progress did not necessarily indicate bad faith dilatory tactics.

The ALRB discredited these Murphy's arguments. Murphy knew that harvest workers would be on his ranch for only three months, so that his failure to provide requested wage data, canceled meetings, and changed negotiators slowed bargaining during this window. In July 1977, Murphy unilaterally raised wages, from a minimum $3.25 to $3.55

per hour—reminding workers that the employer pays their wages. To protest slow bargaining, on September 12, 1977, the pickers began to "pick dirty" (to pick both green and partially red tomatoes, as well as putting dirt and stems in their buckets). In response, Murphy fired union activist Hurtado, and 90 percent of the pickers walked out in protest of what they considered Murphy's unlawful firing of Hurtado.[30] When they returned to work they had to sign a "no strike" pledge, but when they realized that Hurtado would not be rehired, some refused to work and were fired. On September 15, 1977, a labor consultant that Murphy hired offered to rehire 40 of the 150 strikers; they countered that all or none must be rehired.[31] The ALRB found that Murphy had engaged in dilatory or delaying tactics by not responding to the union's proposal or not providing data requested by the union. The ALRB also found that the July 1977 wage increases were unlawful unilateral changes (per se violations of the duty to bargain in good faith) and that the workers who left their jobs on September 12, 1977, were ULP strikers who were entitled to their old jobs, plus back pay.

Surface bargaining is another way to delay reaching agreement and occurs when an employer goes through the motions of good faith bargaining, but never reaches final agreement. Surface bargaining has been described as talking but not agreeing:

> [T]o sit at a bargaining table, or to sit almost forever, or to make concessions here and there, could be the very means by which to conceal a purposeful strategy to make bargaining futile or fail . . . [good-faith bargaining] takes more than mere "surface bargaining" or "shadow boxing" to a draw or "giving the union a run-around while purporting to be meeting for purposes of collective bargaining."[32]

The ALRB examines employer actions to determine if they suggest the employer was merely going through the motions of bargaining, asking questions such as whether the employer systematically opposed all proposals submitted by the union without providing an economic reason. The employer's defense to a union surface bargaining charge is usually the assertion that the employer was engaged in lawful hard bargaining.

In Meyer Tomato, the UFW was certified to represent Meyer's Salinas workers on September 29, 1975, but the first contract was not reached until September 24, 1985, a decade later.[33] Two months before this agreement expired on October 15, 1987, the UFW was certified to represent Meyer's workers outside Salinas as well; most of these workers were in a separate bargaining unit in Visalia. The UFW asked Meyer to negotiate the Salinas and Visalia contracts jointly, and Meyer refused. On November 18, 1987, the UFW met with Meyer and proposed that most provisions of the Salinas contract apply to Visalia, but that Visalia workers receive lower wages and Meyer make smaller contributions to the UFW's RFK health plan and Juan de la Cruz pension plan, since wages in Visalia were generally lower than in Salinas. The UFW on February 22, 1988, requested information from Meyer, and Meyer responded on March 22, 1988, indicating that he was planting sixteen hundred acres of tomatoes in 1988 and that FLCs would harvest the tomatoes.[34] Meyer's negotiators often arrived late and stayed to bargain only one to two hours. During bargaining, the UFW, but not Meyer, offered concessions, with Meyer often insisting that, if the Salinas UFW-Meyer agreement were applied to Visalia, he would stop growing tomatoes in Visalia.

The UFW charged that Meyer was engaged in surface bargaining, and the ALRB agreed. After May 13, 1988, the ALRB found that Meyer was attempting to delay negotiations by not providing an employee list, using negotiators who could bargain for only a few hours, and insisting on extensive "management rights" clauses. Meyer was ordered in 1991 to provide makewhole wages and benefits to its employees from May 1988 until Meyer began to bargain in good faith.

Bertuccio was found to have engaged in surface bargaining by refusing to provide the information requested by the UFW, not giving his negotiator authority to make concessions, and making unilateral changes in wages and working conditions.[35] In Certified Egg/Olson Farms, Inc., after the ALRB found that Olson was a successor to Certified,[36] bargaining was slow, as Jones, the negotiator for Olson, insisted that the parties were negotiating a first contract, not renegotiating a contract with a successor employer, and opposed including a dues checkoff provision.[37] However, Olson also did not want the union to come unto Olson property and collect union dues from workers. The ALJ found, and the ALRB agreed, that Olson was engaged in surface bargaining, as indicated by the delays, unacceptable proposals, and insistence that a mediator join the bargaining—this was insistence on a nonmandatory bargaining topic.

Unilateral Changes and Per Se Violations

Neither employer nor union representatives can walk into the first bargaining session, announce their final offer and say, take it or leave it.[38] Employers need to keep their businesses going during negotiations, so if there is an impasse—an honest deadlock in negotiations—they can make unilateral changes in wages or working conditions. However, if there is no impasse, employer unilateral changes are considered indicators of bad faith because they signal to the employees that the employer can change wages and benefits without the involvement of the union, the workers' exclusive bargaining representative.

Montebello Rose Co. and Mount Arbor Nurseries were two nurseries that bargained jointly with the UFW.[39] Negotiations dragged on without agreement, and both nurseries unilaterally raised wages in order to retain their workers. The UFW charged the nurseries with bad faith bargaining. The issue before the ALRB was whether the nurseries and the UFW were at impasse: if they were not, then the unilateral changes may be bad faith bargaining. The UFW was certified as the bargaining agent for workers at both nurseries on December 3, 1975, and immediately requested job and wage data and negotiations. The UFW met with Mount Arbor in December 1975, but it took three months for Montebello to respond to the UFW. In April 1976, Mount Arbor unilaterally raised wages. Montebello informed the UFW that it would bargain jointly with Mount Arbor, and in May-June 1976, there were several negotiating sessions. In one of these sessions the employers said they could not agree with the UFW's demand for a dues checkoff system because it was too expensive. The two employers made a final offer on June 10, 1976, declared impasse, and broke off negotiations. During the fall of 1976, both Mount Arbor and Montebello raised wages without informing the UFW.[40]

The UFW charged per se bad faith bargaining, citing the unilateral wage increases. The employers responded that the unilateral changes were not a ULP because negotiations were at impasse, and thus the nurseries could lawfully implement the last offer they made at the bargaining table to stay in business. However, the ALJ/ALRB concluded that the cost argument against the dues checkoff—a cause of the impasse—was a pretext because the nurseries never estimated the cost. This means that, during bargaining, they could not say to the union— if you insist on dues checkoff, we must lower the wage increase to offset the dues checkoff cost.[41]

The most famous unilateral-change bad faith cases involved the UFW's efforts to renegotiate contracts with twenty-six Imperial Valley lettuce and vegetable growers early in 1979 (the Admiral Packing case discussed in chapter 3).[42] The UFW made its demands for a 40 percent wage increase plus additional benefits, the employers countered with 7 and eventually 11 percent, the UFW called a strike, and filed ULP changes after employers unilaterally raised wages. The UFW reached agreement with fifteen of the growers while the bad faith bargaining charges were pending, but the ALJ-ALRB considered the case against the remaining eleven growers in September 1979 and agreed with the UFW that the growers had made an unlawful "final offer" when they declared impasse, and thus their wage increases were per se violations. The growers appealed to the Fourth Court of Appeals, which on April 2, 1984, reversed the ALJ-ALRB, concluding that the employers were willing to bargain further, but only if the UFW was also willing to make concessions.[43] The court concluded that the employers could have reasonably declared impasse because of the huge gap between their offer of a 21 percent wage increase and the UFW's demands, which would have raised their labor costs 123 to 190 percent.

The UFW charged that the lettuce producer Bruce Church unilaterally reduced wages and benefits in January 1987 and introduced a new harvesting system without bargaining over its effects on workers.[44] The ALRB rejected the UFW's bad-faith bargaining charges. After a review of Bruce Church–UFW bargaining between the fall of 1985 and mid-1987, the ALRB concluded that Bruce Church, in a timely fashion, had informed the UFW of its intent to reduce wages to rates that other companies were paying and to change its harvesting system. The UFW switched negotiators and did not respond to Bruce Church requests for bargaining sessions, so the UFW could not claim that it was not notified of the proposed Bruce Church changes.

Bargaining Table Misconduct

An employer must bargain to agreement or impasse on all mandatory subjects of bargaining, namely, "wages, hours, and other terms and conditions of employment." NLRB, ALRB, and court decisions have established three broad categories of bargaining subjects—mandatory, permissive, and prohibited. Mandatory subjects are those over which an employer's refusal to bargain, or when an employer makes a unilateral change without bargaining, may be an unfair labor practice. Mandatory wage-related issues include hourly rates of pay, piece-rates, overtime pay, shift dif-ferentials, paid holidays, vacations, severance pay, regular bonuses, pension plans, profit-sharing plans, merit and wage increases, and company-provided meals and housing. Hours of work include regular and holiday work schedules, while other terms and conditions of employment include grievance and arbitration procedures, layoffs, discipline and discharge, the pace of work, sick leave, work rules, seniority promotions and transfers, retirement, union shop provisions, dues checkoff, hiring hall rules, work rules, health and safety procedures, management rights, no-strike clauses, subcontracting, and sometimes mechanization.[45]

Permissive subjects are those that either party may bring up, but the other side may refuse to bargain over without committing a ULP. Employers may not declare an impasse and make unilateral changes if the union refuses to bargain over a permissive topic. Other examples of permissive topics are where the employer will locate the work, the employer's corporate organization, and the size of the supervisory force. Agreements on prohibited subjects are not enforced by the ALRB or the courts. For example, the union and the employer may agree to a closed shop provision, under which a worker must be a union member before being hired, but this provision will not be enforced by the ALRB.

Between the 1950s and the 1970s, the list of mandatory bargaining subjects expanded as unions proposed and employers accepted contract clauses covering health insurance for employee families, supplemental unemployment insurance benefits, and special job security programs. In its Fibreboard decision in 1964, the U.S. Supreme Court encouraged mandatory bargaining over "management decisions" when it ruled that an employer could not contract out its maintenance work without bargaining with the union representing the workers who currently did the work—the decision displaced workers, but did not change the nature or scope of the business.[46] In 1981, the U.S. Supreme Court signaled a return toward management rights in its *First National Maintenance Corp v. NLRB* decision, which concluded that "bargaining over management decisions that have a substantial impact on the continued availability of employment should be required only if the benefit for . . . the collective bargaining process outweighs the burden placed on the conduct of the business."

Thus, there are two extremes on the spectrum of employer decisions that affect employees: subcontracting and partially going out of business. Subcontracting means that the employer wants to have the same work done, but have a third party with his/her own workers do the work, eliminating bargaining unit jobs. Under the ALRA/NLRA, the employer must bargain over (1) the decision to subcontract work, and (2) the effects of the decision on bargaining unit workers, and the employer must notify the union of its tentative decision, give cost or other economic reasons for the decision, and offer to bargain with the union until there is an agreement or impasse. At agreement or impasse, the employer may lawfully implement the decision. After the decision is implemented, the employer must offer to bargain over the effects of the decision on workers and wages, but the union may have little bargaining power.[47] At the other extreme is going out of business for economic reasons, which also eliminates jobs (see table 5.1). An employer may go completely or partially out of business without bargaining over the decision, although the employer must bargain over the effects of the decision; if the employer has gone out of business, unions may have little bargaining power.[48]

Table 5.1. Decision versus Effects-Only Bargaining

Subcontracting: Same work done, but bargaining unit jobs lost (mechanization, use custom harvester)—employer must bargain over the decision and the effects of the decision.

Going out of business (changing crops, closing part of a farm businees): Jobs may be eliminated, but employer needs to offer to bargain only over the effects of the decision.

Many business decisions fall between subcontracting and going out of business for economic reasons. When a union files a ULP charge alleging that a business decision was a mandatory bargaining subject and that the employer committed a ULP by making the decision without bargaining, the ALRB begins by asking whether the employer decision (1) changed the scope and direction of the business and (2) eliminated jobs. If the employer's scope and direction of business is unchanged, but the decision eliminated jobs, it is generally a subject of mandatory bargaining. Thus, mechanization is a mandatory bargaining topic because the employer is still a peach grower; the machine simply eliminates jobs. Similarly, switching from directly hiring workers to hiring workers via a custom harvester is a mandatory bargaining subject, since workers in the bargaining unit lose jobs.

O. P. Murphy Produce Company's decision to mechanize the fresh market tomato harvest was subject to decision bargaining because mechanization would eliminate 80 percent of the bargaining unit jobs, and the business was substantially unaltered in scope or direction—Murphy was still growing fresh market tomatoes.[49] Murphy notified the UFW of his pending mechanization decision—he sent a letter explaining that mechanization was cheaper—and offered to bargain over the decision. The UFW ignored Murphy's letter, believing it was a ploy to get the union to accept a lower piece-rate wage. When Murphy mechanized, the UFW charged bad faith bargaining. The ALRB rejected the UFW's charge, finding that Murphy studied the economics of mechanization, made a tentative decision to mechanize, and offered to bargain over the decision.

Some business decisions do not eliminate jobs, but instead change the wage system, and thus worker earnings. For example, during the 1980s and 1990s, many farm employers began to use conveyor belts in the fields. Workers would walk behind the conveyor belt as it moved slowly through the field and place the lettuce or melon on the belt; workers riding on the machine would pack the commodity into boxes or cartons. Instead of piece rates, most workers employed in "field packing" are paid hourly wages because the employer can control the speed of the machine and thus the pace of work. Employer Vessey notified the UFW that Maggio was considering using conveyor belts to save money harvesting lettuce and offered to discuss the decision and its effects.[50] Vessey began using the wrap machines on December 10, 1979, and the UFW accused Vessey of bad faith bargaining for not bargaining to impasse or agreement over the introduction of the machines. The ALRB reasoned that, since the machines did not eliminate jobs, Vessey did not have to bargain over the decision to switch to lettuce conveyor belts, but did have to bargain over the effects of the lettuce-wrap machines, such as the switch to hourly wages.

The ALRB reached a similar decision in Lu-Ette Farms, Inc., overturning an ALJ decision that Lu-Ette's failure to bargain with the UFW over the introduction of a conveyor belt machine to harvest melons was a ULP.[51] The ALJ called the conveyor belt "mechanization," but the board, citing Maggio, emphasized that no jobs were eliminated, and that the major change for workers was the shift from piece rates to hourly wages.[52] Lu-Ette had an obligation to bargain over the effects of the conveyor belt machine on wages and working conditions, but not over the decision to use the conveyor belt machine.

At the other extreme are employer decisions to go completely or partially out of business for economic reasons. For example, a decision to stop harvesting citrus after a packing shed was destroyed by fire does not require decision bargaining, even if jobs are eliminated. The UFW filed a bad faith bargaining charge against Valdora Produce Company, which closed a citrus packing house for economic reasons without offering to bargain over the decision.[53] A September 1977 fire destroyed Valdora Produce's citrus packing shed, forcing it to pack citrus in rented facilities at higher costs; it lost many of its 110 grower-customers. In May 1980, Valdora quit the citrus business for economic reasons and laid off UFW-represented citrus harvesters (Valdora's grape harvesters were not affected). The ALRB, following the U.S. Supreme Court's 1981 First National decision, concluded that Valdora's decision to close part of its business for economic reasons was not a mandatory bargaining subject. Valdora lawfully offered to bargain over the effects of the closure, but the UFW did not follow up.[54]

The ALRB in the early 1980s first decided that employers must bargain with unions over crop changes that displace workers, but then reversed its position, concluding that changing crops alters the scope and direction of the business and is not a mandatory bargaining subject. The ALRB in a 3–2 decision in December 1982 concluded that Bertuccio's decision to sell garlic in the field to Vessey, thus eliminating garlic harvesting jobs for Bertuccio workers because Vessey workers harvested the garlic, was subject to decision bargaining. In this decision, the ALRB concluded that Bertuccio should have informed the UFW of his tentative decision to sell the garlic to Vessey and negotiated until there was agreement or impasse.[55] This Bertuccio decision caused an uproar in the California legislature, prompting "freedom to farm" bills that would have explicitly declared that crop decisions as not subject to decision bargaining. Before any of these bills were enacted, the ALRB on a 3–2 vote reversed itself in June 1983, deciding in Cardinal Distributing Company that decisions on which crops to grow are not mandatory bargaining subjects.[56] However, an employer's decision to stop growing labor-intensive crops and thus displace workers requires effects bargaining.

Cardinal Distributing was the produce marketing arm of Peter Rabbit farms, whose workers were represented by the UFW. Bargaining for a contract went slowly, and in July–August 1978, Cardinal informed the UFW that it was discontinuing, for economic reasons, the growing of green onions, beets, parsley, and cabbage, which would eliminate 650 jobs, and offered to bargain over the effects of its decision. The UFW alleged that Cardinal committed a ULP by not bargaining over the decision to stop growing labor-intensive crops, but the ALRB disagreed, concluding that "the burden on the employer's right to decide, for economic reasons, which crops to grow or discontinue outweigh the incremental benefit that might be gained through the union's participation on the decision-making process. Such decisions lie at the core of entreprencurial control and do not lend themselves to the collective bargaining process." The ALRB reasoned that the scope of Cardinal's business was altered enough by the crop change that there was no duty to bargain over the decision, only the effects of the decision.

Section 1154(a) (1): Union Threats and Violence at Work and Home

ALRA Section 1154(a)(1) prohibits unions from restraining or coercing employees when they seek to join a (rival) union, engage in concerted activity, bargain collectively, or refrain from these activities. Farm workers or employers who believe that a union or its agents interfered with the labor rights of workers must prove two things: there were acts that interfered with worker rights, and the union or the union's agents were responsible for them. The major issue in most cases is not whether the acts of violence or coercion against workers occurred, but whether union leaders or agents were responsible for them. For example, if a

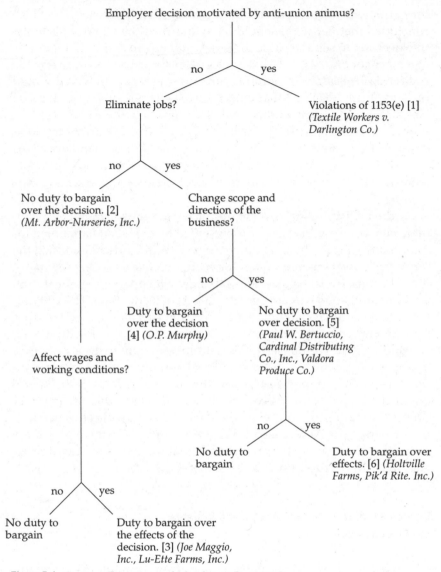

Figure 5.1. Business Decisions and Mandatory Bargaining

union establishes a picket line, it must seek to prevent and minimize violence against workers who elect to exercise their right to refrain from union activities and go to work.

Activities that are 1154(a)(1) ULPs include mass picketing that blocks the entrances and exits to an employer's property, and union agents attacking strikebreaking workers who cross picket lines. In *Western Conference of Teamsters (V. B. Zaninovich and Sons, Inc.)*, Teamsters' business agents committed a ULP by engaging in numerous acts of violence directed at strikebreaking workers and the employer.[57] The union agents threw rocks, bottles, and other objects at strikebreaking workers and Zaninovich supervisors, followed the cars of some strikebreaking workers as they left work in a menacing fashion, and threw Tijuana or three-cornered tacks in front of strikebreaking worker and employer vehicles. Zaninovich, a Tulare County grape grower, was renegotiating a contract with the Teamsters when, on August 24, 1976, the Teamsters called a strike, which reduced the number of pickers from four hundred to less than a hundred. At least a hundred striking workers picketed the entrances to Zaninovich vineyards, and Zaninovich hired security guards, called the Tulare County sheriff to preserve order, and obtained a restraining order from a Tulare County judge ordering the Teamsters not to threaten strikebreaking workers. Zaninovich provided photos, videotape, and affidavits from workers to support allegations that the Teamsters instigated or condoned violence.

The Teamsters acknowledged that there was picket line violence, but said that union agents were not responsible for it, and thus there was no ULP. The board in a 4–1 decision disagreed, finding that some union agents personally engaged in acts of violence and did little to stop violence by picketing workers. The Teamsters were ordered to cease and desist from instigating and tolerating violence and to pay the wages of workers while they listened to an ALRB representative read the notice in which the Teamsters admitted they violated the ALRA and promised not to do so again. However, the Teamsters were not decertified as the workers' representative, as Zaninovich requested.

Cesar Chavez urged nonviolence, but the UFW has been charged on several occasions with allowing or permitting its picket lines to become violent. In Ace Tomato, the UFW won an election in 1983 on a 315–42 vote, with 256 challenged ballots, and because the challenged ballots would not have affected the outcome, was certified in 1986 to represent Ace workers.[58] Ace objected, arguing that the UFW created a "climate of fear" before the election by having UFW supporters and organizers surround labor consultants in their car after having hit the car with dirt clods and unripe tomatoes. According to Ace, they rocked the car as if intending to overturn it and coerced strike-breaking workers to stop work by throwing dirt clods and unripe tomatoes at them. The ALRB agreed with Ace in 1989, overturning a previous decision to certify the UFW because of the preelection violence.

Unions sometimes picket the homes of strikebreaking workers to encourage them not to go to work during a strike. In a 1979 strike in the Imperial Valley, the UFW on three occasions sent thirty to fifty pickets to march outside the homes of strikebreaking workers.[59] The pickets chanted slogans and shouted epithets at the residents for up to four hours a day, prompting Marcel Jojola, the chief of the El Centro police department, to assert that the UFW's picketing of strikebreakers' homes interfered with the rights of workers who decided not to strike.[60] The UFW countered that the picketing was peaceful, and that the UFW had to picket the workers' homes because many farmers fenced their fields and hired security guards, preventing effective workplace picketing. The ALRB, in a 3–0 decision, found that the UFW committed a ULP, and ordered the UFW to cease and desist from mass residential picketing and to send an apology to the residents whose homes were picketed. However, the majority of the board as well as the California courts have refused to outlaw all residential picketing, or even to prescribe in advance exactly how unions should engage in residential picketing. These rulings mean that farm worker unions may picket the homes of strike-breakers, but there are more limitations on picketing at strikebreakers' homes than at workplaces.

ALRA Section 1154(a)(2) prohibits a union from restraining or coercing an employer in the selection of representatives for collective bargaining or the adjustment of grievances. This section prohibits a union from saying, for example, that it will not bargain with a particular management negotiator.

Section 1154(b): Union Security and Discrimination

The ALRA allows a union to negotiate an agreement with a farm employer that requires all workers employed on a farm to join the union after five days of employment and remain union members "in good standing" in order to keep their jobs. Under good standing clauses in collective bargaining agreements, the union decides what it means to be a member in good standing, and the union is the sole judge of whether a particular worker is in good standing.[61] The authority to negotiate a good standing clause is spelled out in ALRA Section 1153, which makes it an employer ULP to discriminate

> in regard to the hiring or tenure of employment, or any term or condition of employment, to encourage or discourage membership in any labor organization. [However] nothing in this part . . . shall preclude an agricultural employer from making an agreement with a labor organization . . . to require as a condition of employment, membership therein on or after the fifth day following the beginning of such employment, or the effective date of such agreement, whichever is later . . . membership shall mean the sat-

isfaction of all reasonable terms and conditions uniformly applicable to other members in good standing.

The relationship between union leaders and members begins with three key concepts: exclusive representation, fair representation, and union security. A union certified to represent the workers on a farm is their exclusive bargaining representative on all issues related to wages and working conditions. This means that individual employer-worker negotiations are banned, and that workers who fail to follow the grievance procedure set out in their collective bargaining agreement when they have a dispute with the employer are not necessarily protected on the grounds that they were engaged in protected concerted activities. For example, when several black employees of the Emporium Capwell store on San Francisco's Union Square alleged that Emporium Capwell discriminated against blacks and picketed the store rather than following the grievance procedure in their collective bargaining agreement, they were fired, and the U.S. Supreme Court concluded they were fired lawfully because they should have pursued their complaint with the help of their exclusive union representative.[62]

Exclusive representation imposes a duty of "fair representation" on the union—the union must represent all workers who file grievances, including antiunion workers. The reason is clear: if a union did not fairly represent all workers in the bargaining unit, the workers would have no lawful means of conveying dissatisfaction to the employer. Unions do not have to act as the worker's advocate for every grievance an employee files—the union can decide that a grievance filed by a worker is frivolous and dismiss it or settle it rather than appealing it through every step of the grievance procedure. The U.S. Supreme Court, in its 1967 *Vaca v. Sipes* decision, concluded that the union, as the workers' representative, can decide that the needs of all workers are more important than those of one. However, if a union fails to appeal a grievance, as a worker requests, the worker can sue the union for damages for not satisfying its fair representation duty.

The third key concept is union security or union shop agreements. About 80 percent of U.S. collective bargaining agreements include a clause that requires all workers to join the union, usually after thirty days of being hired in the nonfarm economy and after five days in California agriculture, and remain union members "in good standing" to keep their jobs.[63] Under the NLRA, good standing is defined as the payment of union dues, fees, and assessments—once members make these mandatory payments, they may campaign against the union's leaders and remain in good standing.[64]

The inherent weakness of farm worker unions was used to justify the ALRA's broader good standing clause: "This history indicates that the Legislature understood and intended that . . . agricultural unions would be able to require a great deal more from their members than simply payment of dues[65] . . . [including] the power to require their members to honor union-authorized strike and picket lines as a condition of continued good standing and continued employment."[66] Good standing is enforced by the union when it requests that an employer dismiss workers the union has found to be not in good standing.[67] Supporters of broad ALRA good standing emphasize that union members have protection from arbitrary union discipline, since the union must establish good standing rules in its constitution via a democratic process, the rules must be equally applicable to all members, and a union's good standing rules are reviewable by the ALRB and the courts. Farm employers, on the other hand, point to thirty potential activities in the UFW constitution that can cause a UFW member to be found not in good standing.[68]

When workers who were found to be not in good standing and fired at the request of the UFW-filed ULP charges, the ALRB has generally upheld the UFW's broad good standing rules, but found in several cases that the UFW did not provide due process to the workers it ordered fired. Due process means that there must be a hearing before a neutral judge in which the accused worker has an opportunity to present evidence on his behalf and the chance to cross-examine the witnesses against him. Several good-standing cases arose from the 1979 vegetable strikes, in which the UFW called strikes and some workers decided to go through picket lines and work. After a new contract, including ALRA good standing clauses, was signed in September 1979, the UFW asked Mann Packing and Sun Harvest to fire several workers who crossed UFW picket lines during the strike and were found to be not in good standing in the UFW.[69] The employers fired these workers, and the fired workers filed 1154(b) charges against the UFW and 1153(c) charges against Mann Packing and Sun Harvest.

When the cases reached the board, there were two major issues: was the UFW's rule that allowed members who cross authorized picket lines to be declared not in good standing lawful, and did the UFW offer the worker-members it ordered fired a due process hearing? Employees Scarbrough and Pasillas returned to Sun Harvest while the strike was in progress, and Martinez, who was employed by Mann Packing, went to work at Growers Exchange, another grower being struck. The three were tried before a UFW ranch committee that included UFW representatives and fellow workers, with the result that Pasillas was found by the UFW to be not in good standing and expelled from the UFW. Sun Harvest fired him November 2, 1979. Employee Martinez appealed the decision that he was not in good standing to the UFW's National Executive Board, and the board reduced his expulsion to a one-year suspension of membership. When the UFW told Mann in January 1980 that Martinez's UFW membership was suspended, Mann fired him. Scarbrough appealed to the National Executive Board, which changed his expulsion from the UFW to a two-year suspension, and Sun Harvest fired him January 8, 1980. Scarbrough appealed the two-year suspension to the UFW's Public Review Board, which restored Scarbrough to full UFW membership—Sun Harvest then rehired him.

The first question was whether the UFW could discipline members who crossed authorized picket lines. The board reviewed this rule and concluded that it was "reasonable" because it helped the UFW to achieve the legitimate goal of solidarity during strikes: "the power [of the union] . . . to expel strikebreakers is essential if the union is to be an effective bargaining agent."[70] The board then turned to each worker. Pasillas, by failing to appeal the ranch committee's decision finding him to be not in good standing, did not exhaust the internal UFW remedies available to him, and his ULP charge against the UFW and Sun Harvest was dismissed. However, the board concluded that Martinez, who had two years education and was illiterate in English and Spanish, did not receive a due process hearing. The ALRB ordered the UFW to restore Martinez to good standing and to provide him with back pay; employer Mann Packing was ordered to reinstate Martinez. Scarbrough's expulsion was reversed by the UFW, which provided him with back pay and had him rehired by Sun Harvest.[71]

Section 1154(c): Union Bad Faith Bargaining

ALRA section 1154(c) requires a union to bargain in good faith with the employer after it has been certified as the elected representative of the employees. The same good faith bargaining standards apply to employers and unions, namely, the union must meet with the employer at reasonable times and places, bargain with the intent to reach agreement, and if agreement is reached, write up and sign the agreement. However, there is an important difference in the remedy for bad faith bargaining. If an employer bargains in bad faith, the ALRB can order the employer to make the affected employees whole for any wages and benefits they lost during the bad faith bargaining period. If a union bargains in bad faith, there is no makewhole remedy for the workers.

It is rare that unions are charged with bad faith bargaining; most unions want to bargain for a new contract as soon as possible to fulfill their promises to workers and to obtain dues income. However, some employers charged that the ALRA's makewhole remedy encouraged the UFW to bargain slowly with particular growers in the expectation that the employer would eventually engage in bad faith bargaining, enabling the UFW could get the wages and benefits it wanted via a makewhole award.

This is what appears to have happened in Maggio, a carrot grower operating in both the Imperial and Salinas valleys. Maggio alleged that the UFW engaged in delaying tactics and surface bargaining to prevent the signing of a contract with wages lower than the UFW won at Sun Harvest.[72] The UFW and Maggio had a contract between June 1977 and January 1979, and when this contract expired, the UFW called a strike against Maggio. In September 1979, the UFW and Sun Harvest signed what the UFW considered to be its standard contract for vegetable growers, and the UFW insisted in July 1981 that Maggio agree to Sun Harvest wages and benefits. Maggio refused, and submitted a counterproposal January 18, 1982, which the UFW rejected. Maggio filed an 1154(c) charge, alleging that the UFW was engaged in bad faith bargaining between 1982 and 1984, citing the UFW's canceling of scheduled bargaining sessions, the UFW's "patently unacceptable" demands, and the UFW's failure to provide information on health and pension plans for which it was requesting Maggio contributions.[73]

The ALRB agreed that the UFW engaged in bad faith surface bargaining by failing to respond to Maggio proposals and canceling bargaining sessions; however, it concluded that there was no ULP when the UFW asked Maggio to pay the highest wages in California agriculture.[74] Maggio asked that the UFW be required to make Maggio employees whole for the wages and benefits they lost during the bad faith bargaining period. However, the ALRB concluded that only employers must pay makewhole, reasoning that the ALRA explicitly allows the ALRB to order unions to provide back pay for workers that the union causes to be wrongly fired, but the ALRA mentions only employers when discussing makewhole.[75]

ALRA Section 1154(d) (1) prohibits unions from threatening or coercing employers or self-employed persons to join a particular union or employer association; 1154(d) (2) restricts secondary picketing, as occurs when a union pickets a grocery store and asks consumers to shop elsewhere because the store sells certain farm products. Strike and boycott activities are covered in chapter 6. Section 1154(e) prohibits excessive or discriminatory union fees, 1154(f) prohibits union "featherbedding," that is, requiring employers to pay workers for services not performed, and 1154(g) and 1154(h) prohibit recognitional picketing— unions can picket an employer only after they are certified to represent the employees, which can happen only after a secret ballot election in California agriculture. Section 1154(i) permits individuals to refuse "to enter upon the premises of any agricultural employer, other than his own employer, if the employees of such employer are engaged in a strike ratified or approved by a representative of such employees whom such employer is required to recognize."

6

Strikes and Remedies

[To remedy an unfair labor practice, the ALRB shall require violators] "to cease and desist . . . to take affirmative action, including reinstatement of employees with or without back pay, and making employees whole . . . for the loss of pay resulting from the employer's refusal to bargain."

ALRA Section 1160.3

Collective bargaining allows the employers and unions closest to the workplace to negotiate agreements to resolve inevitable workplace disputes. Labor relations laws such as the NLRA and ALRA establish a framework for bargaining by laying out the rules under which unions and employers negotiate, and this framework also establishes limitations on the major weapons each party can use to pressure on other. Unions have four major sources of power: strikes, control over the supply of labor, political action, and boycotts. Employers counter these union weapons by hiring replacement workers and maintaining production during strikes or by shutting down production and laying off workers, so that a strike becomes a contest to see whether the loss of wages will force union concessions before the loss of profits leads to employer concessions. Employers also participate in the political process to increase the supply of labor via immigration and support politicians who favor management rights in labor law.

Strikers and Their Jobs

Unions have traditionally relied on strikes—collective refusals to work—to reduce or stop production and profits so that employers agree with or move toward union demands. When a union calls a strike, it normally establishes a picket line in order to build solidarity among the striking workers and to inform potential strike-breaking workers as well as employees of third-party employers that there is a strike. Unions sometimes mount boycotts of the struck employer's products, and picket stores selling the employer's products to urge consumers not to buy the product affected by the strike, putting indirect or secondary pressure on the struck employer.

Between 1935 and 1947, the NLRA permitted unions to strike and picket the employer with whom the union had a dispute over wages, benefits, or working conditions (the primary employer) and to call strikes that induced workers employed by other (secondary) employers to go on strike (sympathy strikes). For example, if manufacturing workers went on strike, a sympathy strike by truckers might make the strike more effective, since the primary manufacturing employer could not move components in or finished goods out of the factory if the secondary truckers refused to cross the factory workers' picket lines. Beginning with the Taft-Hartley Act of 1947, the NLRA was amended to limit the right of unions to engage in secondary strike and boycott activities.

When the ALRA was being debated in the 1970s, the UFW wanted farm worker unions to have 1935 rights to strike and picket, while farm employers wanted them to have more limited post-1947 NLRA strike rights, plus a prohibition on harvest-time strikes. UFW successes between 1965 and 1975 were built on secondary activities such as consumer boycotts, under which the UFW picketed a retail grocery store such as Safeway to put pressure on a farm employer such as wine maker Gallo. A major difference between the secondary activities permitted by the NLRA and ALRA arises from what unions can do while picketing secondary employers such as Safeway that sell Gallo wines. Under the NLRA, the union and its supporters can picket Safeway and ask consumers not to buy Gallo wine (boycott the product), while under the ALRA, the union may ask consumers not to shop Safeway and not to buy Gallo wine (boycott the store and the product).

There are two major types of lawful strikes. Economic strikes are called to pressure an employer to increase wages or benefits or for some other lawful objective. Unfair labor practice (ULP) strikes, by contrast, are called to protest an employer ULP, such as a strike called in response to the employer firing a union activist or to protest the employer's failure to bargain in good faith. During an economic strike, workers lose wages, and the striking workers risk permanent replacement, that is, the employer can hire replacement workers to keep operating during the strike. When the strike is settled, the striking workers may have been replaced—permanently or temporarily. ULP strikers, on the other hand, cannot be replaced permanently. When a ULP strike is settled, the employer must rehire returning ULP strikers, even if rehiring them forces the employer to discharge replacement workers who were hired during the strike. Unfair labor practice strikers are also entitled to the wages and benefits they lost during the strike. The union may announce that it is going on a ULP strike, so that the striking workers believe that they will get back pay and be able to return to their jobs, but the decision as to whether a strike is an economic or ULP strike is made by the ALRB, often a year or more after the strike began. If the ALRB decides that the strike was economic rather than to protest a ULP, strikers may have lost wages and their jobs.

Before the ALRA was enacted, farmers argued that farm worker unions should be prohibited from calling harvest-time strikes, since farmers could lose a year's income if they could not harvest perishable commodities. Many pre-ALRA proposals for a farm labor relations law prohibited farm worker unions from calling strikes if the strike would, in the words of a 1969 proposal, lead to "the loss, spoilage, deterioration, or reduction in grade, quality or marketability of an agricultural commodity in commercial quantities." The ALRA contained no prohibition on harvest-time strikes, and there have been remarkably few. The major economic strike called by farm workers was the 1979 vegetable strike, which boomeranged on the UFW and increased lettuce prices and grower revenues.

Both economic and unfair labor practice strikes are protected worker activities, so an employer may not fire workers for striking. Employers may replace economic strikers permanently, and the employer's assertion that the workers hired to replace strikers are permanent replacements normally ends the issue: the NLRB accepts the employer's word that the replacement workers are permanent hires. When striking workers make unconditional offers to return to work, the employer must put them on a preferential hiring list and hire them as vacancies occur. The ALRB follows this NLRB approach with year-round workers in nurseries and dairies, as well as for irrigators and tractor drivers on crop farms. For example, in Taylor Farms, workers told their foreman that they would not work unless their wages were raised to at least $5.50 an hour on April 30, 1993.[1] Taylor offered smaller wage increases, saying that the workers were already the best paid in the area, and they responded by going on strike. On May 3, 1993, Taylor began to hire permanent replacement workers, informing them that they would not be terminated to open jobs for returning strikers. On May 12, 1993, the striking workers offered unconditionally to return to work. Taylor placed them on a preferential hiring list and began to hire them as vacancies occurred. The returning strikers charged that Taylor committed an 1153(a) ULP by not rehiring them on May 12. The ALJ/ALRB disagreed, concluding that Taylor lawfully replaced striking workers.[2]

Unfair labor practice strikers who refuse to work to protest an employer's violation of the ALRA are entitled to their old jobs back as well as back pay when they return to work. In O. P. Murphy, bad-faith bargaining during the summer 1977 prompted a strike in September 1977.[3] Murphy was ordered to reinstate the fired strikers and give them back pay between September 13, 1977, and October 15, 1977, when Murphy, on the advice of his attorney, offered to reinstate the strikers who made unconditional offers to return to work. Not all of the striking workers were offered reinstatement and back pay: the union representative fired for picking dirty as well as several strikers who threw tomatoes at strike breakers did not receive their old jobs or back pay.

When striking workers make an unconditional offer to return to work, they tell the employer or write a letter saying that they will return to work at current wages. The employer must rehire them or, if they have been replaced permanently, put them on a preferential list to be rehired as job vacancies occur. An employer does not have to rehire returning strikers if the employer can demonstrate that the striking workers committed strike misconduct, such as destroying crops or equipment or engaging in violent picket line activities. Once the employer proves that a returning striker engaged in strike misconduct, the burden of proof shifts to the worker to show that the alleged misconduct did not occur or that the striker did not commit it. If the worker can prove that he did not engage in misconduct, he must be rehired or put on the rehire list.[4]

During the 1980s, several employers sued farm worker unions for damages caused by strikers under California state law (not the ALRA), which allows triple damage claims if the union was guilty of malice or fraud. Although found not guilty of malice or fraud, the UFW was ordered to pay $1.7 million plus interest in damages to Imperial Valley lettuce grower Carl Maggio because some UFW agents were "actively involved in instigating violence" during the 1979–80 vegetable strike. Maggio had videotape of pickets carrying clubs and throwing rocks and collected $2.3 million from the UFW in 1991.[5] In 1989, Teamsters Local 890, representing Dole Food lettuce harvesters, went on strike to protest planned wage cuts. There was violence on the picket line, and Dole sued Teamsters Local 890 for $13.5 million in damages, based on the assumption that, if Dole could have harvested its crops, it would have reaped strike-induced higher prices. Teamsters Local 890 filed for bankruptcy, in part to move the case from state courts, where the Teamsters could have been liable for triple damages if their agents contributed to strike damage, and into federal courts, where they would be liable only for actual damages. Ultimately, Teamsters Local 890 paid $500,000 for actual strike damages and California law was changed to prevent treble damages for strike-caused losses.

Boycotts and Picketing

When unions have a dispute with an employer, they sometimes try to enlist the help of secondary or neutral employers and businesses to put pressure on the employer with whom they have a dispute. The UFW in the late 1960s put pressure on California grape growers by asking grocery stores not to sell California table grapes. If a grocery store such as Safeway continued to sell table grapes, the UFW might picket Safeway and ask customers to shop elsewhere because Safeway sold grapes. The grape boycott was an example of a secondary consumer boycott—the UFW was trying to enlist the support of secondary or neutral grocery stores and their customers in its battle with the primary employer, grape growers.[6] If the secondary employer or business quits handling the product of the primary employer with whom the union has a dispute, the union gains extra leverage over the primary employer.

Union appeals to consumers to boycott particular goods can take two forms under the ALRA: (1) the union can ask customers not to purchase the product of the struck employer and (2) the union can ask customers not to patronize stores that sell the product. For example, suppose the UFW won an election to represent Gallo farm workers, but was having trouble convincing Gallo to agree to the contract provisions it wanted. The UFW, as the certified representative of Gallo workers, could picket Safeway and asked customers (1) not to buy Gallo wine and (2) not to shop Safeway because Safeway sells Gallo wine. The UFW is thus enlisting Safeway and its customers to pressure Gallo—urging consumers not to shop Safeway is a secondary boycott because the UFW is urging consumers to take action that affects a business—Safeway—with whom the UFW does not have a direct dispute. Secondary consumer boycotts were lawful for nonfarm unions between 1935 and 1947, but they were made illegal under the NLRA by the 1947 Taft-Hartley amendments.[7] Secondary strikes, under which the UFW's picketing persuades Safeway employees to go on strike to protest Safeway's sale of Gallo wine, are unlawful under both the ALRA[8] and NLRA.[9]

Boycotts are closely associated with picketing, a form of free speech that enjoys protections under the First Amendment to the U.S. Constitution. However, in 1942 the U.S. Supreme Court drew a distinction between free speech and picketing, declaring that "picketing by an organized group is more than free speech" because picketing is coercive or intimidating.[10] The NLRB and ALRB have wrestled with the proper line between picketing as lawful free speech and unlawful coercive communication. Although it is clear that picketing activities that include violence are unlawful, it has been harder to draw the line on other forms of picketing.[11]

There were two major cases involving UFW picketing and boycott activities in the 1980s and 1990s, and both resulted in ALRB and court decisions that generally reinforced the favorite weapon of the UFW, the boycott. In Egg City, a dispute between the UFW and California's largest egg producer concluded with a ruling that allowed the UFW to picket and urge a boycott of Coco's restaurants because they used eggs from Egg City.[12] Egg City, founded in 1961, was sold several times, including to the Kroger grocery store chain. The UFW had a contract with Kroger-owned Egg City in the early 1980s, and the contract was in force when Kroger sold Egg City in May 1985. The new owners said they were losing money because Egg City paid $2.50 an hour above the prevailing wage. The contract had expired when Egg City filed a Chapter 11 bankruptcy petition in May 1986 and asked the bankruptcy court to cut wages for 240 UFW-represented workers by $2 per hour. The bankruptcy court approved the wage cut, and the UFW called a strike in protest.[13] Egg City hired permanent replacements for most of the 350 strikers, and UFW mounted a secondary boycott that had some success—McDonald's and grocery store chains Ralph's and Von's stopped buying Egg City eggs.

Egg City responded to the boycott by filing ULP charges, arguing that the UFW's secondary boycott activities were unlawful because its eggs were sent to a distributor, Hidden Villa, which bought eggs from several farms. Thus, when UFW pickets followed Hidden Villa trucks to Coco's and established picket lines, they might be wrong—perhaps Coco's was getting no Egg City eggs. The ALRB dismissed the ULP charge, concluding that it is not the union's responsibility to track eggs through Hidden Villa's distribution system to make sure it is targeting the correct restaurant. But the ALRB also ruled that the UFW's picket signs at restaurants being picketed must be truthful, asking customers to eat elsewhere because the restaurant may be serving eggs from a farm where the UFW has a dispute Egg City eggs.[14]

The second boycott involved UFW supporters picketing southern California grocery stores in Hispanic neighborhoods during the union's Wrath-of-Grapes aimed at persuading grape growers not to use certain pesticides. In 1989, the UFW asked Von's, the largest grocery store chain in southern California, not to sell grapes in its nine Tianguis stores, which were Von's stores located in Hispanic neighborhoods. For eight weeks in 1989, Tianguis stores stopped selling grapes. When Tianguis resumed the sale of grapes in summer 1990, the UFW picketed the stores, urging customers to shop elsewhere because Tianguis was selling grapes. Von's charged the UFW with conducting an illegal secondary boycott—the UFW was urging a boycott of Von's to stop the sale of grapes from farms on which the UFW was not certified to represent farm workers.[15] The ALRB agreed with Von's and ordered the UFW to stop picketing, and the UFW and Von's agreed in April 1991 that Von's would stop promoting (but continue selling) grapes, and the UFW would stop picketing Von's.

This Von's-UFW agreement upset the California Table Grape Commission (CTGC), which sued Von's for failing to promote table grapes, prompting Von's to break its agreement with the UFW and promote table grapes. The UFW responded with mass rallies outside Tianguis stores in June–July 1991, during which union supporters at parking lot entrances wore placards that read "Don't Shop Here," "Boycott Grapes," and "No Grapes." Von's CEO later said: "The UFW's efforts were eminently successful, and [sales] volume reverted to free-fall."[16] The CTGC charged the UFW with unlawful boycotting, and the ALRB in November 1993 ruled that the UFW's boycott activities were unlawful because the UFW was trying to involve a secondary employer, Tianguis-Von's, in a primary dispute with table grape growers, but was not certified to represent grape workers.[17] The ALRB emphasized that the UFW could have picketed and urged a boycott of Tianguis-Von's if its placards included the names of the farms on which it was certified to represent grape pickers. The ALRB invited Tianguis-Von's to sue the UFW for damages; it did not do so.[18]

The UFW appealed this ALRB ruling, and a court of appeals overturned the ALRB, concluding that the California Table Grape Commission did not have standing to file unfair labor practice charges with the ALRB, and that the ALRB had no authority to order the UFW to compensate Tianguis-Von's for losses as a result of the grape boycott. The court of appeals ruled that "the ALRB lacks authority to award compensatory damages to persons injured in their property or business by an unlawful secondary boycott."

Hot Cargo Clauses

If unions are certified to represent the employees of two farm employers, but have more bargaining leverage with one farm employer than
the other, they may include a "hot cargo clause" in the collective bargaining agreement with the employer with whom they have more leverage that allows union members not to handle commodities ("hot cargo")
from the other employer. For example, if the UFW was certified at Gallo
and vineyard X, and had more power with Gallo because of its ability
to mount a consumer boycott of Gallo wines, and Gallo bought grapes
from vineyard X to make wine, the Gallo-UFW agreement could include
a clause that allows Gallo's employees to refuse to handle vineyard X
grapes if the UFW has a dispute with X. A hot cargo clause can make it
difficult for an employer with a union contract to do business with certain other employers whose employees are represented by the same
union, but where there is no contract.

Remedies: Reinstatement and Back Pay

ALRA section 1160 empowers the ALRB to order three major types of
remedies to restore the economic status quo after there have been ULPs:
(1) cease and desist orders that order a violator to stop committing
ULPs; (2) orders requiring reinstatement and back pay for workers who
were unlawfully fired, and (3) orders for makewhole payments to employees who lost wages and benefits while an employer bargained in
bad faith.[19] Cease and desist and reinstatement and back pay are standard remedies in both the farm and nonfarm labor markets, although
the ALRB often deals with unique worker circumstances, such as unauthorized workers. The makewhole remedy, unique to California agriculture, has been the source of many hopes and fears, and in 2002 was
deemed ineffectual and augmented by mandatory mediation.

The standard remedy for most unfair labor practices is a cease and desist order, signed by the violator, that admits a ULP was committed and
promises to stop engaging in unlawful conduct. The cease and desist order is included in the Notice to Workers, which is attached to each ALJ
and ALRB decision and explains the charge, the facts, the law, and application of the law to the facts, and the remedy ordered by the ALJ and
ALRB to restore the economic status quo. The notice must be posted at
the workplace, mailed to current workers and those who were employed at the time of the ULP, and read to current workers, usually by

an ALRB agent—the workers are paid their usual wage by the employer or union that committed the ULP while they listen and ask questions. Some employers objected to having the notice read to workers on company time, but reading is considered necessary because of widespread illiteracy among farm workers.

If workers were fired unlawfully in retaliation for their union activities, the ALRB can order them to be reinstated with back pay, even if the employer is required to terminate replacement workers in order to reinstate them.[20] The objective of this remedy is to restore the economic status quo, so the employer must offer the fired workers (discriminatees) "substantially equivalent" jobs if their original jobs no longer exist. Substantially equivalent means jobs with similar wages, hours of work, duration of employment, fringe benefits, duties, responsibilities, and working conditions.

Agriculture is probably the largest U.S. industry that has over 50 percent unauthorized workers, and a major issue is whether unauthorized workers, whose union rights are protected by the ALRA, can be ordered reinstated if they are unlawfully fired. In the 1984 Sure-Tan case, the U.S. Supreme Court confirmed that unauthorized or illegal alien workers are protected by the NLRA: "If undocumented alien employees were excluded from . . . protection against employer intimidation, there would be created a subclass of workers without a comparable stake in the collective goals of their legally resident co-workers, thereby eroding the unity of all employees and impeding effective collective bargaining."[21] However, the Supreme Court reversed an NLRB order requiring Sure-Tan, a Chicago-area tannery, to provide back pay to and rehire unauthorized workers. Sure-Tan had called the INS in retaliation for the workers' prounion vote, and the INS had returned the unauthorized workers to Mexico. The Supreme Court reasoned that, if the NLRB ordered employers to reinstate unauthorized workers who were outside the United States, they would be encouraged to return illegally to the United States for guaranteed jobs; the employer did not have to provide back pay because the workers in Mexico were not available to work.[22]

The ALRB in the 1985 Rigi case decided that the Sure-Tan decision was not an "applicable precedent" because California farm employers historically employed illegal alien workers and the legislature knew about this unauthorized worker employment, but did not exclude unauthorized workers from the ALRA's protections and remedies. Rigi Agricultural Services was a Napa vineyard management company that harvested grapes for Mondavi and had workers who wanted the same working conditions they had at Mondavi. The dissatisfied workers requested a UFW election, which was held in September 1981; the UFW lost by a vote of 20 to 24.[23] Early in 1982, the pro-UFW employees were laid off, and they charged Rigi with an 1153(c) discrimination ULP. The laid-off workers were able to answer yes to the four dual-motive questions: they suffered discrimination (layoffs), they had engaged in union activities, Rigi knew of their union activities, and one reason for their layoffs was Rigi's antiunion attitude (Rigi called meetings during the summer of 1981 and told workers that they did not need a union to represent them). The burden of proof then shifted to Rigi, who showed that the temporary workers among those laid off were not discriminated against—seasonal layoffs were normal for them—but Rigi failed to prove that the five year-round workers would have been laid off if they had not engaged in union activities. Rigi was ordered to reinstate them with back pay.

Rigi protested the reinstatement remedy, arguing that three of the five workers were not legally authorized to work in the United States. However, the ALRB in a 3–2 decision ordered Rigi to reinstate all five workers because they did not leave the United States, as in Sure-Tan, and thus did not have to enter the United States illegally to be reinstated and in 1985 there were no federal sanctions for knowingly hiring unauthorized workers. The two dissenting board members agreed that Rigi should be ordered to reinstate the five unlawfully fired workers with back pay, but would have allowed Rigi to challenge the ALRB's reinstatement order for particular workers, and Rigi would not have to reinstate those under INS deportation orders.[24]

Phillip D. Bertelsen fired fourteen workers on January 31, 1985, for engaging in protected concerted activity—the workers wanted the piece rate for picking oranges raised from $9.50 to $12 a bin.[25] On March 19, 1986, Bertelsen sent them letters offering to reinstate them. When the thirteen workers returned on March 24, 1986, Bertelsen told them that a new hiring policy had been adopted that required all newly hired workers to prove that they were legally authorized to work in the United States. The thirteen returning workers were Salvadorans who had applied for asylum in the United States, and they had letters that prevented them from being deported but did not give them authorization to work in the United States. Bertelsen refused to rehire them. The thirteen stayed in the United States, applied for legalization under the Special Agricultural Worker (SAW) legal status in May 1987, and were rehired by Bertelsen on June 1, 1987.

The ALRB ordered Bertelsen to pay the workers $60,148, or $3,000 to $6,000 each, in back pay to cover the entire January 1985 to June 1987 period because Bertelsen never proved that the workers were in fact unauthorized. Bertelsen appealed the ALRB back-pay remedy to the courts, which sided with the ALRB, concluding that immigration law "does not preempt make whole relief for undocumented workers present in California and physically available for work."

In 1986, the Immigration Reform and Control Act (IRCA) made it unlawful for most U.S. employers to knowingly hire unauthorized workers. IRCA established an employee verification system—newly hired workers must present proof of their authorization to work in the United States, and the employer and worker must sign an I-9 Employee Verification Form that verifies that the worker has presented documentation to the employer showing identity and right to work in the United States; the I-9 Form is kept on file by the employer for INS inspection. The Bertelsen case began before sanctions were enacted, but the ALRB and courts after sanctions were in effect concluded that employers could be required to provide back pay to unauthorized workers because the Supreme Court's Sure-Tan decision applied only to unauthorized workers outside the United States.[26] For example, the Second Circuit U.S. Court of Appeals in 1997 upheld an NLRB order that an employer provide back pay to two unlawfully fired unauthorized workers, reasoning that the purpose of IRCA's employer sanctions was "to reduce the incentive for employers to hire illegal aliens," and not providing back pay might encourage employers to hire unauthorized workers.

Back pay for unauthorized workers ended in March 2002, when the U.S. Supreme Court decided in Hoffman Plastic Compounds that unauthorized workers are not entitled to back pay for the wages they lost after being fired unlawfully for engaging in protected labor activities. The case involved an unauthorized Mexican, Jose Castro, whose real name is Samuel Perez. Castro/Perez presented a false Texas birth certificate to get a job at Hoffman in 1988, was fired unlawfully for handing out union authorization cards to fellow employees, and admitted he was unauthorized when the NLRB's ALJ was determining the remedy for the unlawful firing. The ALJ decided that Castro/Perez was not entitled to reinstatement and back pay, but the National Labor Relations Board partially reversed the ALJ, agreeing that Castro/Perez did not have to be reinstated because he was unauthorized, but ordering Hoffman to provide Castro/Perez with sixty-seven thousand dollars in lost wages for the 3.5 years between his unlawful firing and the time Hoffman learned he was unauthorized.

The U.S. Supreme Court reversed the NLRB's back pay order in a 5–4 decision, with Chief Justice William H. Rehnquist concluding that "awarding back pay to illegal aliens runs counter to policies underlying" immigration law. He continued that back pay "would encourage the successful evasion of apprehension by immigration authorities, condone prior violations of the immigration laws, and encourage future violations," since unlawfully fired workers are required to try to find alternative employment, and any earnings from such employment are deducted from the back pay award. The court emphasized that there are other times when the NLRB does not award reinstatement and back pay, such as to workers who engaged in "serious illegal conduct," including committing violence during strikes.

The Supreme Court implicitly said that being an unauthorized worker in the United States is serious illegal conduct, and thus unauthorized workers whose labor relations rights are violated cannot expect to receive the same remedies as legal workers. The dissenters argued that not providing back pay to unlawfully fired workers might encourage employers to hire them, increasing illegal immigration. The ALRB has not yet applied Hoffman Plastics, but this Supreme Court decision is likely to block reinstatement and back pay for unauthorized farm workers under the ALRA. Some employers may be reluctant to raise unauthorized status as a reason not to reinstate unauthorized workers, since it might reveal to the INS that they have unauthorized workers.

It is often several years before workers who are unlawfully fired are ordered reinstated. Employers or unions violating the ALRA must restore fired workers to the economic status quo they would have had if there had been no ULP. The ALRB calculates the back pay owed to an unlawfully fired worker by answering three questions: when would the aggrieved employee have worked, how much would the worker have earned, and did the fired worker have any interim earnings (deducted from the employer's back pay liability) or job search expenses (added to the employer's back pay liability)?[27] The general formula for calculating back pay is: $Bp = W - (Wi - E) + I$, where Bp is the amount of the back pay award, W is the amount the worker would have earned had he or she not been unlawfully discharged, Wi are any earnings by the worker while unlawfully without a job, E are job seeking expenses, and I is interest—the rate set by the Internal Revenue Service for delinquent taxes.[28] During compliance hearings, the general counsel, representing the fired workers, recommends an amount of back pay, and the violating party (employer or union) has an opportunity to dispute the proposed award.

If the discriminatee was a seasonal worker, back pay is calculated on a daily basis. This means that, for every day in the back pay period, the ALRB must determine if the worker would have worked, his expected wages on days with work, and whether the worker had any interim earnings on days when he would have worked for the offending employer. For each day of work, expected wages (say, one hundred dollars) are determined, interim earnings (say, sixty dollars) are deducted, job search expenses are added to the employer's liability (say, ten dollars), and the employer owes the worker, in this example, fifty dollars. The NLRB uses a quarterly period to calculate expected and interim earnings.[29]

Remedies: Makewhole and Mandatory Mediation

Unions promise workers that they will negotiate higher wages and improved benefits if the union wins the election and becomes the workers' certified bargaining agent. This means that workers are very interested in negotiations for a first contract as well as for contract renewals; they expect each new contract to bring higher wages and improved benefits. If the employer fails to bargain in good faith, the employer can delay wage and benefit increases, thereby benefiting economically from committing a ULP. To prevent this, the ALRA includes a makewhole remedy designed to transfer any economic gains from the violating employer to the workers who were employed during the bad-faith bargaining.

The ALRA is the only labor law that explicitly provides a makewhole remedy for bad faith bargaining, but the ALRB has found it hard to develop consistent rules for making the two major decisions involved in makewhole remedies: when to require the payment of makewhole and how much makewhole to require employers to pay. In Perry Farms, the board decided that makewhole was appropriate *any time* employers bargained in bad faith and workers lost wages and benefits as a result.[30] Perry engaged in a "technical refusal to bargain," meaning that Perry refused to bargain with the UFW in order to get courts to review the ALRB's certification of the UFW as bargaining representative for Perry workers. The UFW filed 1153(e) bad-faith charges, the ALJ/ALRB agreed that Perry bargained in bad faith, and Perry appealed the ALRB's bad-faith decision to the California courts, which allowed the courts to review the ALRB's original certification of the UFW. The ALRB decided, regardless of why Perry refused to bargain, Perry owed makewhole because: "The employees suffer this same loss whether or not the employer's refusal to bargain is designed solely to procure review in the courts of the underlying election issues or is of the flagrant or willful variety." Otherwise, the ALRB reasoned, the employer wins both ways: (1) losing in court would mean no makewhole because the employer was challenging the union's certification and (2) winning in court would mean no makewhole because the election would be set aside and there would be no obligation to bargain.

Perry appealed this ALRB decision to the California Supreme Court, which in 1979 ruled in a similar J. R. Norton case that the ALRB cannot adopt such a blanket makewhole remedy. Instead, the court ordered the ALRB to examine *why* an employer refused to bargain. If the employer was challenging the certification of a union in a "good faith belief" that the board made an error, there should be no makewhole.[31] The ALRB thus developed a two-pronged test to decide when to order makewhole, asking whether the employer's objections to the union's certification were reasonable and then the employer's motivation—was the employer challenging the election in good faith or to delay bargaining.[32]

In 1987 the ALRB's ability to order makewhole was further restricted by a court of appeal decision that, after an employer was found by the ALRB not to have bargained in good faith, the offending employer must be given an opportunity to argue that, even with good-faith bargaining, there would not have been a contract negotiated that increased wages: "Once the Board produces evidence showing the employer unlawfully refused to bargain, the burden of persuasion shifts to the employer to prove no agreement calling for higher pay would have been concluded in the absence of the illegality."[33]

Employer Dal Porto refused to agree to the UFW's demand for a dues checkoff system, but Dal Porto did not determine the cost of implementing such a system, or ask during negotiations that the UFW accept a lower wage increase to offset the cost of a dues checkoff system. According to the ALRB, this indicated bad faith bargaining because "Dal Porto in effect answered 'no' [to the UFW in bargaining] before it knew just what the question was." The court agreed that Dal Porto bargained in bad faith, but ruled that, before calculating a makewhole remedy, the ALRB must give Dal Porto the opportunity to provide evidence that, even with good faith bargaining, Dal Porto would not have negotiated an agreement with higher wages and benefits.[34] The burden of proof in making this no-higher-wages argument is on the employer: "The wrongdoer shall bear the risk of the uncertainty which his own wrong has created."[35]

Saikhon illustrates how an employer can use a Dal Porto defense to eliminate a makewhole remedy.[36] Saikhon bargained in bad faith with the UFW over a two-year period, but avoided paying makewhole by showing, during its Dal Porto defense, that other Imperial Valley growers who bargained in good faith with the UFW did not agree to the wage and benefit package proposed by the ALRB as the basis for Saikhon's makewhole remedy. The ALRB accepted Saikhon's argument that even good faith bargaining would not have produced a UFW-Saikhon contract as long as the UFW demanded that Imperial Valley growers such as Saikhon pay "Sun Harvest" wages—the UFW was able to negotiate its highest wages with firms such as Sun Harvest, which were based in the Salinas Valley, not Imperial. The ALRB agreed with Saikhon that the UFW's strategy "was based on the Sun Harvest contract . . . [the UFW's] position was that this master contract represented the Union's final terms on the major issues of concern, from which the Union was unwilling to bargain."[37] The ALRB nonetheless ordered Saikhon to pay makewhole wages and benefits for the period that Saikhon refused to bargain.[38]

The Dal Porto decision seemed to force the ALRB to break a cardinal rule of labor relations, namely, that government agencies not look inside the bargaining room and review what the parties are saying at the bargaining table. This principle of having the government set the rules but not interfere in the game permits, for example, a union to lawfully press for wages so high that the employer goes out of business. Court decisions that deal with when and how much employers must pay in makewhole remedies force the ALRB to look at employer reasons for not bargaining and to make decisions about what the employer and union would have agreed to during lawful bargaining.

The second makewhole issue is how much employers should pay to the workers who were employed during bad faith bargaining periods. In 1978, when the first makewhole remedies were ordered, there were no regularly published data on the wages and benefits of unionized farm workers. In Adam Dairy or Rancho dos Rios, a Santa Maria, California, dairy with 350 cows and twelve to eighteen milkers and field workers, the UFW won an election on a 5–2 vote in September 1975 and was certified as bargaining representative in December 1975.[39] Adam Dairy failed to provide the UFW with the information it needed to bargain, made unilateral changes in wages, and fired or refused to rehire union activist workers. The UFW charged Adam Dairy with discrimination and bad faith bargaining, the ALRB agreed that Adam bargained in bad faith and ordered Adam Dairy to rehire the fired workers and make its employees whole for the bad faith bargaining.

How much makewhole did Adam Dairy owe its employees? The ALRB decided that, if Adam Dairy had bargained in good faith, it could have been expected to pay the average entry-level wage rate that was negotiated in the thirty-seven UFW contracts signed between 1975 and 1978, $3.13 an hour. Thus, Adam Dairy owed its entry-level workers $3.13 an hour minus the actual wage they received during the bad faith period. In addition, Adam Dairy workers lost the fringe benefits they may have had under a contract, and the ALRB calculated these lost fringe benefits by assuming that wages were 78 percent of total worker compensation, as they were in the U.S. private nonmanufacturing sector.[40] This means that each worker's gross makewhole was $4.01 an hour ($3.13 divided by 0.78), and each entry-level employee should receive the difference between $4.01 an hour and the amount actually paid in wages and benefits during the bad-faith bargaining period. Workers earning 10 percent more than the base wage were entitled to a makewhole wage 10 percent larger, for example, $4.41 rather than $4.01 per hour.

The Adam Dairy method of calculating makewhole raised many questions. For example, the thirty-seven UFW contracts included no dairies, raising questions about using wages negotiated in one commodity to determine a makewhole remedy in another commodity (Martin and Egan, 1989). Concerns about using wages in one commodity to determine what employers would have negotiated in another led the ALRB, in J. R. Norton, to select one or more "comparable contracts" to determine the makewhole remedy.[41] This comparable-contract method of calculating makewhole set off a new round of litigation over which contracts were comparable, and led to charges by the UFW that Republican-appointed ALRB leaders accepted makewhole awards that were far too low.[42]

Makewhole is a remedy designed to encourage good faith bargaining and thus ensure timely negotiations of first and subsequent contracts. Makewhole has been unable to achieve this timely contract negotiation goal; there is often a long lag between certification and first contract, and there are many farms on which a union has won an election and been certified to represent farm workers, but there has never been a contract. As implemented during twenty-seven years in California agriculture, the makewhole remedy seems to have encouraged litigation over whether makewhole is owed and how much, which leads to years and even decades between bad-faith bargaining and makewhole payments to workers. Employers know that turnover in the farm work force is high, giving them an incentive to delay final decisions and payments as long as possible, since awards were made only to workers who can be located, unless there is a settlement that provides otherwise.[43]

The UFW in 2002 declared makewhole a limited remedy for bad-faith bargaining and supported the first amendment to the ALRA to require binding arbitration to obtain a first agreement within six months of a union being certified to represent workers.[44] Farmers bitterly opposed binding arbitration, emphasizing that it is used mostly to resolve disputes when employees cannot strike, such as police and firefighters. Nonetheless, the UFW had a relatively easy time persuading the legislature to approve binding arbitration and applied a great deal of political pressure to get the binding arbitration bill signed into law, making a 150 mile, ten-day "March for the Governor's Signature" from Merced to Sacramento along Highway 99.

A compromise, mandatory mediation, was signed into law. It allows for mandatory mediation of up to seventy-five disputes between 2003 and 2007 involving farms that hire a peak twenty-five or more workers. After a union is certified to represent workers, unions and employers bargain for 180 days for a first contract, and if no agreement is reached, either side can request a mediator to help the parties reach agreement for another thirty days. If mediation fails, the law provides that the mediator must, within twenty-one days, recommend the terms of a collective bargaining agreement to the parties and provide reasons for his recommendations. Either the employer or the union can petition the ALRB within ten days to modify the mediator's recommendations. If this occurs, the ALRB reviews objections and either allows the mediator's agreement to go into effect or modifies it. Either side can appeal the collective bargaining agreement imposed on them by the mediator-ALRB to a state court of appeals or the California Supreme Court.

III UNIONS AND IMMIGRATION

For most of the twentieth century, farm labor reformers wanted to make the farm labor market more like nonfarm labor markets, meaning that farm employers would invest in personnel departments that recruited the best workers, developed remuneration systems to motivate them, and retained them with seniority and fringe benefits. If unions established a strong foothold, union hiring halls could handle recruitment and collective bargaining could determine wages and retention policies. However, instead of farm labor markets becoming more like this nonfarm ideal, many farmers distanced themselves from the workers on their farms, turning to labor contractors to obtain crews of workers. In an ironic twist, some nonfarm labor markets have become more like farm labor markets in the twenty-first century, hiring workers through nonfarm versions of labor contractors, such as temporary help firms.

Farm labor unions began as nontraditional organizations with nontraditional leaders helping nontraditional workers, and these uniquenesses remain. The UFW, for example, continues to rely on member dues for less than a quarter of its budget, raising far more money from donations than from dues and relying on volunteers to help organize increasingly unauthorized immigrant workers. Such a union is also likely to be nontraditional in the strategies and tactics it uses to put pressure on employers, favoring boycotts and politics over strikes and efforts to control the supply of labor.

In chapter 7, I review the economic reasons why farm worker unions are nontraditional, explaining that an inelastic demand for farm commodities may allow strikes to help, not hurt growers, while growing dependence on immigrant workers makes the farm labor market subject to shock adjustments if the immigrants are removed quickly. In chapter 8, I turn to immigration policy, reviewing proposals for a twenty-first-century farm labor policy and their long-run consequences for farm employers, farm workers, and the public interest. I conclude that, in the long run, there is nothing more expensive than cheap food, that the status quo in the farm labor market will prove costly for Americans and their descendants.

7

Nontraditional Farm Worker Unions

Conditions in agriculture are so different . . . that no union should be empowered to act as the exclusive bargaining agent of the workers employed by farmers.

Matt Triggs, American Farm Bureau Federation, testimony before the
U.S. Senate Subcommittee on Migratory Labor, July 8, 1965

Unions play small and declining roles in the U.S. and California farm labor markets, yet low wages, poor working conditions, and unique features of the farm labor market, including immigration and migrancy, keep farm labor issues in the news, reminding Americans that farm labor is a "problem." Most farm employers continue to believe that unions are neither desirable nor inevitable, and most farm workers continue to exit for nonfarm jobs rather than turn to unions for upward mobility in agriculture. Since unions and collective bargaining are not the usual way that workplace disputes are resolved in agriculture, the ALRB has not become an agency farmers and unions look to to make fair and final decisions of labor disputes.

Many farmers complain that they cannot work with the unions that try to organize their workers because they are not traditional business unions, interested in obtaining the best wages and benefits for the workers they represent, but then leaving the employer free to run the business. Traditional unions use strikes to try to put pressure on employers to raise wages, a strategy that farmers can understand and anticipate. Nontraditional unions, by contrast, may use consumer boycotts and political action to pressure farmers, tactics that make it hard for an individual farmer to determine impacts.

Strikes in an ongoing labor-management relationship are often considered akin to disputes in a stable marriage—the parties have every intention of resuming their relationship after the strike is settled. Most economic analyses of strikes assume they are caused by imperfect information between parties that anticipate a long-term relationship: one party does not understand the other's true "bottom line," but during the strike, as costs mount for each side, positions becomes clear, each side makes concessions, and the narrowing of differences eventually leads to a settlement. Economic models of bargaining thus picture negotiations as a process in which the union reduces its demands over time, employers increase their offers, and the falling union resistance curve meets the rising employer offer curve to produce an agreement.[1]

Farmers resisted a farm labor relations laws for decades because they imagined that unions would call strikes when they had their maximum bargaining power, at harvest time. Farmers, who had already invested to produce the crop, would pay up to the price they received for the commodity to get it harvested—preharvest costs were fixed or sunk by harvest time. Thus, much as Japanese crews mounted "quickie" harvest-time strikes to win wage increases, farmers might have to pay very high wages to get their crops harvested because the farmer could not afford to lose an entire year's crop and income. This farmer reasoning ignored the reality that the Japanese quickie strikes aimed to get them the same wages that other farm workers were receiving—as newcomers, they were paid less. It also ignored the fact that a contract for two to three years years could provide assurance that there would be no harvest time strikes.

The ALRA contained no prohibitions on harvest-time strikes, and there have been few. The UFW tried the traditional union weapon, the strike, in 1979 in support of a demand for a 40 percent wage increase from Imperial Valley vegetable growers. But the UFW soon learned that the demand for lettuce, the major commodity affected by the strike, is inelastic, which means that about the same amount is bought at $1 a head as at $1.50 a head. The strike helped to reduce the supply of lettuce by one-third, but the farmers' price tripled, so that winter lettuce revenues doubled during the strike (Carter et al., 1981).[2] The lettuce was already planted when the strike began—farmers did not anticipate a strike, so the normal crop was in the ground—and the UFW strike helped growers as a group because the elasticity of demand for lettuce is 0.2, meaning that a 10 percent increase in the retail price of lettuce reduces demand by about 2 percent.

The boomerang effect of the strike is apparent in figure 7.1. In a normal February, Imperial Valley lettuce growers sold 10.4 million twenty-four-head, or 50-pound, cartons of lettuce at an average price of $3.75 a carton, generating $39 million in revenues (the rectangle formed at *a*). In February 1979, only 6.6 million cartons were shipped, but the grower price was $10.50 a carton, generating $69 million in revenues (the rectangle formed at *b*). A monopoly lettuce producer aiming for maximum profits would have sold 5.8 million cartons at $12 a carton, generating $70 million in revenues (the rectangle formed at *c*).

The UFW's partially effective lettuce strike helped to move the Imperial Valley lettuce industry from *a* to *b*, almost doubling revenues.[3] These additional revenues, of course, were not distributed evenly—the major beneficiaries included Bud (now Dole), which had a Teamster's contract, as well as lettuce producers in Arizona, where there was no strike. However, in markets with inelastic demands, reducing supply increases revenue and is the basis for a marketing system that farmers have lobbied to have federal and state governments enforce, which restricts the supply of farm commodities and raises grower prices and revenues. In order to achieve the same result with labor, the Western Growers Association, which represented most lettuce growers, established a strike insurance program after 1979. Growers paid strike insurance premiums, and those who could not harvest because of a strike received payments.[4]

After 1979, there were very few harvest strikes. One of the few occurred in October–November 1989, when most of the workers employed by Dole's Bud fresh vegetable division in Salinas, and represented by Teamsters Local 890, went on strike to protest Dole's demand for a $0.50 wage cut, from $7.20 to $6.70 an hour, and reduced fringe benefits. Dole, which said it needed to reduce wages and benefits to compete with nonunion vegetable growers, accounted for 15 to 25 percent of California's production of vegetables such as lettuce, broccoli, and celery, and the strike doubled lettuce prices, from the usual fall price of six dollars to eight dollars a carton of lettuce to thirteen dollars to fifteen dollars a carton.[5] Teamsters Local 890—not the local that competed with the UFW to represent farm workers in the 1960s and 1970s—filed for bankruptcy after being ordered to pay $526,692 for damages caused by strikers and pickets.

The UFW has also been involved in more traditional strikes, but most have been very short. Fruits such as citrus can stay on the tree for weeks, and in March 1978, citrus workers in Ventura County went on strike briefly before the employer associations that harvested lemons and oranges agreed to increase wages significantly and give the UFW about twenty contracts in the county, enough to be the dominant influence on wages and benefits. However, the associations passed on the cost of the union contracts to their member growers, some of whom elected to leave the association and have nonunion custom harvesters pick their

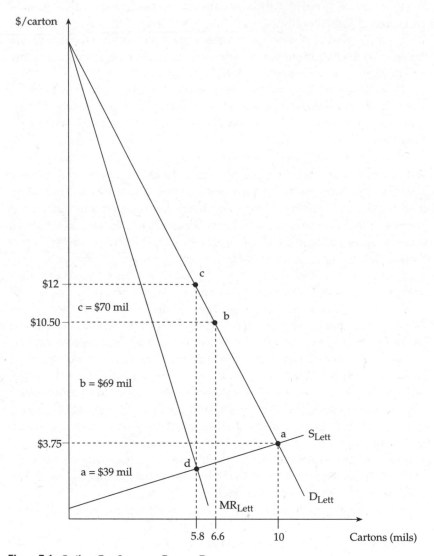

Figure 7.1. Strikes Can Increase Grower Revenues

fruit. When the UFW demanded another significant wage increase in the early 1980s when the 1978 contracts came up for renewal, exits from the associations accelerated and most of these farmer associations eventually collapsed. The UFW was unable to win contracts with the custom harvesters that replaced the associations.

Consumer Boycotts

Since strikes can boomerang and increase grower revenues, farm worker unions tend to rely on nontraditional union weapons, such as consumer boycotts, to put economic pressure on farm employers. Strikes aim to reduce the supply of a commodity, while boycotts aim to reduce the demand for a commodity. If demand is inelastic, and 10 to 20 percent of consumers honor the boycott while supply is unchanged, grower prices and revenues can fall sharply.

From a farm worker union point of view, boycotts are far more effective than strikes: they save the union the cost of paying benefits to strikers, and they allow the union to rely on students, church leaders, and volunteers to mount the boycott. During boycotts, most farm workers keep their jobs and earn normal wages, since farmers will keep harvesting so long as the boycott-lowered price is higher than harvesting costs—the only way that the grower can get this boycott-lowered price is if he harvests the crop, which requires farm workers.

In figure 7.1, a boycott could reduce the demand for the commodity, moving it inward, as from a to d, or from a grower price of $3.75 a carton for lettuce to $2.50, a significant drop for growers. Figure 7.2 illustrates the effects of a consumer boycott on an individual grower. As a result of the boycott, consumer demand falls, and the grower price falls from P0 at a to P1 at b. At the lower price P1, the grower will slightly reduce the amount of lettuce harvested, perhaps by not repicking a field the third or fourth time. However, grower losses in lower revenue are far larger than lost wages—the boycott leaves most farm workers employed, but reduces grower revenue.

The UFW's 1967–69 table grape boycott is an example of a successful consumer boycott. Volunteers did most of the picketing of stores that sold grapes, urging consumers not to buy grapes or shop stores that sold them, and falling per capita grape consumption—from 3.2 pounds per person in 1966 to 2 pounds in 1971–72—reduced grower prices. Most grape pickers kept their jobs and earnings during the boycott. However, the UFW lettuce boycott in the early 1970s largely failed, in part because the UFW did not represent all lettuce workers and urged consumers to "ask for the black eagle" (lettuce picked under UFW contract) and boycott other lettuce, including that picked under Teamster contracts. The UFW's "wrath of grapes" boycott in the 1980s and early 1990s, which relied on mass mailings to consumers also failed: in 1983–84, grape consumption averaged 5.6 pounds per person; in 1999–00, per capita consumption averaged 8.2 pounds per person.

The UFW has sometimes mounted boycotts of a particular firm's

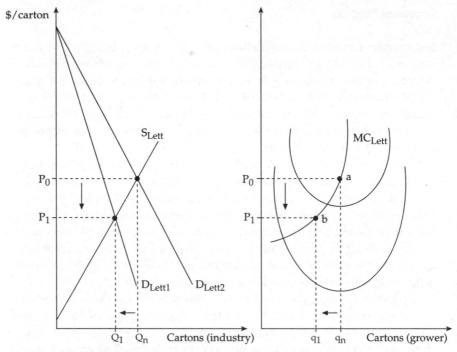

Figure 7.2. Boycotts Can Lower Grower Revenues

commodities. For example, the UFW's boycott of Gallo wine between 1973 and 1978 persuaded some consumers to avoid Gallo wines long after the boycott ended. In other cases, the UFW has threatened to boycott a restaurant that uses commodities from the farm where there is a dispute. For example, the UFW threatened to boycott McDonald's if it continued to buy lettuce from Bruce Church (BCI), which resulted in McDonald's dropping BCI as a lettuce supplier. The UFW has followed a similar strategy at Pizza Hut, asking Pizza Hut not to buy Pictsweet mushrooms because the UFW has a dispute with Pictsweet. During the 1996–2000 strawberry organizing campaign, the UFW did not call for a boycott of strawberries, but it did ask supermarkets to support "fairness for farm workers."[6]

Boycotts aim to reduce the demand for a particular commodity. However, unions sometimes try to increase the demand for particular commodities by asking consumers to "look for the union label," by buying from firms with union contracts. The UFW's largest contract covers one thousand workers employed by Bear Creek, Jackson and Perkins roses. Bear Creek developed two commemorative roses: the Our Lady of Guadalupe rose and the Cesar E. Chavez rose, and the UFW promotes these roses to Hispanics. Bear Creek is one of the largest UFW contracts, covering a peak fourteen hundred workers who earn $6.75 to $15 an hour, receive health insurance, pension benefits, and up to three weeks vacation plus ten paid holidays—including Chavez's birthday.

Farm worker unions outside California also rely on boycotts. The Ohio-based FLOC, for example, threatened a boycott of Campbell's (Vlasic) and Heinz products to persuade these processors of cucumbers to require the Ohio farmers who grow pickles for them to recognize FLOC as the bargaining representative for their farm workers. After seven years, Campbell's (Vlasic) and Heinz agreed in 1885 that growers who grow cucumbers for them must recognize FLOC as bargaining agent for their farm workers and pay the wages agreed to in the FLOC-processor-grower collective bargaining agreement; the processors raised prices to growers to cover the higher wages. FLOC was involved in a similar boycott against Mount Olive Pickle Company in North Carolina in 2000–02, the second-largest processor, but Mount Olive has so far refused to enter into three-way contracts with FLOC, arguing that the "independent farmers" who grow cucumbers are the workers' employers.[7]

The Florida Coalition of Immokalee Workers (CIW) has for several years tried to persuade Taco Bell to get the growers of its tomatoes to raise the piece rate wages they pay to have tomatoes picked in Florida. According to the CIW, tomato pickers receive forty cents to forty-five cents a thirty-two-pound bucket for picking tomatoes in 2000–02. The CIW wants Taco Bell to pay growers a penny a pound more for tomatoes, so that growers raise the piece rate they pay workers to seventy to seventy-five cents a pound. Taco Bell has so far refused to deal with the CIW. However, the Northwest Treeplanters and Farmworkers United union (PCUN in Spanish) ended a decade-long boycott of Norpac, a 240-member farmer's cooperative in Oregon, in 2002 after 21 Norpac grower-members allowed PCUN to organize workers on their farms.

Integration, Trade, and Mechanization

During the heyday of the UFW in the 1970s, inflation was high and many food-related firms and conglomerates, such as oil companies, bought farmland as a hedge against inflation and to earn profits from farming. Fruits and vegetables are high risk but potentially high profit commodities, and the theory of these nontraditional farmers was that, since their firms had multiple income streams, they could earn the higher than average profits from FVH commodities. Some pundits expected most produce to have brand names by the 1980s, so that consumers would expect Dole or Sunworld labels on their fruits and vegetables as marketers also became growers. Vertical integration and brand names were expected to also increase the power of unions, since the money spent advertising a brand name could also increase that brand's vulnerability to a boycott.

Firms such as Dole have developed brand names, but most fruits and vegetables continue to be sold without labels. Many firms with brand names, such as Driscoll strawberries, are no longer farmers, preferring to buy produce from "independent farmers" who agree to grow fruits and vegetables according to their specifications. Many of the oil companies sold their farmland in the 1980s, and the insurance companies and other investors who bought much of this land leased or sold it to "independent farmers" who were less vulnerable to boycotts. Cesar Chavez was undaunted by this reorganization of labor-intensive agriculture, arguing that the UFW would represent farm workers regardless of who owned the land. However, the UFW has found it much harder to put pressure on growers who do not have nonfarm businesses and brand names.

Union-led boycotts of fruits and vegetables are also getting more difficult because imports have taken a growing share of the produce market. The United States has been a net exporter of farm commodities for decades, and in recent years has exported commodities worth about $50 billion a year, and imported commodities worth $40 billion a year—U.S. farm receipts are about $200 billion a year, so about 25 percent of U.S. farm commodities, by value, are exported. The United States has more balanced trade in fruits and vegetables—exports and imports are each about $8 billion a year—and it is sometimes said that, if unions succeed in pushing up U.S. farm wages, U.S. farm workers would be displaced by imports or machines. Higher U.S. farm labor costs would encourage more food marketers to buy or "source" fruits and vegetables abroad, but transportation costs and seasonality put limits on imports. For example, Mexican fruit and vegetable production peaks in the winter months, when U.S. consumption is lowest.

The mechanization threat is more immediate. If unions were to push up U.S. farm labor costs, farmers might mechanize more tasks, reducing farm worker employment. The mechanization of tomato harvesting in response to rising wages after the end of the *bracero* program was expected to be the first of many harvests that would be mechanized. Lawsuits that restricted the expenditure of tax monies on mechanization research, plus rising illegal immigration and stable wages, slowed mechanization research. Fluctuating farm prices also discourage mechanization, since farmers know they will have to pay for the machine even if prices dip so low they do not plant or harvest a crop. There are prototype machines available to do most farm labor tasks, but they are not adopted widely until rising wages put them into action, then practical experience leads to refinements and cooperation with packers and processors that allow the entire commodity to mechanize.

Instead of mechanization eliminating farm jobs, some nonfarm jobs became farm jobs in the 1990s. Nonfarm unions pushed wages in the nonfarm packing sheds where broccoli and melons were packed into cartons to twice field worker levels, prompting integrated grower-packers to close packing sheds and pack commodities in the field, usually by having workers follow slow-moving conveyor belts. In this case, farm workers both pick and pack commodities, which increases the number of farm jobs. Lettuce grower-packers in the 1950s eliminated the high-wage jobs of workers who packed lettuce into wooden cartons, which were loaded onto rail cars and packed with ice for shipment to East Coast markets. By packing lettuce into cardboard cartons in the fields, and using portable vacuum tubes that sucked the air out of the lettuce to cool it quickly, the jobs of high-wage lettuce shed workers were eliminated (Padfield and Martin, 1965).

The interaction of food chain integration, trade, and mechanization make it difficult to predict the trajectory of the farm labor market. However, for at least the next several decades, there will continue to be millions of often short-duration farm jobs that will require workers to stoop and pick crops, or climb ladders and pick fruit into bags that hang over their shoulders. Stooping and climbing lead to frequent injuries from falls and back strains, which explains why most harvesters are young men. Women and older workers are more common among the workers who follow conveyor belts, where there is less lifting of heavy bags or boxes. If the immigration of young men slowed, there could be a renewed interest in mechanical aids, which are devices to make farm work easier and reduce injuries. Many nonfarm tasks that require great effort or repetitive motions have been mechanized, and it would be possible to, for example, use hydraulic lifts instead of ladders to pick fruit from trees, so that workers do not have to balance on a ladder with a heavy bag.

The mechanical aids most likely to be used widely are those that are not expensive to the employer and do not slow down workers aiming to maximize earnings under piece rate wages. One successful example of a mechanical aid is a smaller tub for picking winegrapes. If workers repeatedly bend and stoop to pick up tubs that weigh more than fifty pounds, back injuries mount; if the weight is below fifty pounds, there are far fewer back injuries. Ergonomics researchers replaced the standard fifty-five-pound tub into which high-quality wine grapes are hand picked with a forty-six-pound tub. The cost of the plastic tubs was low, and workers' earnings did not fall much from the slightly more trips they had to make to dump full tubs, and the smaller tubs were quickly adopted (http://ag-ergo.ucdavis.edu). As employer costs for injuries rises, and ergonomics research among farm workers becomes more common, there may be more such "back-saving" innovation.

Politics and Unions

Cesar Chavez was a master at gaining favorable media coverage, with most stories portraying the UFW's activities as a David versus Goliath struggle of poor farm workers taking on corporate agribusiness. The UFW held rallies to draw attention to its boycotts and attracted both media coverage and local politicians who supported UFW causes. The high-water mark for the UFW came in 1974, when the UFW's early support for Jerry Brown gave Chavez a dominant role in the preparation of the Agricultural Labor Relations Act, ensuring that it included items the UFW wanted: contractors cannot be employers, unions must have broad good standing authority over members, and secondary boycott activities by farm worker unions are lawful. The UFW, which never claimed more than seventy thousand members, many of whom were not U.S. citizens and thus could not vote, nonetheless became an organization whose endorsement politicians sought, and whose political action committee (PAC) funds they wanted. Federal, state, and local candidates often invited Chavez to their rallies and were photographed with Chavez to show their sympathies for farm workers and, more broadly, Hispanics.

By the mid-1980s, the UFW had shrunk, Republican governors were making appointments to the ALRB, and Chavez began to call the ALRA-ALRB an obstacle to the farm workers. The UFW, described as "one of the biggest contributors to Democratic legislative election campaigns" in 1986, asked that the ALRB be defunded.[8] Most farm labor reformers disagreed, urging Chavez to renew organizing activities among the new generation of farm workers in the fields, immigrants who knew nothing of the struggles of the 1950s and 1960s. The UFW refused, asserting that organizing was useless in a political environment in which the ALRB had become a progrower agency and workers who expressed prounion sympathies were unlawfully fired. Instead, the UFW turned to the Wrath-of-Grapes boycott, which was based on mass mailings. George Higgins, who helped Chavez negotiate the first table grape contracts, questioned the usefulness of this boycott, asking: "Let's assume the boycott solves the pesticide issue. . . . How would that organize workers?"[9]

California had Republican governors making appointments to the ALRB between 1983 and 1999. When Arturo Rodriguez became president of the UFW in 1994, he reestablished links to the AFL-CIO, church groups, Hispanic organizations, as well as the Mexican government— most of these groups look to the UFW as a leading representative of working Hispanics. The honors and memorials to Cesar Chavez after his death helped to solidify the position of the UFW as the leading voice of powerless Hispanic workers. The UFW supported Democratic candidates in the 1990s, but its candidates for statewide office often lost, such as Democrat Kathleen Brown's loss to Pete Wilson in the race for governor in 1994. The UFW has also been unable to persuade the majority of California voters to agree with its position on ballot initiatives or propositions affecting Hispanics: California voters approved Propositions 187 (clamping down on illegal immigration) in 1994, 209 (limiting affirmative action) in 1996, and 227 (ending bilingual education) in 1998, despite strong UFW and other Hispanic and union opposition.

The UFW's successes in the 1960s and 1970s inspired farmers to step up their own political activities: many grower-funded PACs that deal with farm labor were begun in response to the passage of the ALRA in 1975 and the fight over the access rule in 1976. By the early 1980s, the farm labor fight shifted from Sacramento to Washington, and farmer contributions were credited with winning congressional approval of a special guest worker program for agriculture in the Immigration Reform and Control Act of 1986. So long as farmers had the upper hand in Congress, and newcomer immigrants continued to arrive in California fields, it was hard for the UFW to organize farm workers and win wage increases in California, whether the ALRB was administered in a prounion or progrower fashion.

Perhaps the major legacy of the UFW and Cesar Chavez will be the generation of Hispanic leaders who were trained in social activism by the UFW. The UFW welcomes volunteers, and many Hispanic political and labor leaders in California spent time with the UFW, including Joe Serna, Jr., the first Hispanic mayor of Sacramento who renamed a downtown park Cesar Chavez Plaza. Miguel Contreras, head of the Los Angeles County Federation of Labor, the umbrella organization for four hundred unions with a claimed membership of 700,000 workers, proudly recounts his eighteen arrests for violating antipicketing injunctions in the summer of 1973 as a UFW volunteer. Contreras credits Chavez for teaching a generation of Hispanic labor leaders who came to power in the 1990s "that the imaginary shackles you have to your employer are always there unless you as a worker have a feeling of self-worth, [unless] you know that you can go get a job somewhere else and still make a living. Cesar taught us to break those imaginary shackles. That's the greatest lesson I've learned, clearly."[10]

The major legacy of Cesar Chavez and the UFW in its first forty years may well be the activists who were trained for the leadership positions they have begun to assume in a growing and changing California. In this growing and changing California, the power of the UFW in the future is likely to hinge on four major factors: demography, mechanization, trade, and alliances. The demographic influence of Hispanics is growing. On April 1, 2000, Census day, the U.S. population was 281 million, including 35 million Hispanics. This count indicated that for the first time more Hispanics than blacks lived in the United States. One third of these Hispanics are in California, and two-thirds are Mexican-born or Mexican-Americans. Chavez envisioned the UFW as a labor organization to help Hispanics to help themselves by enlisting nonfarm workers to support farm worker causes, so the growing number of Hispanics should increase the number of Americans sympathetic to UFW appeals.

The counter argument is that, even if the number of Hispanics rises, the power of the farm worker unions may not increase, especially if most farm workers are recently arrived immigrants, and most Hispanics are urban residents with no links to the farm labor market. Urban Hispanics, this argument runs, will have higher priorities than helping farm workers—they will want good jobs and schools, affordable housing, and convenient transportation. Many urban Hispanics have relatively low incomes which, critics of the rising-Hispanic-population-equals-more-farm-worker-union-power argument assert, may make them reluctant to support farm worker causes that could increase their food costs.

Mechanization can similarly enhance or reduce farm worker union power. The traditional economic prediction is that union power decreases as opportunities to replace workers with machines increase—in such cases, pushing up wages presents unions with a jobs-wages trade off. However, mechanization in fruit and vegetable commodities has been limited not only by an ample supply of workers that held down wages, but also by consumer preferences for fresh produce, the type that is most difficult to handle mechanically. Offsetting the loss of jobs to machines may be new field worker jobs created when previously nonfarm jobs in packinghouses move into the fields.

If the major farm worker union weapon continues to be appeals to consumers to boycott a firm's produce, the growth of brand names should facilitate union-called boycotts. This means that, if Safeway wants to buy grapes and other fruit from Sunworld, and wants to obtain a premium price for Sunworld-labeled fruits, then a union-Sunworld dispute that leads to a Sunworld boycott could have severe impacts on Sunworld, especially if it led Safeway to switch suppliers. If, on the other hand, a brand name such as Sunworld is applied to produce grown in California as well as in other countries, mounting boycotts of brand-name produce may be more difficult.

Agriculture in California was shaped by government policies on land, water, trade, and marketing, many of which are being questioned on environmental and other grounds. Except for pesticides, the UFW has not been active in most of the public policy debates that shape agriculture. As environmental and other groups increase their scrutiny of water and land policies, farm worker unions could find powerful allies in their attempts to put pressure on farm employers. In most industries, pressure from outside groups, such as environmental or consumer groups, tends to unite employers and unions, as in the auto industry where unions and car makers jointly opposed higher mileage standards. In California agriculture, a history of mistrust between employers and unions may persuade unions to form alliances with outside groups.

The UFW took a recent step toward cooperation with employers in its Bear Creek (Jackson & Perkins Rose) contract. Producing roses is analogous to an industrial process, but the flower industry employs workers who are like other farm workers in education, immigrant status, and other characteristics. The UFW formed a "partnership" with Bear Creek that, according to the union, increased the quality of the bare-root roses produced by about a third in a few years. So far, the UFW has not been able to extend this partnership model to other farms with UFW contracts.

Immigration and Unions

Most farm workers are immigrants from Mexico, and many Mexican immigrants with nonfarm jobs had their first U.S. job in agriculture. Mexican immigration and farm labor are inextricably intertwined, so policy decisions on immigration affect the trajectory of farm worker unions. The United States is a nation of immigrants, but it has been debating immigration's impacts for two centuries. During the 1990s, there was an effort to quantify the economic impacts of immigrants, and the central conclusion—that immigrants have a small but positive effect on the size of the U.S. economy—makes it unlikely that immigration will be curbed. However, the growing dependence of agriculture on immigrant farm workers may be changed, which could dramatically alter the number and type of farm worker employed. This section summarizes the economic analysis of immigration and alternative farm labor adjustment scenarios.

Immigration has two major economic effects: it increases the supply of labor and reduces wages or the growth in wages. Also the increase in employment due to immigration raises national income. The wage and employment changes due to an influx of immigrants are illustrated in figure 7.3. Before immigrants arrive, the U.S. economy is at E, with about 125 million U.S.-born workers earning $13 an hour. Total national income is $AE\ L0$, with the rectangle illustrating the wages paid to workers, and the triangle showing the share of national income going to owners of capital and land. Suppose 15 million immigrant workers are added to the U.S. labor force, shifting the labor supply to the right, to 140 million at F, and lowering hourly wages by 3 percent to $12.60.

The movement from E to F creates two rectangles, C and D, as well as triangle B. Rectangle C represents reduced wages paid to U.S. workers; they do not disappear into thin air, but are transferred to the owners of capital and land in the form of higher profits and rents—rectangle C. Because of immigration, total U.S. employment and wages expand by rectangle D and triangle B, with immigrants getting most of the benefits of this expansion in the form of their wages (D). The net gain from immigration is triangle B, and its size can be estimated in percentage-of-national-income terms as $1/2$ x 3 percent decrease in U.S. wages due to immigration x 11 percent immigrant share of U.S. labor force x 70 percent share of labor in U.S. national income, or $1/2$ x $0.002 = 0.001$. Thus United States national income increases about 1/10 of 1 percent due to immigration, which in dollar terms was $8 billion of the $8 trillion U.S. GDP in 1997. To put the immigrant effect in perspective, if the U.S. economy grows by 2 percent a year, it expands by $160 billion, so $8 billion is equivalent to about twenty days of economic growth.

The increase in national income due to immigration—triangle B—will be larger if there are more immigrant workers and if the wage depression effect of immigrant workers is larger. For example, if the immigrant wage-depression impact doubled to 6 percent, and the immigrant share of the work force doubled to 22 percent (as in California in the late 1990s), national income would increase due to immigration by $1/2 \times 0.06 \times 0.22 \times 0.7 = 0.005$, or 5/10 of 1 percent, which is about $40 billion. The size of triangle B is larger still in labor-intensive agriculture.

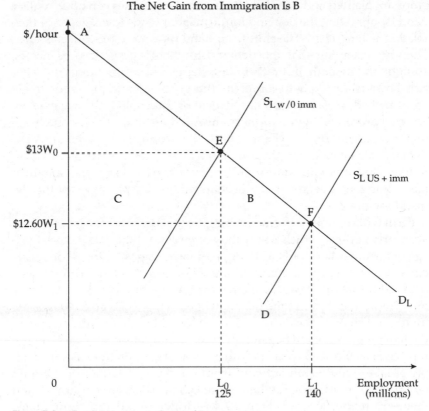

Figure 7.3. The Net Economic Gains of Immigration

In fruit and vegetable agriculture, wages may be 50 percent lower due to the presence of immigrant workers, 95 percent of farm workers are immigrants, and labor's share of revenue is about 30 percent, so the increase in revenue in fruit and vegetable agriculture could be: $1/2 \times 0.5 \times 0.95 \times 0.3 = 0.07$, or 7 percent of the $35 billion in annual FVH revenues, with immigrants accounting for about $2.5 billion. This gain in FVH revenues due to immigration helps to explain why growers are willing to invest considerable sums in lobbying government to keep border gates open for farm workers.

Farm worker unions often face two distinct types of demand for labor curves. In the short-term, the demand for labor is usually inelastic (inflexible), since farmers who have planted lettuce or peaches to be hand picked cannot easily use machines to pick their crops if workers go on strike—they will pick their crops so long as the price they receive exceeds harvesting costs. However, given several years to change how crops are planted and handled after harvest, machines can often replace hand labor, so that the demand for farm labor tends to be elastic or flexible in the long term. The shift from hand picking to machines is often "lumpy," meaning that the demand-for-labor curve may be not be straight and smooth, but rather stair-stepped or segmented. As wages rise, farmers are likely to complain, but go ahead and pay more to get crops picked. However, at some critical or threshold high wage, farmers and processors agree to mechanize harvesting, which usually requires cooperation to change both harvesting and packing. The demand-for-labor curve thus appears to be nearly vertical at first— farmers hire about the same number of workers as wages rise, and then has a horizontal segment, as mechanization sharply reduces the demand for labor.

Farm worker unions normally imagine that demand-for-labor curves are nearly vertical, which is why they often assert that "there is no shortage of farm workers, only a shortage of farm wages." Most economists agree, imagining the response to higher wages as a (slightly) reduced demand for labor—fewer workers employed—but a larger total wage bill. Unions had a hard time raising wages in the 1980s and 1990s as the immigrant share of the farm work force rose, but what would happen if the federal government began to enforce immigration laws and did not replace unauthorized workers with guest workers? In this case, the supply of labor would shift leftward from e in figure 7.4, and there would be a new equilibrium at b, where more U.S. workers are employed, and they earn higher wages.[11] Figure 7.4 is drawn to reflect a common assertion—all available U.S. workers are hired first, and then immigrants are hired.

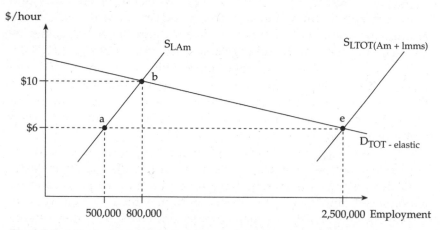

Figure 7.4. Adjustments to Fewer Immigrants: Smooth

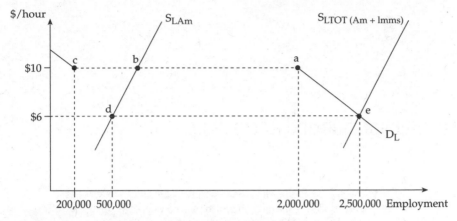

Figure 7.5. Adjustments to Fewer Immigrants: Segmented

The alternative lumpy-adjustment scenario assumes that the demand for farm labor is segmented or kinked—at a critical high wage, the demand for labor falls sharply as growers mechanize or quit growing hand-harvested commodities. Figure 7.5 illustrates a segmented labor demand curve. Beginning again at e, where 2.5 million farm workers, 80 percent immigrants, are employed at an average wage of six dollars an hour, the number of immigrants is reduced via enforcement. At first, there is a smooth adjustment to fewer workers, reflected in the movement from e to a. However, at ten dollars an hour, the critical threshold wage, the demand for labor falls sharply—from 2 million to 200,000—reflecting mechanization or farmers stopping production. In this example, the employment of U.S. workers also falls, so that at the new equilibrium c, U.S. farm worker employment has fallen from 500,000 to 200,000, but wages for the remaining U.S. workers rise from six dollars to ten dollars an hour.

Which is the more likely farm labor adjustment scenario? The mechanization of most commodities is segmented, the result of cooperation between growers and packinghouses or processors to fundamentally change the way in which the crop is grown, harvested, and handled after it leaves the farm. The segmented or lumpy nature of labor-saving mechanization in fruit and vegetable agriculture means that it can be very difficult to predict exactly how or when the demand for labor will fall as wages rise.

8

Immigration and Agriculture

The brightest hope for the welfare of seasonal agricultural workers lies
with the elimination of the jobs on which they now depend.
Lloyd Fisher, *The Harvest Labor Market in California*, 1953

The farm workers of tomorrow are growing up today outside California, a fact that has not changed much in the past one hundred years. At
the dawn of the twenty-first century, the major farm labor issue is
whether immigrant newcomers will continue to be the mainstay of the
seasonal farm work force for another century. The answer to this question will largely determine whether California can keep its 1975 promise
to bring "peace and justice" to the fields.

The availability of newcomers without other job options has an economic consequence: land prices are raised by low wages, giving land
owners an incentive to maintain agricultural exceptionalism—exemptions from immigration and labor laws. The reasons why farmers argue
that "agriculture is different" have not changed much over the years—
at the whim of unpredictable weather, they grow perishable commodities; the only costs farmers can control are wages, and Americans want
low food prices—but the consequences of agricultural exceptionalism
may be more serious. Will newcomers with less than half as much education as the average American be able to achieve upward mobility after working a decade as farm workers? What will happen to their
children?

During the twentieth century, newcomers with slightly less education
than Americans could have their first jobs in the fields, but they and
their children later found nonfarm jobs in the state's fast-growing economy. But newcomers to the fields today, such as the non-Spanish-speak-
ing indigenous peoples of southern Mexico and Central America, are

more "foreign" than ever, and they may find upward mobility far more difficult to achieve in a restructured U.S. economy that offers declining wages for those with little education. By importing the rural poor from abroad to fill seasonal farm jobs, the United States risks creating a new rural poverty that may be very hard to extirpate (Taylor, Martin, and Fix, 1997).

This chapter has three purposes. First, it reviews the exceptions for agriculture that were included in the Immigration Reform and Control Act (IRCA) of 1986, provisions that accelerated the arrival of newcomers and increased the isolation of the farm labor market from mainstream nonfarm labor markets. Second, it outlines the features of the twenty-first-century guest worker program being debated in Congress, which is likely to include "earned legalization," or allowing foreigners to become immigrants if they do farm work for four to seven years. Third, it estimates the benefits of newcomers in the fields to consumers—the average household saves about ten dollars a year on fresh fruits and vegetables because of wages held down by immigrants—and outlines the alternatives, including mechanization and rising imports.

IRCA: Exceptions for Agriculture

After the ALRA was enacted in 1975, many farm labor reformers thought that the farm labor problem had been solved. It was only a matter of time, reformers thought, until the UFW would transform the farm labor market with hiring halls and high wages, just as longshore and construction unions had transformed the labor markets in which they operated. There would be mechanization in response to these higher wages, but everyone would be better off with fewer, higher-wage workers operating machinery. The remaining task for reformers was to help farm workers and their children to make the transition from farm to nonfarm jobs, so employment and training programs were expanded and community development efforts undertaken to create nonfarm jobs for those exiting the "migrant stream." For the fewer farm workers, there were to be job ladders, annual worker plans, and modern personnel management programs.

These 1970s assumptions of a "new era" in farm labor proved to be wrong. Instead of farm wages and benefits rising under union pressure, they began to stabilize and fall, and the 30 percent jump in apprehensions of unauthorized Mexicans in the United States between 1982 and 1983, after Mexico devalued the peso, suggested that the influx of newcomers was accelerating. In 1984, Sun Harvest gave up its leased farmland, signaling the exit of companies that hired large numbers of workers directly and were vulnerable to union-called boycotts.[1] The UFW began "losing" strikes—after the UFW called a strike in support of a wage increase in Ventura County in 1982, many farmers turned to labor contractors who hired unauthorized workers, and a unionized harvesting association that had fifteen hundred UFW members was disbanded. Around the state, the percentage of unauthorized farm workers was creeping upward, reaching 20 to 30 percent by the mid-1980s.

The United States began to debate what to do about illegal immigration in the early 1970s, when union-friendly committees in the House of Representatives enacted sanctions on employers who knowingly hired illegal workers (the UFW testified in support of sanctions), but grower-friendly committees in the Senate refused to act (U.S. House of Representatives, 1971, 1984). Farm labor became less important as the immigration reform debate heated up in the late 1970s and early 1980s—the U.S. Commission on Immigration Reform (CIR) estimated in 1981 that only about 15 percent of the unauthorized workers were employed in agriculture. When Congress began debating the CIR's recommendations in 1982, there was little testimony about farm labor. A general consensus emerged that immigration reform should be based on the twin pillars of employer sanctions to reduce illegal immigration and legalization of the unauthorized foreigners who had developed an equity stake in the United States.

During the early immigration reform debates, California farmers were more concerned about union activities than they were about immigration reform. Interest in the farm labor aspects of immigration reform was strongest in Florida and other eastern states that imported workers under the H-2 program to cut sugarcane and harvest apples. The chief concern of H-2 users was that, in any immigration reform, Congress not make H-2 admissions more difficult or employer costs higher. As the momentum for immigration reform gathered steam in 1983, eastern and western farmers met to decide whether to work together to make the H-2 program more employer-friendly for growers, or whether western growers should push for an alternative guest worker program (FLA, 1986). Western growers, who did not have the on-farm housing required to employ H-2 workers, and who feared that advertising for workers as required by the H-2 program would result in pro-UFW workers responding, decided to seek a new guest worker program. Any new guest worker program, growers decided, could have no requirement for housing and no role for the U.S. Department of Labor to certify or review farmer efforts to recruit U.S. workers.

To get this new guest worker program, the Farm Labor Alliance (FLA) was formed. In what *The New York Times* called one of the top-ten political stories of 1984, the FLA persuaded the House of Representatives, where opposition to guest workers was strongest, to approve a new farmer-friendly program. The so-called Panetta-Morrison program satisfied the two key demands of western growers—no housing and no certification—by creating a new class of "P visas" for foreign workers who could "float" from farm to farm, legalizing the status quo, since most of the P visas would have gone to unauthorized workers already in the United States. In 1985, Senator (later governor) Pete Wilson, a Republican from California, persuaded the Senate to approve a similar guest worker program offering "O visas" to guest workers. The success of the FLA in Congress brought condemnation from legislators who were trying to reduce illegal immigration. Senator Alan Simpson, a Wyoming Republican, one of the leaders in immigration reform, decried P and O visas as efforts to "legalize the status quo of illegal labor in agriculture" (Congressional Record September 12, 1985, S11326).

Western growers had demonstrated that they had the political clout to get Congress to approve a farmer-friendly guest worker program. Without a compromise on agricultural guest workers, there would be no immigration reform, prompting Representative (now senator) Charles Schumer of New York to broker a compromise in the summer of 1986 that had three important elements. It made the H-2 program slightly more employer-friendly; created a legalization program for unauthorized farm workers, the Special Agricultural Worker (SAW) program; and if SAWs quickly left agriculture, producing labor shortages, allowed them to be replaced by Replenishment Agricultural Workers (RAWs), an earned legalization program that included P and O visa features. The clear message sent by the Schumer compromise was that immigration reform would not force agriculture to reverse its growing dependence on foreign workers.

The primary goal of IRCA was to legalize unauthorized foreigners and reduce illegal immigration (U.S. House of Representatives, 1986). Many proponents of immigration reform hoped for other effects as well, including more success for unions, as it was believed that now-legal farm workers, no longer fearful of the INS, would have the confidence to push for higher wages. Rising farm wages, in turn, were expected to lead to a new round of mechanization, as farmers tried to reduce labor costs at a time of rising imports.

However, IRCA's agricultural exceptions in fact accelerated the spread of unauthorized Mexican workers throughout U.S. agriculture in the 1990s and reduced rather than increased real farm wages (Martin, 1994).

One reason was a change in enforcement practices. Before IRCA, immigration enforcement in agriculture was often a people chase; workers fled when they saw Border Patrol vans driving into fields and vineyards, and agents attempted to apprehend those who tried to run away. In nonfarm industries, by contrast, INS had to present evidence to a judge that there were likely to be unauthorized workers in the workplace and get a search warrant to conduct a raid. Farmers argued that "open fields" were really "open air factories," and the INS should be required to obtain search warrants before checking for unauthorized workers. Congress agreed, and IRCA required the INS to obtain search warrants to check farms for unauthorized workers.[2]

Enforcement changes made it harder for the INS to inspect farms for unauthorized workers, while the SAW program made it easier for unauthorized workers to obtain legal immigrant status. There were two separate legalization programs in 1987–88: the main one for unauthorized foreigners in the United States since January 1, 1982, and the agricultural, or SAW program, for unauthorized foreigners who did at least ninety days of work on crop farms in 1985–86. The congressional authors of these programs expected that 1.5 to 2 million foreigners would apply under the main program, and 350,000 to 400,000 foreigners would apply under the SAW program.[3] In fact, about 1.7 million foreigners applied under the main program, and 1.3 million under the SAW program.

Why were there three times more SAW applicants than expected? Primarily because the SAW program was the "easy legalization program." A foreigner could have entered the United States illegally much later, in 1986 rather than 1981, and did not have to remain in the United States to be legalized as a SAW—many foreigners applied for SAW legalization abroad. However, the major reason why so many foreigners applied for SAW legalization was that it included a unique feature for federal immigration law: the burden of proof was on the INS to disprove the unauthorized foreigner's assertions in the application. This meant that, once a foreigner applied for SAW legalization by submitting a letter (affidavit) from a U.S. employer asserting that the worker did at least ninety days of qualifying work (most worker applications were accompanied by one sentence letters from labor contractors that said: "Juan Gonzalez picked tomatoes in Stockton for ninety-four days between May 1, 1985 and May 1, 1986"), the burden of proof was on the INS to show that Juan Gonzalez did not pick tomatoes for ninety-four days in Stockton. This could have been done—the tomato picking season does not last ninety-four days in Stockton—but the INS did not develop effective antifraud teams, and approved 90 percent or 1.2 million SAW applications. Since there were only 350,000 to 450,000 qualifying unau-

Table 8.1. IRCA Legalization Applicants

Characteristic	Pre-1982[a]	SAW[b]
Median Age at Entry	23	24
1. Age 15 to 44 (%)	80	93
2. Male (%)	57	82
3. Married (%)	41	42
4. From Mexico (%)	70	82
5. Applied in CA (%)	54	52
Total Applicants	1,759,705	1,272,143

Source: INS Statistical Yearbook, 1991, 70–74.
[a]Person filing I-687 legalization applications.
[b]Person filing I-700 legalization applications.

thorized farm workers, the SAW program was "one of the most extensive immigration frauds ever perpetrated against the U.S. government."[4]

Once they were legalized, SAW farm workers could live and work anywhere in the United States without fear of the INS. The expectation was that most would keep their families in rural Mexico, where living costs were lower, and commute to seasonal farm jobs in the United States, much as green card commuters did in the 1960s and 1970s. The data suggested that cross-border commuting would be feasible, since 80 percent of the SAWs were working-age Mexican men (table 8.1), over 40 percent were married, and many had large families in rural Mexico whose status was not legalized. Most SAWs did not finish primary school, and their average U.S. earnings in the mid-1980s were $3.50 to $4.50 an hour, or $3,500 to $4,500 a year (the federal minimum wage was $3.35 an hour in the 1980s).

The third IRCA-inspired change in agriculture sent farmers the signal that there would be guest workers available in the future. Farmers in the eastern United States could import guest workers under the H-2A program with which they were familiar, and the Replenishment Agricultural Worker (RAW) program could supply additional foreign workers under rules suited to western growers, although both programs could in fact be used anywhere in the United States. The RAW program did not require farmers to have their need for foreign workers certified the U.S. Department of Labor and allowed foreigners who worked as agricultural guest workers to "earn" an immigrant status. Farmers with two channels to import guest workers believed correctly that they did not have to change wages and working conditions in order to get seasonal farm workers.

IRCA: The Legacy in the 1990s

The SAW program initially attracted few applicants, and there were fears that IRCA was ushering in a new era for farm labor, an era of fewer workers and higher wages. But 1987 fears of labor shortage ended with massive labor surpluses, as workers streamed north to become *rodinos*, the term many Mexicans used for SAWs.[5] In some cases, so many workers sought seasonal harvest jobs that there were reports of workers simply going to work in the fields and hoping they would be paid. Farmers, who were cautious about planting labor-intensive crops in the mid-1980s because they feared labor shortages and higher wages, realized that labor would be readily available and planted as much as they thought they could sell—the acreage of fruits, vegetables, and nursery crops surged between 1987 and 1997 (see table 8.2).

IRCA established a Commission on Agricultural Workers (CAW) to review nine farm labor questions, which suggested the areas expected to be affected by immigration reforms. After four years of studies and hearings, CAW concluded that, although the SAW program legalized virtually all eligible farm workers, and many more as well, the ample supply of labor due to the continued availability of illegal workers prevented the newly legalized SAWs from obtaining improvements in wages and benefits, so that most farm workers still had below-poverty level earnings: two hundred dollars weekly or five thousand dollars for twenty-five weeks of farm work in the early 1990s (CAW, 1992). The CAW recommended additional steps to develop a legal farm work force, to improve social services for farm workers and their families, and to improve the enforcement of labor and immigration laws.

Perhaps the most important effect of immigration reform was to spread unauthorized workers from the Southwest to the rest of the

Table 8.2. US FVH Expansion: 1987–97

	1997 Acres	1987–97 Change (%)
Vegetables	3,539,670	8
Fruits, Nuts, Berries	5,158,064	3
Nursery & Greenhouse		
Nursery	1,234,510	113
Greenhouse (sq. ft.)	1,027,000	35

Source: 1987 Census of Agriculture Tables 27–30, pp. 353–404.
1997 Census of Agriculture, Tables 29–33, pp. 462–517.

Table 8.3. CAW's Mandate

1. Conduct an overall evaluation of IRCA's Special Agricultural Worker (SAW)
   provisions and recommend appropriate changes.
2. Review the impact of the SAW program:
   • on the wages and working conditions of U.S. farm workers
   • on the adequacy of the supply of labor
   • on the ability of agricultural workers to organize
   • on the international competitiveness of U.S. crops
   • on whether SAWs stay in the farm work force
   • on whether employer sanctions affected the supply of farm labor
3. Determine the extent:
   • to which agriculture relies on a temporary workforce
   • of unemployment and underemployment among U.S. farm workers
   • to which farmers are unable to find workers because they do not use modern labor-
     management techniques
   • to whch the supply of farm labor is adequate
   • to which certain geographic regions need special programs to secure labor

country. Before immigration reform, Mexican-born legal and unauthorized farm workers were found largely in the western states, Texas, and
Florida; Mexican-born workers in other states were rare. SAWs, as legal
immigrants, were free to travel in search of higher wages and more
hours of work, and many wound up in midwestern and southeastern
fields and farm-related meat and poultry processing jobs. Pioneer SAWs
served as anchors for the unauthorized workers who continued to arrive in the United States from their hometowns, giving rise to phrases
that described Mexican immigration as "changing the face of" or "La-
tinizing" rural America. Case studies of labor markets found few examples of employers making the changes hoped for by immigration
reformers: raising wages and improving working conditions, but found
lots of evidence of farmers hiring workers through contractors and eliminating fringe benefits (Martin et al., 1995).[6]

The switch by employers to hiring unauthorized workers through labor contractors was a major defeat for farm labor reformers. Instead of
centralizing information about seasonal jobs and seasonal workers, so
that the fewest number of workers could fill the jobs, job matching became even more decentralized. In the 1990s, contractors whose major
asset was their ability to assemble crews of workers proliferated, but
few understood or obeyed complex laws regulating contractors, and
none was large enough to achieve efficient job matching. The switch to
contractors left many workers worse off, since contractors pay less per
hour, and workers who had lived on the farm when they were hired directly by the farmer now had to pay for off-farm housing and rides to
work, which reduced worker earnings by 30 to 40 percent.

Today, contractors are the glue that binds seasonal workers and jobs (Thilmany, 1994). As the contractor share of farm employment rises, the ability of the government to regulate the farm labor market declines. Effective labor and immigration law enforcement depends on complaints, and contractors tend to hire newly arrived and unauthorized workers who are not familiar with their U.S. workplace rights. They also need a variety of services, including false work documents, housing, and rides to work, that the contractor, for a fee, often provides. These extensive contractor-worker interactions make it unlikely that workers will complain to enforcement agencies and unlikely that the agencies will penetrate worker-contractor relationships.

Twenty-first-Century Guest Workers?

During the 1990s, the percentage of unauthorized workers in the crop labor force increased fourfold, from 10 to 15 percent at the beginning of the decade to 50 to 60 percent at the end (U. S. Department of Labor. 1990–2001). If immigration laws were to be enforced, there would be shortages of "legal workers," at least until there were significant adjustments in the farm labor market and production practices. The rising share of unauthorized farm workers meant that farm labor lobbyists could keep fears of farm labor shortages alive among growers, and they developed proposals for a new round of guest worker programs. The first proposal, the Alternative Agricultural Temporary Worker Program, would have allowed farmers to simply attest or assert that they needed foreign workers, and the foreign guest workers would then be admitted to the United States. In order to encourage them to return to Mexico, 25 percent of their U.S. wages would have been deducted and returned to the workers in Mexico.

There were many problems with this proposal, with critics asserting that history demonstrates clearly that growers cannot be trusted to determine their "need" for foreign workers. Critics noted that wage deductions from *bracero* workers in the 1940s led fifty years later to suits against the U.S. and Mexican governments and U.S. and Mexican banks seeking billions of dollars in damages on behalf of ex-*braceros* who never had their forced savings returned to them. The Alternative Agricultural Temporary Worker Program was defeated in the House on a 242–180 vote in March 1996.

A 1997 Senate proposal took a different tack to avoid DOL checking on whether a farmer tried to find U.S. workers by shifting recruitment from employers to the government. Under this proposal, a farmer would apply to the Employment Service for, say, a hundred workers. The Employment Service would register legal workers seeking farm jobs and, if the ES registry could refer just thirty workers, the farmer would be "certified" automatically as needing seventy guest workers. Critics noted that this proposal would lead to new bureaucracies in each state and would shift the "blame" for not finding U.S. workers despite high unemployment rates in agricultural areas from growers to the government.

To narrow the differences between growers and worker advocates over a new guest worker program, congressional allies of growers and workers agreed to have the General Accounting Office study the farm labor market. Its much-anticipated report, released in December 1997, sided with worker advocates: the GAO concluded that no new guest worker program was needed because there is "no national agricultural labor shortage . . . [and] a sudden, widespread farm labor shortage requiring the importation of large numbers of foreign workers is unlikely to occur in the near future." The GAO acknowledged that the percentage of farm workers who were unauthorized was 35 to 40 percent and climbing, but downplayed concerns that stepped up enforcement could lead to farm labor shortages. The INS, the GAO noted, was focusing on locating and deporting criminal aliens, not conducting workplace raids—only seven hundred unauthorized workers were removed from U.S. farms in the 1997 fiscal year. Furthermore, eleven of the twenty largest U.S. agricultural counties had unemployment rates of more than twice the U.S. rate of 5.2 percent in June 1997, suggesting plenty of workers (GAO, 1997).

The GAO report, plus strong opposition to a new guest worker program from President Clinton, bolstered worker advocates. However, as the unemployment rate dropped, and with grower-friendly Republicans in control of Congress, the House Immigration Subcommittee in March 1998 approved a pilot program for twenty thousand free-agent farm workers, with the major control device a 25 percent wage deduction to induce their return to Mexico. The full Senate followed with the approval of the Agricultural Job Opportunity Benefits and Security Act (AgJOBS) in July 1998 by a surprising 68–31 vote, suggesting that most senators would approve a program that did not require farmers seeking guest workers to obtain certification of their need for foreign workers.[7] AgJOBS included the ES registry method to give growers access to foreign workers and, in a bid for worker advocate support, included earned legalization—guest workers could "earn" an immigrant status by doing at least six months of farm work for four years after being registered as guest workers. However, most worker advocates condemned

AgJOBS as worse than the *bracero* program, calling earned legalization "indentured servitude." Reflecting the concerns of worker advocates, U.S. secretary of labor Alexis Herman sent a letter to Congress that said "the President has been and remains opposed to establishing a new agricultural guestworker program . . . if [AgJOBS] were presented to the President, I would recommend that he veto it" (*Rural Migration News,* "No Guest Workers," January 2001).

The year 2000 marked a turning point in the quest for a new guest worker program. The three major issues were certification, who (farmers or the government) would be given control of the border entry gate; housing (would the government require employers to provide housing for out-of-area US workers and guest workers?); and legalization (could "new guest workers" earn immigrant status?). The certification argument was about the appropriate hurdle between farmers and foreign workers. Farmers argued that they should be able to open the door to guest workers with little government interference, while worker advocates wanted a border gate that would be opened for guest workers only when proven necessary. In legislative terms, the border gate issue was whether any new guest worker program should continue to require the U.S. Department of Labor to certify a farmer's need for foreign workers on a job-by-job basis, or whether farmers could be trusted to look for workers without oversight, so that their attestations that they needed foreign workers would be sufficient.

Foreign workers are from outside the area. Should the farmer have to provide housing for these out-of-area workers? The answer in the H-2A program, and in European guest worker programs, is yes, under the theory that foreign workers new to the area cannot be expected to arrange their own housing, especially if they are unskilled workers arriving to fill seasonal jobs. A history of abuse of out-of-area farm workers has led to fairly detailed regulations of the farm worker housing that growers are currently required to provide. However, rising farm worker housing standards and enforcement prompted many farmers in California to close their on-farm housing—California farmers provided fewer than 25,000 beds for 800,000 farm workers in 2000—and most do not want to "get back into the housing business." To deal with housing, farmers proposed that they provide a housing allowance of $125 to $150 a month to guest workers, and let them find their own housing in nearby communities.[8]

The third issue was the fate of new guest workers. United States immigration law draws a sharp line between immigrants and nonimmigrants—nonimmigrant tourists and guest workers cannot "earn" credits for immigrant status by coming frequently to the United States.

On the contrary, foreigners seeking to visit the United States for tourism, temporary work, or study must convince a consular officer that they intend to return home. Working without authorization, or overstaying a nonimmigrant visa by more than six months, can lead to fines and prevent a foreigner from entering the United States legally for ten years. In an application of this distinction between immigrants and nonimmigrants, unauthorized farm workers became immigrants under the SAW legalization program, but some legal H-2 guest workers did not qualify for legalization. The RAW program introduced the earned legalization or probationary immigrant concept for farm guest workers—RAWS would have earned an immigrant status by doing farm work for at least four years—but the RAW program was never used, since there were no farm labor shortages in the early 1990s.

Earned legalization became the middle ground for growers who wanted guest workers and worker and ethnic advocates who wanted legalization. As discussions proceeded, Mexico urged the United States to legalize unauthorized Mexicans, and worker and ethnic advocates accepted the substitution of ES registries for certification and housing allowances instead of housing, and argued in favor of an earned legalization program that would not require "AgJOBS workers" to do too much farm work to earn an immigrant status. In the summer of 2002, the proposals being debated require AgJOBS workers to do 60 to 120 days of farm work a year for three to six years, which means currently unauthorized farm workers could become immigrants by doing an additional 180 to 720 days of farm work. Instead of ending agriculture's role as a port of entry for unskilled workers, AgJOBS would make the agricultural port of entry more important than ever, the only unskilled job that would qualify a foreigner for immigration to the United States.

Whither Agricultural Exceptionalism?

A new guest worker program would represent governmental acceptance that farmers will normally reach outside U.S. borders for workers, continuing agricultural exceptionalism. Throughout the twentieth century, farm labor reformers acknowledged that the structure of western agriculture—large farms, specialization, and seasonal workers—developed as a result of historical accident, and they argued that ending these exceptions would encourage farm labor markets to resemble the nonfarm labor markets in which most Americans worked. Farmers countered the reformers with the argument that agriculture was different. A major dispute was seasonality, or the fact that farmers wanted workers available for a few months a year and wanted to pay them only when they were employed. A presidential commission noted that logging, shipping, and construction offered seasonal jobs that required hard work under unpleasant conditions, but "only in agriculture [has seasonal] . . . labor become a problem of such proportions and complexity as to call for repeated investigations by public bodies" (President's Commission, 1951, 1).

Seasonality was expected to diminish as the labor supply tightened, pushing up wages, spurring mechanization, and producing fewer but better-paid farm workers. In the virtuous circle that developed in the 1960s and 1970s, there were relatively few immigrant strike breakers, and growers proved that they could raise wages and introduce fringe benefits to get seasonal workers. In the late 1970s, the ALRB asserted that the UFW negotiated entry level wages that were twice the minimum wage, so that if an employer failed to bargain in good faith, the ALRB could order the employer to pay a makewhole wage twice the minimum wage, the equivalent of $13.50 an hour in 2002. Farm work was changing from a job to a career, and two leading farm labor economists wrote that "the concept of a career in hired farm work is becoming increasingly recognized" (Fuller and Mamer, 1978; Fuller, 1991, 167).

However, the virtuous circle of the 1970s gave way to contractors and newly arrived Mexican workers in the 1980s and 1990s. There were many reasons for the unraveling of efforts to transform the farm labor market. There were UFW leadership failures, especially the early 1980s decision to stop organizing and replace non-Hispanic UFW staff members with relatives of Chavez. The UFW also made the mistake of assuming that the ALRB, using state funds, would take care of worker and union interests, and squandered much of its funds and good will in political infighting that left it poorly positioned when Republicans began to make appointments to the ALRB. But even if UFW leadership had remained close to farm workers, and even if the leadership of the ALRB had not changed, continued immigration would have undermined the UFW and other farm worker unions. Immigration reform in 1986 seemed to offer a chance for farm worker unions to reinvigorate themselves in spite of these setbacks, and the UFW and growers established competing organizations to help unauthorized farm workers apply for SAW status, under the theory that helping workers to legalize would earn their loyalty. However, fewer than one in twelve SAWs used either labor or grower assistance organizations, and the growers' organization helped ten times more SAWs than the UFW.

Continuing immigration was the main reason that, in the 1990's, contractors and other agricultural service firms could undermine unions by organizing and deploying workers on farms. It is doubtful that more effective union leadership and continued proworker ALRB appointments could have prevented the demise of collective bargaining in California agriculture, which also occurred in nonfarm labor markets. Continuing immigration had union-displacing effects in nonfarm labor markets that were not affected by union leadership failures and political appointments, such as construction, but these nonfarm sectors began with a higher percentage of workers covered by contracts. They also retain factors that increase union strength, including relatively skilled workers, apprenticeship programs that teach construction skills, and government contracts on which prevailing union wages must be paid.

Immigration exceptions for agriculture have made agriculture a major port of entry for unskilled Mexican immigrants. Since immigration policy allows the unification of families, U.S. farm jobs have played an important role in moving about 10 percent of the persons born in Mexico to the United States, half in the 1990s. What are the consequences of continued agricultural exceptionalism? Growers argue that, without immigrant farm workers, food prices would rise. This argument may have held more sway when working families spent 30 to 40 percent of their earnings on food, but today the cost of food eaten at home accounts for less than 8 percent of the average household's annual expenditures, and most of this spending is not for fresh fruits and vegetables picked by immigrant workers.

In 2000 the average "consumer unit," as the government calls households, spent 15 percent more on alcoholic beverages, $372, than on fresh fruits and vegetables, $322. When considering the argument that, without immigrant workers, Americans would no longer be able to afford lettuce or grapes, it is important to remember that the average household spends $6.20 a week on fresh fruits and vegetables, less than the cost of a movie ticket. Farmers do not get all of the money spent on fresh fruits and vegetables. In fact, even though strawberries are picked directly into the containers in which they are sold, and iceberg lettuce gets its film wrapper in the field, farmers received an average 16 percent of the retail price of fresh fruits in 2000, and 19 percent of the retail price of fresh vegetables, so the $322 paid by a typical household for fresh produce includes $56 for the farmer. Farmers do not pay all of this $56 to farm workers. Farm labor costs are typically less than a third of farmer revenue, meaning that farm worker wages and benefits are less than $18 per household per year, less than one half of one percent of average annual spending. Consumers who pay $1 for a pound of apples, or $1 for a head of lettuce, are giving 16 to 19 cents to the farmer, and 5 to 6 cents to the farm worker.

If the influx of immigrant workers were slowed and farm wages rose, and the increases in farm labor costs were passed through to consumers, what would happen to fruit and vegetable prices? We first need to know how much farm wages might rise. In 1966, after the *bracero* program ended, the fledgling United Farm Workers union won a 40 percent wage increase for table grape harvesters. Average farm-worker earnings were $7.56 an hour for U.S. field and livestock workers in 2000, according to a USDA survey of farm employers, and a 40 percent increase would have raised them by $3 to $10.58 an hour. If this wage increase were passed fully to consumers, the 5 to 6 cent farm labor cost of a $1 pound of apples or a $1 head of lettuce would have risen to 7 to 8 cents, and the retail price would have risen by 2 to 3 cents. For a typical household, a 40 percent increase in farm labor costs translates into a 2.4 percent increase in retail prices, and total spending on fruits and vegetables would rise $8, from $322 a year to $330 a year. This small increase would, however, produce a big improvement in the earnings of a typical seasonal farm worker, whose earnings would rise to $11,200 a year, up from $8,000.

Such wage increase could have two other effects, labor-saving mechanization and increased trade, both of which would reduce the demand for immigrant farm workers. Labor-saving mechanization in fruit and vegetable agriculture is often lumpy, reflecting the fact that all growers must switch the way in which they grow, prune, and harvest crops, so that packing sheds and retailers can handle them. The tomato harvester demonstrates the importance of having the government be the honest broker between growers and processors to expedite the lumpy mechanization process. In 1960, 80 percent of the forty-five thousand peak harvest workers used to pick the 2.2 million tons of the tomatoes rendered into catsup in California were *braceros*, and growers testified that "the use of *braceros* is absolutely essential to the survival of the tomato industry." The *bracero* program ended in 1964, and thirty-five years later, five thousand workers ride machines to sort 12 million tons of tomatoes. Labor-saving mechanization was spurred by the disappearance of *bracero* workers and facilitated by the state government, which established random sampling stations to test machine-harvested tomatoes and determine the price paid to the grower. Processing tomatoes are worth about 2.5 cents a pound. When tomatoes were picked in fifty-pound lugs, and each lug was worth $1.25, the loss was relatively minor if a lug was rejected for having too many green tomatoes or too much dirt. But with machine-picked tomatoes arriving in twenty-five-ton truck loads, each load is worth $1,250, the state-run random sampling stations were crucial to overcome the perennial struggle between growers and packers over deductions for poor quality.

There are machines available to harvest almost all of the fresh fruits and vegetables grown in the United States, but as the tomato example highlights, one farmer in isolation cannot usually put labor-saving machines in the fields (Brown, 1984). Instead, farmers must work with scientists to change the plant or tree, engineers must fine tune their machines under field conditions and, most importantly, growers and packers must renegotiate their agreements on the price and handling of commodities. Without leadership to make these incremental and often complex changes, growers find it easier to lobby for the labor status quo, as is apparent in the single most labor-intensive agricultural activity in North America—harvesting raisin grapes. Some five thousand growers have 125,000 to 150,000 acres of raisin grapes around Fresno California, and each August to September, some forty thousand to fifty thousand workers, an estimated 75 percent unauthorized, are involved in the six-week harvest, cutting bunches of green grapes, laying them on paper trays to dry in the sun, turning them, and then picking up the trays of raisins (Mason, 1998). About 4.5 pounds of green grapes are dried into one pound of raisins.

There are several mechanization options, including a dried on the vine (DOV) system developed by the major raisin growers' cooperative, Sun Maid, which involves cutting the canes on which grapes grow so that the grapes can dry into raisins while still in bunches on the vine.[9] Drying the raisins on the vines allows them to be harvested by a machine outfitted with rotating fingers that shakes them off the vines and catches them in a bin, reducing the number of harvesters needed and increasing the need for pruners in winter, when many farm workers are unemployed. One machine can harvest about fifteen acres of raisin grapes a day, equivalent to what a crew of forty workers can harvest by hand,[10] so several hundred machines operating around the clock could replace one of the major ports of entry for newcomer immigrants. Retro-fitting raisin vineyards for DOV harvesting costs about $1,500 per acre. Why are most raisin growers pushing for guest workers rather than converting to mechanical harvesting? One reason is that U.S. raisin prices are low, less than a thousand dollars a ton, due to overproduction in the United States and increased imports. With raisin prices declining, many growers are reluctant to make capital expenditures to retrofit vineyards and buy harvesting machines. Instead, many raisin growers attempt to maximize their variable costs—costs that do not have to be paid if there are no raisins to pick—by hiring immigrant workers.

If the United States closed the agricultural port of entry, there would likely be higher farm worker wages and more mechanization, as in the 1960s. But in the twenty-first century, there would also be more imported fruits and vegetables. Over the past forty years, imports have increased their share of many consumer markets, from autos to TVs, but it is sometimes argued that food is different, that the United States needs to grow its own food to ensure that it is safe to eat and guarantee food security in the event of war. This argument is flimsy for several reasons, including the fact that the United States imports virtually all its tropical fruits such as bananas, and because it is easy to substitute one food for another, as apples or oranges for bananas. If the U.S. government argues that Europe should accept genetically modified corn and wheat because U.S. safety studies consider these commodities safe, it is hard to argue against Chilean grapes or Mexican tomatoes, which must pass U.S. safety tests, on the grounds that imported commodities are not safe.

Mechanization and imports are alternatives to agricultural exceptionalism. Closing the port of entry for farm workers would allow market forces to push up wages, which would increase mechanization and imports, and leave the United States with a smaller but better paid farm work force. Agricultural exceptionalism has left a legacy of farm worker poverty, and the efforts to mitigate that poverty with assistance programs and special labor laws seem as doomed to fail in the twenty-first century, as they did in the twentieth century. Farm labor has been an uncomfortable topic in U.S. history. For most of its first 150 years, agriculture was the largest single U.S. industry. Farming in most of the United States was a family affair, with family members doing most of the work on the nation's farms, but farming in California has become a foreign affair, in the sense that immigrants are doing more and more U.S. farm work. If agricultural exceptionalism is allowed to continue, it will produce farm labor problems today, and urban poverty tomorrow.

Notes

1. NAWS data apply to workers employed on crop farms. In the March 2000 Current Population Survey, 17 million (or 12 percent) of the 140 million persons in the civilian labor force were not born in the United States.

1. California Farm Labor

1. There is a list of family farm definitions at http://www.ers.usda.gov/briefing/FarmStructure/Questions/familyfarms.htm.

2. In these data, workers hired by two farm operators are counted twice, but workers brought to farms by contractors and other intermediaries are not counted at all—only the money that the farmer paid to the contractor is counted.

3. Delano Farms, another major table grape grower, shipping 1.7 million boxes of grapes in 1996, is a division of Anderson & Middleton, a Hoquiam, Washington, timber concern.

4. Bud is not considered a "farm operation" in the Census of Agriculture because it signs agreements with growers that limit its role to "harvesting, packing, and marketing crops." Bud has contracts with farmers, who plant, cultivate, apply pesticides, weed and thin, and irrigate crops for harvesting by Bud, which does not own farm land. Dole has other farming operations, including a citrus operation in southern California, a grape and tree fruit operation in central California, and a nut operation in central California. Dole in February 2001 laid off nineteen hundred workers from its nonunion table grape operations and announced that it would obtain workers through farm labor contractors instead of hiring workers directly.

5. Contractors, but not temporary help companies, usually supervise the farm workers they bring to a farm. This produces the seemingly contradictory situation of the temporary help firm being responsible for workers compensation insurance for the workers it hires and sends to various employers, even though the companies to which Manpower or Labor Ready send workers are responsible for safety issues.

6. Contractors can and usually are considered employers in their own right under immigration, minimum wage, and other labor laws—if these laws are violated, liability rests with the contractor, not the farm on which workers are working. In an effort to tighten

farmer oversight over the contractor who bring workers to their farms, a California law effective in 2002 requires farmers to keep a copy of the licenses of FLCs they use for three years and verify that the license is valid. Failure to do so may make the farmer jointly liable with the contractor for labor law violations.

7. The Congressional Budget Office estimates that agriculture-related spending accounted for one-third of the $28 billion in federal expenditures to support business in 1995—about $8 billion for the Commodity Credit Corporation, which buys grains and other commodities if market prices are too low, and $2 billion for the Conservation Reserve Program, which pays farmers to retire land that is prone to erode if farmed (1995, xi). The dependence of farm incomes on government payments and programs has made farmers among the most generous contributors to political campaigns. Fruit and vegetable farmers, who claim to get no government subsidies because they do not get checks for wheat, corn, or cotton, contribute heavily to political campaigns to influence immigration, water, pesticide, and marketing decisions.

8. California's $6 billion in livestock sales exceed the farm sales of most states, and hired workers have become essential to large-scale dairy and poultry production in California.

9. Between 1992 and 1997, FVH commodities increased their share of U.S. crop sales from 31 to 33 percent; in California, FVH commodities accounted for 40 percent of the state's crop sales in 1992, and 44 percent in 1997.

10. California had 37,549 FVH farms in 1992, and they sold vegetables worth $2.4 billion, fruits and nuts worth $4.8 billion, and horticultural specialties worth $1.6 billion, for a total of $8.8 billion or 52 percent of California's $17 billion agricultural sales. Small farms had sales less than $50,000 in 1992.

11. For example, about 12 percent of the strawberries and 30 percent of the oranges produced in California in 1997–98 were exported.

12. It is hard to determine the exact number of persons employed on farms each year because some individuals use two or more social security numbers, while in other cases two or three workers may be employed under one number.

13. Botanists consider tomatoes a fruit because its stems, leaves, and roots are not edible. However, the U.S. Supreme Court in an 1893 trade case declared tomatoes to be a vegetable, reasoning that many tomatoes were cooked and served as vegetables.

14. For example, table grape growers obtain an average nine hundred to one thousand twenty-one-pound boxes of grapes an acre, and receive about ten dollars a box or fifty cents a pound for grapes. Labor costs are about 33 percent of the grower's price, but only 9 percent of the average retail price of $1.70 a pound in 1997.

15. The major winter activity on California farms is pruning—cutting branches and vines to promote the growth of fewer but larger fruit. Pruning accounts for 10 to 40 percent of the hours of labor used in many tree and vine crops, but occurs over several months, so fewer workers are involved.

16. The NAWS interviewed 4,199 workers between October 1, 1996, and September 30, 1998, in eighty-five counties across the United States (U.S. Department of Labor, 2000).

17. The characteristics of workers born in Mexico changed in the 1990s to include more Indians, such as Mixtecs and Zapotecs, from southern Mexican provinces such as Oaxaca.

18. A survey of California farm workers that conducted physical exams found generally poor health: high blood pressure, high serum cholesterol, and a high prevalence of anemia; it also reported that 81 percent of the men and 76 percent of the women were overweight (CIRS, 2000).

19. Workers with "two jobs at least 75 miles apart" may not stay away from their "usual home" overnight to do farm work. Instead, they may commute long distances to the two jobs.

20. The quarterly USDA publication, *Farm Labor*, reported higher average hourly earnings and hours worked—an average $6.98 an hour for field and livestock workers in 1998, and forty hours a week. USDA obtains data from employers; NAWS from workers.

21. The federal minimum wage rose from $4.25 to $4.75 on October 1, 1996, and to $5.15 on September 1, 1997. At $5.15 an hour, workers earn $206 a week.

22. Only about one-third of California's crop workers were hired through a FLC in 1990–91 (U.S. Department of Labor, 1993b), but bilingual foremen do most of the recruitment of the two-thirds of the workers who are listed in surveys as being hired "directly" by growers.

23. The USDA's Farm Labor Survey, for example, asks farm employers to report the gross earnings of all workers for the week containing the 12th of the month and their total hours worked, so that average hourly earnings in the USDA survey are simply gross earnings divided by total hours worked, a method that weights most heavily the earnings of workers who work the most hours. For example, one tractor driver employed 72 hours a week at $10 an hour earns $720, while two piece-rate peach pickers working 6 hours a day and earning an average $6 an hour work a total 72 hours and earn $432. This farm would report average field worker earnings of $8 an hour (1152/144).

24. The Farm Labor Survey collects earnings data from employers; NAWS collects earnings data from workers. Between 1995 and 1997, when the Farm Labor Survey reported that the average hourly earnings of field and livestock workers in California were $6.24, the NAWS reported average hourly earnings of $5.69, about 10 percent less.

25. Workers employed 160 hours a month at $6 an hour earn $960 a month, and an additional $160 for health insurance adds 17 percent; a $14 an hour worker earns $2,240 a month, and $160 for health insurance adds 7 percent. Nonfarm U.S. employers paid an average $1 an hour for health insurance in 1998, or $2 an hour for if their workers were union members.

26. California's Department of Housing and Community Development saw its farmworker housing budget increase from $3.5 million in 1999–2000 to $53.3 million in 2001–02, as Governor Gray Davis said: "Farmworkers do some of the most backbreaking work in our society, and the fruits of their labor are vital to our economy. This administration is committed to increasing the supply of safe, decent, and affordable housing for agricultural workers and their families." In November 2002, voters approved an initiative, Proposition 46, that will provide $200 million for farm worker housing.

2. History of Farm Labor

1. *Notes on Virginia* Q.XIX, 1782. ME 2:229, http://etext.virginia.edu/jefferson/quotations/jeff1320.htm.

2. The Roman statesman Cato expressed a similar sentiment: "It is from tillers of the soil that spring the best citizens."

3. Fogel and Engerman argued that slavery was economically efficient because plantation owners paid a great deal of attention to labor management: "The organization of slaves into highly disciplined, interdependent teams capable of maintaining a steady and intense rhythm of work." At one point, they asserted that slaves working on plantations were comparable to a "modern assembly line."

4. Historian Hubert Bancroft wrote thirty-nine volumes on the history of the Pacific coast, from Alaska to Panama, and his research materials were the basis of the University of California Berkeley Bancroft Library.

5. Enos, in a swipe at large farmers, continued: "If the size of their landed estates and the mode of cultivating them preclude the employment of civilized labor under civilized conditions, it is better that such estates lay waste, than that they be made a means of perpetuating the coolie system" (quoted in Fuller, 1967, 434).

6. Historians believe that fruit replaced wheat as interest rates fell (it took several years to get a crop) and as farmers learned how to grow fruit—the lack of labor did not hold back the expansion of fruit production.

7. This is one of the reasons why, even today, farmers want to own land: a large Cali-

fornia farmer was quoted in 1979 as saying that "farming in California is a means to an end, and that end is owning land" (Jack Anderson, *Sacramento Bee*, November 6, 1979).

8. London and Anderson (1970, 8) report that forty thousand mostly young Japanese men employed in agriculture were enumerated in the 1910 California Census of Population in California.

9. In 1894, the Japanese offered to work for $0.50 per day while the Chinese expected $1.00, and whites got $1.25 to $1.75 daily (Fuller, 1940, 19833).

10. Many of the persons imported from present-day India and Pakistan were Sikhs from the Punjab region, but all immigrants from South Asia in the early 1900s were called "Hindoo" or "Hindu" regardless of religious affiliation.

11. The so-called "ninth proviso" exemption to section 3 of the 1917 Immigration Law was extended to railroad maintenance workers and coal miners in June 1918. Between May 1917 and June 1920, some fifty-one thousand Mexicans entered the United States under these exemptions, and 80 percent were farm workers (Fuller, 1940, p. 19853).

12. Herbert Hoover in 1918 argued for removing all restrictions on Mexican immigration by asserting that "we need every bit of this labor that we can get and . . . we will need it for years to come." The Mexican Consul in Arizona countered that many Mexicans and Mexican-Americans in that state were unemployed, so that "there is an abundance of labor here and what is lacking is a good wage and above all good treatment" (quoted in Kiser and Kiser, 1979, 14–15).

13. In 1924, for example, the labor supply was estimated to be 102 percent of normal and labor demand was 85 percent of normal (Fuller, 1940, 19860).

14. Vagrants were often arrested for being public nuisances, much as drunks and prostitutes. California's vagrancy laws of 1933 and 1937 were declared unconstitutional in 1941 (*Edwards v. California*).

15. For example, while Steinbeck was visiting the Arvin camp, local farmers threatened to disrupt the regular Saturday night dance. If they had succeeded, a precedent may have been established for local law enforcement to override the authority of federal camp managers, who were far more sympathetic to migrants than local sheriffs. The federal Weedpatch camp near Lamont had several hundred families living in one-room cabins and tents, and a poster in its community hall that read: "California. Cornucopia of the World. Room for Millions of Immigrants. A Climate for Health and Wealth. Without Cyclones or Buzzards."

16. The Mexican government did not permit *braceros* to be employed legally in Texas during World War II because of discrimination against Mexicans.

17. The commission recommended "legislation be enacted making it unlawful to employ aliens illegally in the United States" and that "legalization for employment purposes of aliens illegally in the United States be discontinued and forbidden" (p. 180).

18. In 1951–52, there were five apprehensions per *bracero* admission; by 1956–57, there were five *bracero* admissions per apprehension.

19. One of the most contentious issues was prevailing wages. Farmers had to offer U.S. and *bracero* workers at least the minimum or prevailing wage, whichever was higher. However, when the President's Commission in 1951 tried to determine how prevailing wages were determined, it concluded: "As best we could determine, the prevailing wage . . . is arrived at somewhat in this manner: farm employers meet . . . and decide on the wage they intend to pay [without considering] whether the wage agreed upon is sufficient to attract the labor supply needed" (1951, 59).

20. "Harvest of Shame," produced by Edward R. Murrow, is one of the most acclaimed U.S. documentaries. CBS followed up with a documentary, "Legacy of Shame," which aired July 20, 1995, that emphasized how little the farm labor system has changed since 1960 because "it works."

21. The bus, a converted truck, was owned by Demco Farms of Salinas (Galarza, 1977).

22. In 1964, for example, foreign workers accounted for an estimated one-eighth of the man-months of labor used in twelve labor-intensive crops. Some of these foreign workers

were H-2 workers in sugarcane and tobacco, and tomatoes accounted for almost one-fourth of the Mexican foreign workers (Hirsch, 1967, 6).

23. Secretary of Labor Wirtz interpreted the decision to terminate the *bracero* program as signifying congressional intent to reduce or eliminate the presence of temporary foreign workers in U.S. agriculture. Under December 19, 1964, DOL regulations, U.S. employers wishing to receive DOL certification to import H-2 workers had to attempt to recruit U.S. workers by offering the highest of the three wages, free housing, and round-trip transportation. If the employer could not recruit U.S. workers under these circumstances, DOL could certify his need for H-2 workers for a maximum of 120 days, because "the only justification for bringing in labor is to meet the peak conditions of the highly seasonal agricultural industry" (Congressional Research Service, 1980, 65).

24. In January 1967, there were sixty-five thousand Mexican green card commuter farm workers (London and Anderson, 1970, 10).

25. Farmers often asserted that half or more of their workers were unauthorized. In 1983, the University of California cooperated with the Employment Development Department to interview thirteen hundred farm worker households—at least thirty households around each of the forty-three EDD offices that had farm worker representatives, and found that 80 percent of the farm workers were foreign-born, but most were legally authorized to work in the United States—only 24 percent were believed to be unauthorized.

26. Farmers and unions competed to help unauthorized farm workers become legal immigrants. The farmers' organization—Alien Legalization for Agriculture—proved the most successful, helping about 5 percent of SAW applicants, but most farm workers became SAWs and thus legal immigrants without help from farmers or unions.

3. Farm Worker Unions

1. Economist Paul Taylor, one of the Big Four farm labor reformers of the 1930s, thought that the combines that replaced migrants during the 1920s in the grain harvest could be encouraged as a way to reduce the appeal of radicals in rural communities (Taylor, 1937).

2. Hops produce cones that are one to two inches long, with papery green scales that turn yellowish when ripe. At the base of these scales are small yellow lupulin glands resembling pollen that contain the alpha and beta acids that give each type of hops its characteristic bittering or flavoring properties.

3. Varden Fuller disputed the commission's finding, noting that poor housing and seasonal employment had been integral features of the farm labor market for decades without causing labor unrest. Fuller believed that labor unrest in Wheatland was due to urban unemployment, which drove into the fields white workers who were not accustomed to the prevailing living and working conditions of the Chinese and Japanese farm workers who did most of California's harvest work.

4. Historian David Vaught challenged the view that the Durst ranch's recruitment practices were typical. He emphasized that most fruit and nut farms were under one hundred acres in 1910, so that the "average orchard or vineyard might be characterized more accurately as a workshop rather than a factory" (1997, 166). However, Vaught's later discussion of citrus production makes it clear that, even if farm production occurs in small-sized units, labor can be organized in an industrial way by the packinghouses, which have long dominated citrus harvesting. For example, Sunkist, with sixty-five hundred members in California and Arizona in 2000, accounted for about half of U.S. fresh citrus sales, meaning that the average citrus farm is thirty or forty acres. Farmers are responsible for getting their oranges and lemons picked, but packinghouses usually coordinate harvesting with "custom harvesters," often labor contractors with fork lifts who are considered to be farm employers under federal and state labor laws.

5. There were only three thousand farms in California in 1930 with annual sales of thirty thousand dollars or more, but they were one-third of all large U.S. farms. Wages were about one-third of cash expenditures on such large farms (U.S. Senate, 1942, Part 47, 17226).

6. The bureau first established a standard or going rate for each task, and then estimated the supply and demand of farm labor at that wage. If the supply was judged to be inadequate, the bureau recruited additional workers by advertising for workers, asking the Employment Service to find additional workers, or appealing to the U.S. government to import foreign workers (Fisher, 1952, p. 101).

7. Tejon Ranch Company, founded in 1843 (http://www.tejonranch.com/), is a 270,000-acre ranch in Kern County; its stock trades on the New York Stock Exchange as TRC.

8. The CAWIU gained experience with farm worker protests through its involvement in ten farm labor strikes throughout California between 1930 and 1932 (Jamieson, 1945, 80).

9. The chairman of the House committee said that "we hope that agricultural workers eventually will be taken care of . . . but just now I believe in biting off one mouthful at a time" (Fuller, 1968, 434). As of 2003, farm workers remain excluded from the NLRA, but most farm workers have been included under the FLSA and Unemployment Insurance since the 1960s and 1970s. Workers compensation insurance, which provides payments to cover medical expenses and disability payments in the event of on the job injury, is a state-by-state program that initially excluded farm workers in most states. As of 1994, eleven states did not require farm employers to carry workers compensation insurance for farm workers.

10. The failure of farm worker unions to take root during the 1930s when factory workers joined unions influenced subsequent analyses. For example, writing in 1952, Morin emphasized that farm workers turn to unions when they cannot escape to the nonfarm labor market to better themselves (Morin, 1952, 101).

11. Galarza worked with his family during the summer months around Sacramento. He graduated from Sacramento High School, and earned a Ph.D. in economics from Columbia in 1947.

12. Galarza went on to write several books on the *bracero* program, including *Strangers in the Fields* in 1956, *Merchants of Labor* in 1964, *Spiders in the House* and *Workers in the Field* in 1970, and *Farmworkers and Agribusiness* (1977).

13. *Bracero* workers were excluded from eligibility for Teamsters membership, the usual practice. When the *bracero* program unexpectedly ended, many ex-*braceros* became immigrants and Teamster union members.

14. Vacuum cooling involves putting cartons of lettuce into portable tubes that can be sealed, removing the air, and cooling the lettuce in less than one hour. Antle was bought by Dole in 1978.

15. According to Chavez, by spring 1965 the NFWA had about twelve hundred members, but only two hundred paid dues (Daniel, 1987, p. 365).

16. Contemporary reports indicated that five hundred of two thousand table grape pickers did not pick in support of a demand for a raise from $1.20 and $0.10 per twenty-five-pound box of grapes to $1.40 and $0.25. The crop was large in 1965 and prices were low, so some grapes were not picked because of low prices, "causing the strikers to think that they were being extremely effective." The 1965 strike was referred to in a grower newspaper as "one of the most widely publicized strikes that is not a strike" (*The Packer*, October 9, 1965).

17. The many books and articles that describe the rise of Cesar Chavez and the UFW include Kushner, 1975; Jenkins, 1985; Levy, 1975a; Majka and Majka, 1982; Taylor, 1975; Sosnick, 1978.

18. The Catholic church provided moral and financial support to the farm worker movement. Pope Leo XIII's 1891 encyclical, *Rerum Novarum*, held that workers had a

moral right to a living wage and the right to organize and bargain collectively to obtain a living wage.

19. Throughout the 1960s, the U.S. Senate had a standing Subcommittee on Migratory Labor. In its annual reports, it called for the extension of collective bargaining rights to farm workers by simply removing the language from the NLRA that said farm workers were not covered employees. In the 1969 report, extending collective bargaining rights to farm workers was the first of fifteen goals (U.S. Senate, 1969, 19).

20. The federal minimum wage was $1.25 an hour in 1966, $1.40 in 1967, and $1.60 in 1968.

21. The National Farm Labor Union Local 218, led by Ernest Galarza, was on strike against DiGiorgio from 1947 to 1950.

22. The DiGiorgio contract is available at http://www.lib.berkeley.edu/~ljones/ UFW/digiorgio/indexdigiorgio.html.

23. The UFW signed a six-year agreement with E. & J. Gallo Winery that expired in March 1973, when Gallo shifted the contract covering 500 workers to the Teamsters. By 1969, the UFW had twelve contracts covering 5,000 wine grape harvesters, a significant accomplishment, but only a small fraction of the peak 500,000 farm workers.

24. The September 1975 Harris poll asked: Have you stopped buying and eating/drinking . . . grapes . . . to support the efforts of Caesar Chavez to organize farm workers into his union or not? 12 percent said yes. When asked the same question about lettuce, 11 percent said yes, and when asked about Gallo wine, 8 percent said yes. In this poll, respondents were asked if wages paid to farm workers were "average," and 24 percent agreed, or "below average," 58 percent agreed.

25. Political pundits credit Chavez for helping Robert Kennedy to narrowly defeat Hubert Humphrey in race for the Democratic presidential primary in California in 1968. UFW leader Dolores Huerta was with Kennedy when he was killed in Los Angeles after the polls closed.

26. The UFW called on field workers to strike in late August 1970 to protest their representation by the Teamsters without elections, prompting lettuce growers to seek an injunction to stop the UFW's picketing. The California Supreme Court, in *R. T. Englund et al. v. Cesar Chavez et al.* on December 29, 1972, concluded that local courts should not have prevented the UFW from picketing. On August 30, 1970, Inter Harvest, which had signed an agreement covering field workers with the Teamsters on July 27, 1970, signed a collective bargaining agreement with the UFW after an August 23, 1970, card count showed that a majority of workers favored UFW representation.

27. The UFW said these twelve contracts covered 6,500 workers, which would have implied an average 542 covered by each contract; a $1.6 million strike fund that had been provided to the UFW by the AFL-CIO had been spent by the end of 1973.

28. In 1966, Cesar Chavez testified about the "great need for having farm workers covered under the [NLRA]" (U.S. Senate Subcommittee, 1966, p. 367).

29. Cambridge Reports, National Omnibus Survey, October 1976.

30. The short-handled hoe (*el cortito*) was preferred by some farmers because, they said, workers closer to the ground did more careful work; opponents emphasized that hoes with handles shorter than four feet caused back problems.

31. The UFW also demanded a 60 percent wage increase for tractor drivers and irrigators, from $3.75 to $6 an hour, and a 53 percent increase in the piece rate for harvesting lettuce, from $0.57 per twenty-four-head carton to $0.87 per carton, and an increase in the celery piece rate of 64 percent, from $0.86 to $1.41 a box. The UFW also demanded five more paid holidays, a COLA, and standby and reporting pay.

32. The eleven growers against whom the UFW struck lost $6 to $10 million, while the seventeen who continued to harvest lettuce had windfall profits from higher lettuce prices.

33. Admiral Packing 7 ALRB 43 (1981). The ALRB cited part of an ad placed by growers in a Mexicali newspaper as take-it-or-leave-it bargaining. The ad read: "The contract

is complete in each of its clauses and it is already accepted and signed by the 27 affected companies. Now, the Union must sign it so that you can return to work."

34. Sun Harvest in the early 1980s owned no farm land; it went out of business by not renewing its leases.

35. Hollywood producer Ed Lewis bought and gave to the UFW-affiliated National Farm Workers Service Center a former sanitarium in La Paz about one hour southeast of Bakersfield. Chavez reportedly wanted to move out of Delano to foster independent decision making and local leadership among farm workers, so that all issues were not directed to him for decision. However, after Chavez in the early 1980s befriended Charles Dederich, the founder of Synanon, a drug rehabilitation organization, he reportedly fired or encouraged the resignation of non-Hispanic UFW officials. *New York Times*, April 24, 1993.

36. About 10 percent of the 350 delegates walked out, and Chavez vowed that "they would never get their jobs back" even after a federal court in 1982 ruled that they could not be fired. Majka and Majka observed that "the UFW has had a persistent problem in handling internal dissent" (1982, 274).

37. Stirling was quoted as saying: "When I came over here the agency was biased for the UFW. . . . Chavez thought he owned the agency, and he did." Ronald B. Taylor, "UFW Takes Risky Shift in Focus after a Long Decline," *Los Angeles Times*, October 30, 1988.

38. Growers commissioned a study, published in 1982, that concluded the ALRB was biased because it deviated from NLRB precedent only to help unions, not growers, helping to set the stage for court reversals of ALRB decisions (Lieberman, 1982).

39. UFW membership data are inconsistent. In 1981, the UFW claimed a peak 105,000 members, although an internal report discussed 30,000 "regular dues-paying members" (Majka and Majka, 1982, 271). One partial explanation for the discrepancy is that, after the UFW was decertified on a particular farm, it continued to claim as members non-dues-paying members as long as it pursued claims that the employer was unlawfully involved in the decertification election.

40. The five pesticides were Dinoseb, Captan, methyl bromide, Parathion, and Phosdrin. The Wrath-of-Grapes boycott was officially ended November 21, 2000. In 1983/84, when the UFW launched its high-tech boycott of table grapes, consumption averaged 5.6 pounds per person; in 1999/00, per capita consumption averaged 8.2 pounds per person.

41. In September 1984, UFW convention materials reported that there were twenty-seven thousand members employed under 161 contracts, and that thirty-six thousand more workers were employed on farms on which there had been an election won by the UFW but no contract. (*BNA Daily Labor Report*, September 7, 1984).

42. Data reported in *Los Angeles Times*, September 4, 1985, part IV, 1. Per capita grape consumption was 8.5 pounds in 1989–90, although some of the increase may have reflected rising imports.

43. For example, Msgr. George Higgins said: "Let's assume the boycott solves the pesticide issue. . . . How would that organize workers?" quoted in Ronald B. Taylor, "UFW Takes Risky Shift in Focus after a Long Decline," *Los Angeles Times*, October 30, 1988. In an op-ed piece, Jerome Cohen wrote that "we should render unto Cesar what is Cesar's—namely, the responsibility for the UFW's failure as yet to fulfill its promise" by resuming organizing activities. "UFW Must Get Back to Organizing," *Los Angeles Times*, January 15, 1986. The UFW had twenty organizers in the mid-1980s, down from two hundred in the late 1970s.

44. In August 1993, the UFW "claimed 22,000 farm workers work under UFW contracts in a year, while others estimate the number of jobs covered by UFW contracts at 9,000 or less." *BNA Daily Labor Report*, August 20, 1993.

45. Farm operator BCI closed in fall 2000, giving up leases on land used to grow lettuce and selling its farming equipment. The UFW-BCI agreement ended with $650,000 distributed to the workers. Fresh Express, the packaged salad firm that began as an adjunct to BCI, became the focus of the company and was sold to Performance Food Group, a food-service distributor in 2001. Fresh Express buys lettuce from many growers, and thus is less vulnerable if a UFW-BCI dispute led to another boycott.

46. The saga of the UFW-CBFWC is recounted in Marc Lifsher, "How Anger toward UFW Led to Rise of Rival Union," *Wall Street Journal*, June, 9, 1999. The UFW version is at: http://www.ufw.org/paper1.htm.

47. Proposition 187 would have restricted the access of unauthorized migrants to state-funded services; 209 ended state affirmative action programs; and 227 ended bilingual education.

48. In fall 1995, the UFW reported that forty farm employers were paying premiums into its Juan de la Cruz pension fund, and that the fund, with $72 million in assets, was distributing 1,500 pension checks a month that averaged $167 each. According to a union press release, the UFW in 1994 was paying pension benefits to 11,000 retired farm workers in California—in one case, $90 per month. However, the UFW has been unable to contact and pay almost one in five retired workers eligible for UFW pension benefits—some two thousand workers are eligible, but have not applied for benefits. (*Sacramento Bee*, September 21, 1994, B8).

49. If the average UFW member earned $12,000 annually, and paid 2 percent union dues or $240 a year, then the UFW's $1.7 million dues income would be generated by 7,083 members. If the average UFW member earned $6,000, an average $120 in dues would indicate 14,167 members.

50. There are a number of not-for-profit and for-profit organizations associated with the UFW. The not-for-profit organizations include the Cesar Chavez Foundation and the National Farm Workers Service Center. The for-profit organizations include ETG Specialty Advertising, Ideal Mini Mart, and American Liberty Investments. In 1993, profits from these affiliated organizations contributed about as much as worker dues to the union's $3.8 million income (UFW, 1994).

51. The first Teamsters contract was signed with Bud Antle, Inc., in 1961, but all field workers were not covered by this Teamsters contract until July 16, 1970—before 1970, harvest workers were covered, but not hoers, irrigators, and tractor drivers.

52. In addition to Bud-Dole workers, the Teamsters represent workers at several nurseries.

53. Farm worker unions seem to be splintering rather than consolidating. In July 1995, three large industrial unions—the United Auto Workers union with 800,000 members, the United Steelworkers of America with 700,000 members, and the International Association of Machinists with 490,000 members—announced plans to merge by 2001. All three unions have lost about half their members since the mid-1970s. In 1994, there were 16.7 million union members in the United States, including 13.3 million members of seventy-eight unions affiliated with the AFL-CIO. The largest U.S. union is the National Education Association, a non-AFL-CIO affiliate with 2.2 million members.

54. Increased employment through contractors also reduced farm worker take-home pay in the 1990s, since most contractor employees have to pay for housing and rides to work

55. The monthly Current Population Survey (CPS) collects data on whether workers in particular industries and occupations are union members. There are few unionized farm workers: in 1992, the CPS reported that about 2.5 percent of the 1.5 million agricultural wage and salary workers were union members, and that 5 percent of the 1.8 million persons with farming, forestry, or fishery occupations were union members, reflecting the higher degree of organization in these latter two industries.

During the 1970s, the CPS reported no unionized farm workers in major farm worker states such as Washington and North Carolina. Several Midwestern states had 3 to 5 percent of their "farm workers" in unions, but these are more likely to be hired hands in integrated farming and grain elevator operations than seasonal field workers. The CPS in the 1970s reported that 7 percent of California farm workers were union members.

Analyses of the effects of unions on wages using 1970s CPS data often found large union wage premiums: unionized farm workers, these studies suggested, earned 40 to 60 percent more than nonunion farm workers (Perloff, 1986). However, sample sizes are so small that it is not clear to what subgroup the CPS data refer.

56. In 2000, the International Longshore and Warehouse Union, which split from the East Coast-based International Longshore Association in 1937, reported forty-two thousand members in sixty local unions in the states of California, Washington, Oregon, Alaska, and Hawaii (www.ilwu.org). About half of the ILWU members in 2000 are in Hawaii and many work in hotels and restaurants.

57. Mary Otto, "Migrants Make 'War' to Achieve Peace," *Miami Herald*, September 6, 1998.

58. In June 2000, it appeared that Vlasic, which was spun off from Campbell in 1998, might be sold or go out of business; its stock fell from twenty-seven dollars in 1998 to two dollars in 2000.

59. Under the FLOC contracts, pickle harvesters received about $1,500 an acre for harvesting, plus $5.50 an hour for preharvest work, in 2000. FLOC members pay of 2.5 percent of their wages in dues.

60. The AERB in the early 1990s had a full-time staff of four and an annual budget of $150,000 (AERB, 1991).

61. Kansas and Idaho have similar farm labor relations laws that, inter alia, outlaw secondary boycotts, the Idaho Agricultural Labor Act and the Kansas Agricultural Employment Relations Act.

62. Year-round workers at Chateau Ste. Michelle were paid in June 1995 an average $7.50 per hour, and their pay ranged from $6.75 to $10.30. In addition, they received company-paid medical benefits, two to five weeks of vacation annually, and eleven paid holidays. The eighty temporary workers hired during the grape harvest were paid an average $5.40 hourly.

4. The ALRA, ALRB, and Elections

1. The ALRB had a staff of forty to forty-five and a budget of $4–$5 million in the late 1990s to protect the rights of the 700,000 to 800,000 individuals employed on thirty-five thousand California farms sometime during the year; administering the ALRA cost five dollars to six dollars a worker. The NLRB, by contrast, administered the NLRA with a staff of two thousand and a FY02 budget of $215 million to cover about 100 million private-sector, nonsupervisory U.S. workers, a cost of two dollars a worker.

2. On the other hand, workers can vote in elections on several farms, which reduces the number of farm workers casting ballots.

3. On the basis of 361 "conclusive" elections in which a union was certified or received a clear majority of the votes cast, Segur and Fuller note that there were an average 89 votes per election, and that more than half of all elections (208) involved vegetable operations (1976, 28). The UFW won 198 and the Teamsters 115 of these first elections.

4. There are about thirty-five thousand ULP charges filed annually with the NLRB.

5. The NLRB permits (but does not require) employers to recognize a union representative for its workers by a card check, i.e., the union presents union authorization cards signed by more than 50 percent of workers.

6. The access issue remains unresolved in the nonfarm labor market. In 1992, the U.S. Supreme Court in *Lechmere v. NLRB* ruled that a Connecticut department store could prohibit all handbilling in a parking lot owned by the store. In this particular case, UCFW organizers talked to employees in a public area as they were entering the store-owned parking lot, and this access was approved by the U.S. Supreme Court.

7. The California Supreme Court upheld the access rule on a 4–3 vote in March 1976, and the U.S. Supreme Court refused to hear the growers' appeal. *Superior Farms (Pandol) v. ALRB*, 429 U.S. 802 (1976) (Hg. den.).

8. A *posse comitatus* is an armed group of men organized by a sheriff to maintain the peace.

9. Western Tomato Growers & Shippers, Inc. 3 ALRB 51 (1977).

10. The assault probably is also a violation of criminal laws that the district attorney

could prosecute. Perry was found to be acting on behalf of two tomato companies, and the ALRB ordered the two companies to mail and read a notice to all their employees explaining that the company and its agents violated the ALRA by interfering with union organizers attempting to take access to workers.

11. Examples of access rules include: *Vista Verde Farms v. Agricultural Labor Relations Bd.*, (1981) 29 Cal.3d 307 [complete exclusion of union organizers from the labor camp]; *Karahadian Ranches, Inc. v. Agricultural Labor Relations Bd.* (1985) 38 Cal.3d 1, 8 [210 Cal.Rptr. 657, 694 P.2d 770] [union organizer lawfully present in the camp kitchen]; Silver Creek Packing Company, 3 ALRB No. 13 (1977) [exclusion of outsiders from locked and guarded camp; also, workers actually housed in separate cabins]; Anderson Farms Company, 3 ALRB No. 67 (1977) [all access to camp barred except between 5:30 p.m. and 8:30 p.m.]; Merzoian Brothers Farm Management Company, Inc., 3 ALRB No. 62 (1977) [complete denial of access to camp by locking gates at night].

12. *Sam Andrews' Sons v. ALRB*, California Supreme Court, November 17, 1988

13. Ranch 1, Inc. SPUDCO 5 ALRB 36 (1979).

14. The ALRA is the only labor law that explicitly excludes FLCs from its definition of employer. Under the federal Migrant and Seasonal Agricultural Worker Protection Act (29 U.S.C.1802), which regulates farm worker recruitment, transportation, housing, and payroll practices, "the term 'farm labor contractor' means any person, other than . . . an employee of an agricultural employer, who, for any money . . . performs any farm labor contracting activity." Farmer-employers can be joint employers with FLCs, meaning that both the employer and the FLC are liable for violations. If the FLC cannot pay a fine, the employer must. Under the U.S. Immigration Reform and Control Act, the FLC can be solely responsible for verifying the legal status of each worker in the crew.

15. In many cases, the farm employer sets the piece rate wage for FLC workers, and the FLC negotiates only the commission or overhead fee for worker recruitment and supervision services. For example, the farmer might agree to pay seven dollars an hour to FLC workers, and a 30 to 40 percent commission to cover the FLC's costs of social security and other payroll taxes.

16. Kotchevar Brothers 2 ALRB 45 (1976). The ALRB started issuing decisions in 1975, so 2 ALRB 45 case means that this was the 45th ALRB decision issued in the second year of ALRB activity, or in 1976.

17. Sutti Farms 6 ALRB 11 (1980). In this case, the International Union of Agricultural Workers filed a petition for an election at Sutti Farms on July 16, 1979. During the July 23, 1979, election, Sutti challenged all the ballots cast by the employees of Zepeda, a FLC who, according to Sutti, has "exclusive control over his entire work force." Zepeda received a flat fee per acre or pound to cover the cost of the workers he provided, plus 30 percent for payroll taxes and his commission.

18. ALRA Section 1156.4 says: "Recognizing that agriculture is a seasonal occupation for a majority of agricultural employees, and wishing to provide the fullest scope for employees' enjoyment of the rights included in this part, the board shall not consider a representation petition or a petition to decertify as timely filed unless the employer's payroll reflects 50 percent of the peak agricultural employment for such employer for the current calendar year for the payroll period immediately preceding the filing of the petition. In this connection, the peak agricultural employment for the prior season shall alone not be a basis for such determination, but rather the board shall estimate peak employment on the basis of acreage and crop statistics which shall be applied uniformly throughout the State of California and upon all other relevant data."

19. A farm may have several payrolls, e.g., field workers paid weekly and office staff monthly. In such situations, the ALRB has ruled that employment must be calculated by adding up both groups of workers and dividing by employment on a "representative" or average work day to compute average daily employment.

20. Mario Saikhon, Inc. 2 ALRB 2 (1976); the body count terminology was used in Triple E Produce Corp. (1990) 16 ALRB 14.

21. In most cases, employers after an election assert that the election must be redone

because there should have been two or more elections rather than one election. For example, the UFW received 72 votes against 67 no-union votes in a September 9, 1983, election at Pappas and Company. Pappas challenged 103 votes, arguing that most of these votes came from workers employed by Pappas Enterprises, and should not be counted. In Pappas and Company, 10 ALRB 27 (1984), the ALRB ruled that Pappas Enterprises grew melons, and Pappas and Company harvested and packed them, and the Pappas family owned both companies, and thus all their farm workers should be included in one bargaining unit.

22. Bruce Church 2 ALRB 38 (1976).

23. Holtville Farms, Inc. 10 ALRB 49 (1984).

24. Prohoroff Poultry Farms 9 ALRB 68 (1983).

25. Until 1979, pullets were raised and eggs were produced at the main ranch location in San Marcos, but in 1980, these functions were separated on two ranches.

26. Most of the employees at the main San Marcos ranch gathered eggs for an hourly wage that was based on previous piece rate productivity of thirteen to sixteen cases per hour. Egg gatherers' wages averaged $5.44 per hour in 1983. Laborers in San Marcos averaged $5.09 per hour, versus $4 to $4.15 in Potrero, ninety miles closer to the Mexican border.

27. Coastal Berry Company 26 ALRB 2 (2000).

28. R. C. Walters and Sons 2 ALRB 14 (1976).

29. Joe Maggio Inc. 5 ALRB 26 (1979).

30. The rule was that 20 percent produce from other growers made the packer or processor a commercial operation, and the employees of the packing shed nonfarm employees.

31. Camsco Produce Co., 297 NLRB 157 (March 15, 1990).

32. The NLRB regional director ruled "that the Employer's [Produce Magic's] employees are not agricultural laborers" except when they cut lettuce. 1992 NLRB Dec. 17973; 311 NLRB 173; 1993 NLRB 144 L.R.R.M. 1001. In this case, Produce Magic sought to have employees usually considered farm workers to be classified as nonfarm workers to head off the UFW-sought election.

33. Associated-Tagline, Inc 25 ALRB 6 (1999).

34. General Shoe Corporation (1948) 77 N.L.R.B. 124 at p. 127.

35. Hollywood Ceramics Company, Inc. (1962) 140 N.L.R.B. 221; Midland National Life Insurance Co. (1982) 263 N.L.R.B. 24.

36. Quoted in Sakata Ranches 5 ALRB No. 56 (1979).

37. NLRB v. Gissel (1969) 395 U.S. p. 575, 617. The ALRB asserted that "employees are entitled to receive information relevant to their decision to vote regardless of whether the information comes from the union, the employer or third parties, so long as it is not coercive or otherwise unlawful, so that they can make an informed as well as a free choice." D'Arrigo, Inc. (1977) 3 ALRB 37.

38. Oasis Ranch Management 18 ALRB 11 (1992) 12.

39. Hansen Farms 2 ALRB 61 (1976).

40. Anderson Farms Company, 3 ALRB No. 67 (1977).

41. Giumarra Vineyards Corp. & Giumarra Farms Inc. 7 ALRB 24 (1982).

42. Even though the UFW said it had majority support among workers as evidenced by authorization cards, a farm worker union cannot be certified until it wins a secret-ballot election.

43. In *NLRB v. Burns International Security Services, Inc* 406 U.S. 272 (1972) the U.S. Supreme Court asserted that, when Burns took over the contract to provide security services to Lockheed, it did not have to hire Wackenhut employees. However, since it did hire Wackenhut employees, Burns had an obligation to bargain with the United Plant Guard Workers union.

Under some circumstances, the new owner can plead financial hardship and seek to modify wages and working conditions in an existing contract. Some scholars believe that the new buyer in the nonfarm labor market has no duty to bargain with the existing union unless and until the new buyer hires at least 50 percent of the old employer's workers, so that it is apparent that the workers employed want the union to represent them.

44. Highland Ranch and San Clemente Ranch 5 ALRB 54 (1979), modified and remanded, 29 Cal. 3d 874 (1981), modified, 8 ALRB 11 (1982).

45. Certified Egg Farms and Olson Farms Inc. 16 ALRB 7 (1990).

46. Certified/Olson were separate businesses with the same family ownership and management when the union election of September 11, 1975, resulted in the Teamsters being certified as the bargaining agent for Certified's workers on three egg farms in Gilroy, California, on November 19, 1975. At the time of the stock transfer in April 1986, the Teamsters and Certified were in the middle of the three-year February 15, 1984, to February 14, 1987, contract that automatically renewed each February unless one party gave notice. In April 1986, Certified's stock was transferred to Olson, and in May 1986, Certified/Olson stopped forwarding dues to the Teamsters, and in July 1986 refused to discuss a grievance filed by the Teamsters protesting Certified's hiring of nonunion workers. In November 1986, Certified refused to provide the Teamsters with the information that it wanted to bargain for a new contract. Certified argued that, because it had ceased to exist in April 1986 when its stock was transferred to Olson, there was no longer a contract between it and the Teamsters.

Certified bought 5 to 10 percent of its eggs from other farmers, so its processing plant employees would fall within the traditional definition of agriculture. In Egg City (see chapter 7), by contrast, almost 30 percent of the eggs processed were bought from other farmers; Egg City was reclassified as a nonfarm employer in the late 1980s.

47. Gourmet Harvesting and Packing and Gourmet Farms 14 ALRB 9 (1988).

48. If no contract has ever been signed, and the other conditions are satisfied, then a decertification petition requires signatures from at least 50 percent of the workers in the bargaining unit.

49. Cattle Valley Farms, 8 ALRB 24 (1982).

50. Abatti Farms 7 ALRB 36 (1981).

51. The ALRB finding that Abatti interfered with the 1978 decertification election is Abatti 7 ALRB 36 (1981). In Abatti 16 ALRB 17 (1990), the ALRB dismissed Abatti's petition for an opportunity to present a "Dal Porto" defense that even if Abatti has bargained with the UFW after 1978, no contract with a higher wage would have been signed. If Abatti could not present a Dal Porto defense (because it refused to bargain at all), Abatti asked that the ALRB base makewhole on the wages offered by an Imperial Valley employer who bargained with the UFW to impasse or with the wages Abatti and the UFW agreed to in a 1986 contract; under either of these measures, Abatti owed no makewhole.

The ALRB found in this case that Abatti owed its employees about 10 percent more than they were actually paid during the bad faith bargaining period. This 10 percent make whole remedy reflected wage trends in UFW contracts during the early 1980s.

52. Cattle Valley Farms 9 ALRB 65 (1983).

5. Employer and Union Unfair Labor Practices

1. Bruce Church Inc. 16 ALRB 3 (1990).
2. Arnaudo Brothers Inc. 3 ALRB 78 (1977).
3. Oasis Ranch Management 18 ALRB 11 (1992).
4. Merzoian Brothers Farm Management 3 ALRB 62 (1977).
5. Triple E Produce, 23 ALRB 8, (1997).
6. Concerted activities usually involve two or more employees acting on behalf of a group of employees. Complaints by a single employee to state officials about safety conditions on the job were considered protected concerted activities until 1986, when the NLRB ruled that a safety complaint by one nonunion truck driver was not protected concerted activity. The NLRB case, Meyers Industries 281 NLRB 118 (1986), overturns Foster Poultry Farms 6 ALRB 15 (1980) and Miranda Mushroom Farms, Inc. 6 ALRB 22 (1980).

OSHA and other safety laws may prohibit employers from firing workers who make safety complaints, but the NLRB does not consider a single worker making a safety complaint to be engaged in protected concerted activity.

7. See *NLRB v. Washington Aluminum Co.*, 370 U.S. at 17 (1962).

8. NLRA section 10(e) is equivalent to Cal. Lab. Code §1160.3.

9. Pappas & Company 5 ALRB 52 (1979).

10. The melons (cantaloupes) were harvested by workers who bend over, pick them, and put them in a sack that hangs over their back—when filled with fifteen to twenty-five melons, the sack can weigh seventy-five pounds. Workers carry full sacks to a truck at the end of the field, walk up a plank that is dragged behind the truck, and dump their bags behind a rising wooden barrier. The crew shares a piece rate wage that reflects how many feet of truck(s) they filled with melons.

11. Unionized workers employed under a collective bargaining agreement may be fired if they walk out during the life of the agreement without, e.g., first filing a grievance.

12. Anthony Harvesting 18 ALRB 7 (1992).

13. Pantoja was the driver of the slow-moving conveyor belt that moved through broccoli fields and on which cut broccoli is cut and put into boxes. He was out of his seat stapling together the boxes in which harvested broccoli is placed for shipment to market, and thus unable to stop the harvester in an emergency, when an OSHA inspector conducted an inspection on November 11, 1990. The slow-moving conveyor belt could be stopped with ground-level safety switches, but they were broken on this machine. Pantoja (and his supervisor) were fired on November 11, 1990, and the ALJ/ALRB ruled that the firing was lawful—even though Pantoja engaged in PCA, he disobeyed instructions to remain in the driver's seat, and thus it was lawful to fire him.

14. Stamoules Produce 16 ALRB 13 (1990).

15. Workers complained about poor labor camp conditions and the company's refusal to pay them for commuting time, which was sometimes four hours daily.

16. If the pro-UFW crews also had the least seniority, and they were not hired because of the reduced melon acreage, it would have been difficult for the UFW to prove that failure to rehire was to retaliate for union activities.

17. Springfield Mushroom 14 ALRB 10 (1989). During picking, some of the mushroom stems fall back unto the bed; the stems must be cleaned up to keep the other mushrooms growing properly.

18. One reason given for not rehiring the three workers in 1985 was that Springfield believed they were not authorized to work in the United States. Springfield employed eight to ten full-time pickers and several part-time pickers, and obtained workers by having the bilingual foreman recruit Mexican immigrants, including illegal aliens. These workers sometimes changed their names and social security numbers upon their return after seasonal layoffs, so it was hard for Springfield to argue that fired workers were never rehired because they were illegal aliens.

19. Jack G. Zaninovich 4 ALRB 82 (1978); Royal Packing Co 5 ALRB 31 (1979), aff'd, 101 Cal. App. 3d 826 (4th dist. 1980).

20. E. & J. Gallo Winery 7 ALRB 10 (1981).

21. U.S. Congress, Senate, Committee on Education and Labor, 1935, 9–11.

22. *NLRB v. Cabot Carbon Co.*, 360 U.S. 203 (1959).

23. Electromation, Inc., 309 NLRB 990 (1992), enf'd, 35 F.3d 1148 (11th Cir. 1994).

24. Anderson Farms Company 3 ALRB 67 (1977).

25. This is the so-called Wright Line test. Once the employee has shown that his union activities were a motivating factor in the employer's decision to discharge him, the burden shifts to the employer to show that discharge would have occurred in any event. If the employer fails to carry his burden in this regard, the NLRB is entitled to find that discharge was improper. *NLRB v. Transportation Management, Inc.*, (1983) 462 US 393 [113 LRRM 2857].

26. Nishi Greenhouse 7 ALRB 18 (1981).

27. *NLRB v. Insurance Agents' International Union.* 361 U.S. 477 (1960).

28. The chairman of the Senate Committee on Education and Labor in 1935 described the government's role in establishing only the rules which the union and employer must obey as follows: "When the employees have chosen their organization, when they have selected their representatives, all the bill proposes to do is to escort them to the door of the employer and say, 'Here they are, the legal representatives of your employees.' What happens behind those doors is not inquired into, and the bill does not seek to inquire into it." Cox, Archibald, 1958, 1401.

29. O. P. Murphy Produce Co., Inc. 5 ALRB 63 (1979).

30. Most of the fresh tomatoes sold in the United States are "mature greens," picked when they are green, and then gassed with ethylene to make them ripen. Tomatoes handled in this manner can be sold over a two-week period, versus less than one week for most vine-ripened tomatoes. Even though mature green tomatoes were hand-picked into five-gallon buckets for about fifty cents per bucket in the early 1990s, about 25 percent were found unusable after being washed and sorted in packing sheds before being sent to market.

31. Murphy began to rehire strikers only after a Monterey County judge on October 13, 1977, ordered him to rehire them in response to an ALRB order.

32. *NLRB v. Herman Sausage, Inc.*, 275 F. 2d 229, 232 (5th Cir. 1960).

33. Meyer Tomato, 17 ALRB 17 (1991).

34. The FLCs had oral agreements to harvest the tomatoes for $47 a ton, or about 2.35 cents a pound.

35. Paul W. Bertuccio 8 ALRB 101 (1982).

36. Olson Farms/ Certified Egg Farms Inc. 19 ALRB 20 (1993).

37. A checkoff provision means that workers' union dues are automatically deducted from workers' pay and forwarded to the union.

38. In 1960, General Electric made a "final offer" during the first bargaining session, and "Boulwarism," named after the GE vice president who developed it, was considered per se evidence of bad faith bargaining.

39. Montebello Rose Co. and Mount Arbor Nurseries 5 ALRB 64 (1979), aff'd, 119 Cal. App. 3d 1 (5th dist., 1981). Mount Arbor Rose Company was in McFarland. In Sam Andrews' Sons 9 ALRB 24 (1983), significant issues had not been discussed, few meetings had occurred on the disputed issues, and the union had not assumed an uncompromising attitude on the key issue.

40. The ALRB failed to extend the UFW's one-year certification after December 1976, and Mount Arbor and Montebello assumed the UFW no longer represented the employees—several UFW supporters were laid off.

41. The employers also claimed to be representing their employees' best interests by opposing the good standing provision the UFW wanted, which would have required workers to join the UFW and to remain members of the UFW in good standing in order to continue to work for Montebello and Mount Arbor. The ALRB found that an employer who opposes union good standing on the grounds that the employer is protecting workers from the union they selected to represent them has rejected the ALRA's purpose of permitting workers to select their exclusive bargaining representative.

42. Admiral Packing 7 ALRB 43 (1981), 10 ALRB 9 (1984).

43. The court of appeals concluded that "neither party can be said to be solely responsible for the impasse." *Carl Joseph Maggio, Inc. et al., Petitioners, v. Agricultural Labor Relations Board, Respondent.* Court of Appeal of California, Fourth Appellate District. 154 Cal. App. 3d 40; April 2, 1984.

44. Bruce Church 17 ALRB 1 (1992).

45. A union shop provision in the agreement could require all the workers employed on a farm to join the union after five days and remain union members in good standing to keep their jobs.

46. 379 U.S. 203 (1964).

47. During the life of an agreement, the union can protect itself by writing a clause into the contract that regulates subcontracting. If there is no agreement, the union can call a strike to protest.

48. Business closures cannot be runaway shops, as occurs when an employer closes a union business and opens a nonunion business nearby. The complete closure of a business, even for antiunion reasons, is not subject to ALRB/NLRB review. Textile Workers v. Darlington Co., 380 U.S. 263 (1965).

49. O. P. Murphy Produce Co., Inc. 7 ALRB 37 (1981).

50. Joe Maggio, Inc. 8 ALRB 72 (1982).

51. Lu-Ette Farms, Inc. 8 ALRB 91 (1982).

52. Pickers put melons into bags that have fourteen to eighteen melons each and are carried up a gangplank into a truck with sides that are about five feet high. The entire crew divides a per foot of melons on the truck piece rate. The conveyor belt system involves some workers picking the melons in front of the machine and placing them in a row. Other workers pick up these melons and put them on the conveyor belt, which conveys them to a waiting truck. The speed of the conveyor belt regulates the pace of work, so most employers who use conveyor belt harvesting systems pay their workers hourly wages. Eliminating the bags also enables women to work in the melon harvest.

53. Valdora Produce Company 10 ALRB 3 (1984).

54. Valdora was guilty in this case of subcontracting its citrus harvesting to a FLC without offering to bargain over the decision. The Lara crew did most of the picking, usually working five to six days weekly for up to ten months annually. The Yanez crew was the backup crew. The Lara crew was first to sign up and support the UFW. In the summer of 1979, the UFW learned that Yanez was harvesting citrus in Escondido with a FLC rather than a UFW crew. The UFW filed a grievance with Valdora, charging breach of the collective bargaining agreement. Valdora argued that the switch from having Yanez as foreman to Yanez as an independent FLC was not a mandatory bargaining subject. The ALRB disagreed, and found Valdora in this instance guilty of not bargaining in good faith. Holtville Farms, Inc. 10 ALRB 101 (1984).

55. Paul W. Bertuccio 8 ALRB 101 (1982).

56. Cardinal Distributing Company, Inc. 159 Cal. App. 3rd 758 (4th dist. 1978). Cardinal was found to have committed an 1153(e) ULP by failing to provide the information needed by the UFW to bargain, and by unilaterally raising the wages of carrot bunchers without offering to bargain with the UFW over the raise.

57. V. B. Zaninovich and Sons, Inc. 3 ALRB 57 (1977).

58. Ace Tomato Company, Inc/George B. Lagorio Farms, 15 ALRB 7 (1989) 12 ALRB 20 (1986).

59. United Farm Workers of America, Jojola, 6 ALRB 58 (1980).

60. "The essence of coercion or restraint is that a person is forced, according to the dictates of another against his or her own judgment and will, to act or to refrain from acting in a certain way," p. 4.

61. A typical UFW good standing clause is: "Union membership shall be a condition of employment. Each worker shall be required to become a member of Union immediately following five (5) continual days after the beginning of employment, or five (5) days from the date of the signing of this Agreement, whichever is later; and to remain a member of the Union in good standing. Union shall be the sole judge of the good standing of its members. Any worker who fails to become a member of the Union within the time limit set forth herein, or who fails to pay the required initiation fee, periodic dues or regularly authorized assessments as prescribed by Union, or who has been determined to be in bad standing by the Union pursuant to the provisions of the Union's constitution, shall be immediately discharged or suspended upon written notice from the Union to the Company [Name of Employer], and shall not be re-employed until written notice from the Union to the Company of the worker's good standing status."

62. In *Emporium Capwell Co. versus Western Addition Community Organization*, 420 US 50 (1975), black employees charged that the Emporium Capwell department store was dis-

criminating against minority employees, and that the filing of individual grievances under the union contract would be too slow to resolve their complaints. Four employees picketed the store, demanding that the company president meet with them to end discrimination against minorities in hiring and promotion. The NLRB held that the protesting employees were not engaged in protected concerted activity, and thus could be fired lawfully, because they had a union contract and a grievance procedure to deal with their complaints. The fired employees appealed, arguing that there should be a limited exception to the union being the exclusive bargaining representative if the purpose of the protest was to root out racial discrimination. The U.S. Supreme Court disagreed, reaffirming the exclusive bargaining role of elected union representatives to deal with wages and working conditions.

63. Other types of union security clauses are the closed shop, which requires the employer to hire only union members, the preferential shop, which requires the employer to give preference to union members when hiring, and maintenance of membership, which requires employees to maintain their union membership throughout the collective bargaining agreement if they join.

64. The U.S. Supreme Court in 1963 reaffirmed approval of union security or union or agency shop clauses in collective bargaining agreements that require employees to be union members in good standing, but noted that, if "it is permissible to condition employment upon membership ... [then] 'membership' as a condition of employment is whittled down to its financial core," i.e., only the repayment of dues and fees.

65. United Farm Workers of America (Pasillas, Martinez, Scarbrough) 8 ALRB 103 (1982), 14.

66. UFW-Sun Harvest 9 ALRB 40 (1983), 8. In the nonfarm sector, the U.S. secretary of labor and the federal courts have the primary responsibility for regulating the relationship between unions and their members.

67. A federal district court in 1985 ruled that the good-standing clause of §1153(c) was unconstitutional as a violation of a worker's first amendment rights to free speech and association: "Mere union strength and industrial peace are insufficient goals to justify abridgement of rights which union members hold." *Beltran v. State of California* 617 F. Supp. 948 (S. D. Cal. 1985).

68. Jordan Bloom, testifying May 21, 1975, before the Senate Industrial Relations Committee for farm employers on SB1, the bill that became the ALRA, made legislators aware of the implications of broad ALRA good standing by citing examples of farm employers ordered to fire UFW members who "refused to go to a demonstration" under pre-ALRA UFW contracts. Bloom wanted the ALRA to have NLRA good-standing criteria, which give unions less authority to discipline members.

Articles 18 to 21 of the UFW constitution spell out the union's disciplinary procedures. They allow UFW members to charge other members with violating good standing rules within sixty days of the event. The accused member must have at least seven days to prepare a defense to the charges and the UFW's ranch committee acts as the judge between the charging and defending UFW members. Ranch committee decisions can be appealed to the UFW's National Executive Board and then to the UFW's Public Review Board. United Farm Workers of America 12 ALRB 16 (1986).

69. United Farm Workers of America (Pasillas, Martinez, Scarbrough) 8 ALRB 103 (1982).

70. United Farm Workers of America (Pasillas, Martinez, Scarbrough) 8 ALRB 103 (1982), 14.

71. Scarbrough died in early 1983, and the ALRB ordered the UFW to provide back pay to his estate.

72. UFW (Maggio) 12 ALRB 16 (1986).

73. In August 1982, when Maggio was paying general field workers $4.12 per hour, the company proposed increases to $4.53, $4.89, and $5.28 over three years, and the UFW demanded $6.80 an hour—the highest UFW rate at that time was $6.65 at Sun Harvest.

74. The ALRB concluded that the UFW's high wage demands were not unreasonable,

since (1) Maggio had previously agreed to pay the prevailing wage in the Salinas Valley and (2) the UFW could have been trying to "take wages out of competition" for all vegetable growers.

75. The major author of the ALRA, Rose Bird, testified that makewhole applies "only where an employer bargains in bad faith." Quoted in UFW (Maggio) 12 ALRB 16 (1986), 15.

6. Strikes and Remedies

1. Taylor Farms, 20 ALRB 8 (1994).

2. The ALJ/ALRB also found that Jose Lomeli and Antonio Rangel quit their jobs; they left work with UFW flags and joined workers who were picketing, although they did return to work to get their tools.

3. O. P. Murphy and Sons 5 ALRB 63 (1979).

4. Bertuccio Farms 10 ALRB 52 (1984).

5. Dan Morain, "U.S. Justices Refuse to Hear the Union's Appeal of a $1.7–Million Judgment Awarded an Imperial County Grower," *Los Angeles Times*, October 8, 1991.

6. The word *boycott* comes from an economic war waged by Irish farmers in the 1880s against an English land agent, Charles Cunningham Boycott, who refused to cut rents during a time of poor crops. Their subsequent refusal to work his land or sell him goods forced him to return to England.

7. National Labor Relations Act Section 8(b)(4)(ii)(B) makes it an unfair labor practice for a union to "threaten, coerce or restrain any person," with the object of "forcing or requiring any person to cease using, selling, handling, transporting, or otherwise dealing in the products of any other producer . . . or to cease doing business with any other person."

8. Cal. Lab. Code S1154(d).

9. National Labor Relations Act §8(b)(4)(B) 29 U.S.C. §158(b)(4)(B) (1982).

10. *Bakery and Pastry workers Local 802 vs. Wohl* 315 U.S. 769 (1942).

11. *Bertuccio vs. Superior Court* 118 Cal. App. 3d 363 (1981). Unlawful primary picketing can be enjoined by state courts at the request of either the ALRB or the employer, after the employer has filed an unfair labor practice charge with the ALRB.

12. United Farm Workers of America 15 ALRB 10 (1989).

13. A Japanese company loaned Egg City $14 million in exchange for a 40 percent equity stake to bring Egg City out of bankruptcy.

14. Some of the UFW's picketing went beyond truthful advertising of the dispute, alleging that the eggs served were old or bad, and these signs made that picketing unlawful. In addition, it was unlawful for UFW pickets to induce a secondary strike at the Long Beach port, where longshoremen refused to load Egg City eggs. A decertification election was held at Egg City on November 3, 1986; workers voted 105 for no union and 79 to retain the UFW. Egg City filed a suit against the UFW, alleging that the UFW's boycott activities had cost it $6.6 million. During the summer of 1993, the UFW and Egg City privately settled this suit.

In June and September 1986, Egg City filed charges against the UFW with the NLRB. The second of these charges resulted in an NLRB complaint against the UFW, and a November 1986 settlement between the NLRB and the UFW agreed that the UFW was not a labor organization under the NLRA, and that it had no interest in representing Egg City employees who were deemed by the NLRB to be nonfarm workers. Egg City paid all its workers as if they were farm workers until January 1987, e.g., it paid time-and-a-half overtime wages only after ten hours on a single day, not after eight hours. Egg City said that, even before the June 1986 UFW strike, it had begun buying eggs from other farms and processing them, so that all of the workers engaged in processing eggs were nonfarm workers.

15. Table grape production is concentrated; the largest five growers account for about

half of the 50 to 60 million twenty-two-pound lugs of grapes produced in California each year.

16. Eventually, most Tianguis stores were converted into regular Von's, and Von's was later bought by Safeway.

17. United Farm Workers 19 ALRB 15 (1991).

18. The California Table Grape Commission sued the city of San Francisco for refusing to serve grapes at Candlestick Park, despite a June 1994 agreement to promote grapes in exchange for a sponsorship fee. The CTGC argued that the California Department of Food and Agriculture found grapes to be safe, and that the ALRB had found the UFW's grape boycott to be unlawful, so that San Francisco should not be supporting an "illegal boycott." A California judge ruled that the CTGC had been empowered by the Legislature to promote grapes, not to litigate labor issues, and in 1995 dismissed the suit.

San Francisco canceled the grape sponsorship arrangement, and in 1988 agreed not to allow public funds or facilities to be used to buy or promote grapes.

19. Section 1160 permits the board "to issue an order requiring [the violator] to cease and desist from such unfair labor practice, to take affirmative action including reinstatement of employees with or without back pay, and making employees whole, when the board deems such relief appropriate for the loss of pay resulting from the employer's refusal to bargain, and to provide such other relief as will effectuate the policies of this part."

20. *Phelps Dodge Corp v. NLRB*, 313 U.S. 177 (1941).

21. *NLRB v Sure-Tan, Inc.* 467 US 883(104 S.C.2803) (1984).

22. Congress in the late 1990s tried to restrict the labor relations rights of unauthorized workers. For example, the U.S. House of Representatives approved an amendment to the Fiscal Year 1997 NLRB appropriation that would have prohibited the agency from expending funds to protect the labor relations rights of an employee not lawfully entitled to be present and employed in the United States. The Senate-House conference committee dropped this restriction on NLRB activities.

23. Rigi Agricultural Services 11 ALRB 27 (1985).

24. This would be analogous to a Dal Porto defense to an order for a makewhole remedy.

25. Phillip D. Bertelsen. 12 ALRB No. 27 (1986).

26. In this case, A.P.R.A. Fuel Oil Buyers Group, Inc., a Brooklyn heating-oil company, was ordered to reinstate two illegal workers wrongfully fired for their union activities with back pay. A.P.R.A. hired the two workers in 1989–1990, knowing that they were not authorized to work, they signed Teamster authorization cards, and A.P.R.A. fired them in January–February 1991. The NLRB concluded the firings were unlawful retaliation for the workers' union activities, and in 1995 ordered A.P.R.A: (1) to provide back pay to the two workers from the date of their unlawful discharges until either they were reinstated by A.P.R.A. or failed to produce work authorization documents and, (2) to reinstate the men if they produced work authorization documents.

27. The Labor Law Reform Act of 1977 would have allowed the NLRB to require employers who fired workers in retaliation for union activities to give double back pay.

28. Lu-Ette Farms, Inc. 8 ALRB 55 (1982).

29. Abatti Farms, Inc. and Abatti Produce, Inc. 9 ALRB 59 (1983).

30. Perry Farms 4 ALRB 25 (1978), rev'd on other grounds, 86 Cal. App. 3d 448 (3d dist. 1978).

31. *J.R. Norton Co. v Agricultural Labor Relations Board* (1979) 26 Cal 3d 1, 39.

32. J. R. Norton 6 ALRB 26 (1980).

33. *Dal Porto and Sons v. ALRB*, 191 Cal. App. 3d 1195 (3d dist. 1987). "Make-whole relief may be imposed only where the parties would have entered into a collective bargaining agreement providing for higher pay in the absence of the employer's refusal to bargain" (p. 1205).

34. Employers may mount a Dal Porto defense to avoid makewhole only if they have bargained with the union, not in technical refusal to bargain cases.

35. *Dal Porto and Sons v. ALRB*, 191 Cal. App. 3d 1195 (3d dist. 1987). 1207.

36. Mario Saikhon, Inc. 15 ALRB 3 (1989). Mario Saikhon took over sole ownership of Mario Saikhon Inc at age thirty in 1962. In September 1992, he was convicted of criminal tax evasion, and sentenced to 6.5 years in prison and $22 million in fines, the largest individual criminal tax case in U.S. history. In 1992, Mario Saikhon Inc farmed fifteen thousand acres acres in California, Arizona, and Mexico, and had twenty-two hundred employees in the Imperial Valley.

37. Vessey & Co. et al. 13 ALRB 17 (p. 18).

38. Before the ALRB calculated this amount, the case was settled for $2.1 million in 1993.

39. Adam Dairy 4 ALRB 24 (1978).

40. The 78 percent figure was from the Bureau of Labor Statistics publication, Employee Compensation in the Private Nonfarm Economy (1974). The board in 1983 reduced the fringe benefit percentage of total compensation from 22 to 15.7 percent by excluding mandatory employer contributions for social security and unemployment insurance, which were 6.3 percent of total compensation in 1974 (they are not subject to bargaining) Robert H. Hickham 9 ALRB 6 (1983). An analysis that calculated the value of fringe benefits paid on a hourly basis (e.g., an employer's dollar an hour contribution to the RFK health plan) and made assumptions about the eligibility of workers for other fringe benefits, found that the benefits in UFW contracts added 14 to 17 percent to the hourly wages of unionized California farm workers between 1976 and 1987 (Martin, Egan, and Luce, 1988).

41. J. R. Norton 4 ALRB 39 (1978), rev'd and remanded on other grounds, 26 Cal. 3d 1 (1979).

42. Holtville Farms, Inc. 10 ALRB 13 (1984); Kyutoku Nursery 8 ALRB 73 (1982).

43. In January 2002, the ALRB created an Agricultural Employee Relief Fund into which monies owed farm workers are deposited. If workers owed money cannot be found, the monies are left in the fund and paid to workers in cases in which other farm workers eligible for monetary awards can receive payouts from the fund, ending the incentive of employers to use worker turnover to reduce makewhole payments.

44. Between 1975 and 2002, the ALRB ordered $34.2 million in makewhole remedies, and employers paid $4.4 million.

7. Nontraditional Farm Worker Unions

1. The number of major U.S. strikes—those involving a thousand or more workers—dropped from a record high 470 in 1952 to 29 in 2001.

2. The eleven growers against whom the UFW struck lost $6 to $10 million, while the seventeen who continued to harvest lettuce had windfall profits from higher lettuce prices.

3. If 100 heads of lettuce are normally sold at $1 each, total revenue is $100. With an elasticity of -0.2, raising the price by 10 percent reduces quantity demanded by 2 percent, so that 98 heads are sold at $1.10, but total revenue rises to $108.

4. Quail Street Casualty is a Bermuda-based insurance company established by WGA to provide harvest-time strike insurance. In 1988, Quail Street collected $1.5 million in premiums to insure against strike-caused losses on thirty-seven thousand acres of fruits and vegetables in California and Arizona, about $40 an acre, and one of the twenty-seven participating growers collected an insurance payout. *Western Grower and Shipper*, September 1989, 19. (www.quailstreet.com/QSM_QSC.HTM).

5. "Bud Strike Shakes Deal," *The Packer*, November 11, 1989, 1 and 6A. Teamsters 890 was the local that competed with the UFW to represent farm workers in the 1960s and 1970s, and filed for bankruptcy in 1990 after being order to pay $526,692 for damages in the 1989 strike.

6. Safeway, for example, on September 15, 1997, pledged its support for the "issues

raised by the UFW on behalf of strawberry workers' right to organize, seek enforcement of the laws . . . and to work in a discrimination-free environment."

7. Mount Olive said: "Our company does not employ farm workers—farmers do—and it is unfair for our company to influence farmers or farm workers to sign labor contracts. . . . We do not want to interfere in the relationship between employer and employee."

8. Leo C. Wolinsky, "Senate Democrats Move to Cripple Farm Labor Board," *Los Angeles Times*, April 11, 1986.

9. Quoted in Ronald Taylor, "UFW Takes Risky Shift in Focus after a Long Decline," *Los Angeles Times*, October 30, 1988. 3.

10. Ted Rohrlich, "Miguel Contreras. A Boss for a New Generation Broadens Big Labor's Appeal," *Los Angeles Times*, January 31, 1999.

11. Figure 7.4 is drawn to reflect the common employer assertion—all available U.S. workers are hired first, and then immigrants are hired.

8. Immigration and Agriculture

1. Sun World bought a 50 percent interest in Interharvest in 1978 and renamed it Sun Harvest.

2. However, farmers simultaneously argued that, unlike factories, agriculture was extraordinarily dependent on unauthorized workers and won a deferral of employer sanctions enforcement while the SAW legalization program for farm workers was underway, until December 1, 1988.

3. The 350,000 figure became the limit for Group I SAWs, who did at least ninety days of crop work in each of the years ending in May 1, 1984, 1985, and 1986. Group II SAWs, by contrast, did ninety days of crop work only in the year ending May 1, 1986. Over 90 percent of all SAW applicants were in the Group II category. Some 88,000 unauthorized farm workers were legalized under the pre-1982 program.

4. Robert Suro, "Massive Fraud in Amnesty Effort," *New York Times*, November 12, 1989, A1. About 100,000 SAW applications were rejected, often after they told preposterous stories. For example, some SAW applicants in New York City, when asked about the qualifying farm work they did, said they climbed trees to pick strawberries.

5. Rep. Peter Rodino (D-NJ) was chair of the House Judiciary Committee who favored legalization over guest workers.

6. Hourly wages rose with the minimum wage (from $3.35 to $4.25 in California on July 1, 1988; from $3.35 to $3.80 in the United States on April 1, 1990 and to $4.25 on April 1, 1991), but piece rate wages generally remained unchanged between 1985 and 1990.

7. AgJOBS required each state to establish a registry to which legally authorized farm workers seeking jobs would report to indicate their availability, and a farmer's need for guest workers would be determined by the farmer calling the registry and requesting, e.g., a hundred workers. If the registry had only twenty-five workers available, the farmer would be certified to have seventy-five guest workers admitted.

8. The housing allowance was one-fourth of the HUD Section 8 housing allowance for the region, based on four workers sharing a two-bedroom apartment.

9. The key to DOV is pruning—the fruiting vines (this year's crop) are separated from the renewal vines (next year's crop). After the grapes mature, the fruiting vines are cut so that the grapes begin drying while still on the vine, so that vineyards often appear as alternating green and brown zones. Under the Sun Maid system, fruiting vines are on the south side of the trellis and renewal vines on the north side.

10. One machine operating sixty days can harvest nine hundred acres a season; equivalent to the work of a crew of forty.

Bibliography

Adams, R. L., and T. R. Kelly. 1918. "A Study of Farm Labor in California." Berkeley, Calif.: Giannini Foundation of Agricultural Economics.

AERB (Agricultural Employment Relations Board). 1991. "Sunset Review: Report 91–1 to the Arizona Legislature Committee of Reference." Phoenix. September 6.

ALRB (Agricultural Labor Relations Board). "Annual Report to the Legislature." Sacramento.

Alston, Julian, James Chalfant, Jason Christian, Erika Meng, and Nicholas Piggott. 1997. "The California Table Grape Commission's Promotion Program. An Evaluation." Giannini Foundation Monograph 43. November.

Bancroft, Hubert. 1890. *History of California*. San Francisco. The History Company.

Bardake, Frank. 1993. "What Went Wrong with the UFW?" *Nation*, reprinted in the *Sacramento Bee*, August 1, 1993, F1, F6.

Barr, Evan. 1985. "Sour Grapes: Cesar Chavez Twenty Years Later." *New Republic* 193 (November 25): 20.

Billikopf, Gregorio. 2001. "Labor Management in Agriculture. Cultivating Personnel Productivity." University of California Agricultural Issues Center. Available at http://are.Berkeley.edu/APMP/.

Bishop, Charles E., ed. 1967. *Farm Labor in the United States*. New York: Columbia University Press.

Briggs, Vernon. M. 1973. *Chicanos and Rural Poverty*. Baltimore: Johns Hopkins University Press.

———. 2001. *Immigration and American Unionism*. Ithaca: Cornell University Press and Institute of Labor and Industrial Relations.

Briggs, Vernon M., J. Walter Fogel, and Fred Schmidt. 1977. *The Chicano Worker*. Austin: University of Texas Press.

Brissenden, Paul F. 1920. *The I.W.W.: A Study in American Syndicalism*. New York. Columbia University Press.

Brown, Galen. K. 1984. "Fruit and Vegetable Mechanization." In *Migrant Labor in Agriculture: An International Comparison*, ed. P. Martin, 195–209. Berkeley, Calif.: Giannini Foundation.

California Senate. 1961, 1963. Senate Fact Finding Committee on Labor and Welfare.

"California's Farm Labor Problems: Report of the Senate Fact Finding Committee On Labor And Welfare." Parts I and II. Sacramento.

Cargill, B. F., and G. E. Rossmiller, eds. 1969–70. *Fruit and Vegetable Harvest Mechanization*. 3 vols. East Lansing: Rural Manpower Center.

Carter, Colin, Darrell Hueth, John Mamer, and Andrew Schmitz. 1981. "Labor Strikes and the Price of Lettuce." *Western Journal of Agricultural Economics* 6, no. 1 (July): 1–14.

CAW (Commission on Agricultural Workers). 1992. *Final Report*. Washington, D.C.: Government Printing Office.

CDFA (California Department of Food and Agriculture). "Annual: California Agricultural Overview." Sacramento. Available at http://www.cdfa.ca.gov/docs/CAStats01.pdf.

CIRS (California Institute for Rural Studies). 2000. "Suffering in Silence: A Report on the Health of California's Agricultural Workers." Available at http://www.calendow.org/frm_pub.htm.

COA (Census of Agriculture). USDA. National Agricultural Statistics Service. Available at http://www.nass.usda.gov/census/.

Commission on the Future of Worker-Management Relations (also known as the Dunlop Commission). 1995. Final Report and Recommendations. Washington, D.C. January.

CRS (Congressional Research Service). 1980. "Temporary Worker Programs: Background and Issues." Washington, D.C. February.

Craig, Richard B. 1971. *The Bracero Program: Interest Groups and Foreign Policy*. Austin: University of Texas Press.

Daniel, Cletus E. 1981. *Bitter Harvest: A History of California Farmworkers, 1870–1941*. Berkeley: University of California Press.

———. 1987. "Cesar Chavez and the Unionization of California Farm Workers." In *Labor Leaders in America*, ed. Melvyn Dubofsky and Warren Van Tine, 350–382. Urbana: University of Illinois Press.

Dunne, John Gregory. 1967. *Delano: The Story of the California Grape Strike*. New York: Farrar, Straus & Giroux.

Eagle, Tracy E. 1998. "The ALRB—Twenty Years Later." *San Joaquin Agricultural Law Review* 8.

Edid, Maralyn. 1994. *Farm Labor Organizing: Trends and Prospects*. Ithaca: Cornell University Press.

Fisher, Lloyd. 1953. *The Harvest Labor Market in California*. Cambridge, Mass.: Harvard University Press.

FLA (Farm Labor Alliance). 1986. "Working with Immigration Reform." Grower Bulletin. December.

Fogel, Robert, and Stanley Engerman. 1974. *Time on the Cross: The Economics of American Negro Slavery*. Boston: Little, Brown.

Fogel, Walter, ed. 1985. *California Farm Labor Relations and Law*. Los Angeles: University of California Los Angeles, Institute of Industrial Relations.

Freeman, Richard, and James Medoff. 1984. *What Do Unions Do?* New York: Basic Books.

Fuller, Varden. 1940. "The Supply of Agricultural Labor as a Factor in the Evolution of Farm Organization in California." Ph.D. diss., University of California, Berkeley, 1939. Reprinted in "Violations of Free Speech and the Rights of Labor." Education and Labor Committee [The La Follette Committee]. Washington, D.C.: Senate Education and Labor Committee. 19778–19894.

———. 1991. *Hired Hands in California's Farm Fields*. Berkeley, Calif.: Giannini Foundation.

Fuller, Varden, and John Mamer. 1978. "Constraints on California Farm Worker Unionization." *Industrial Relations* 17, no. 2 (May): 143–155.

Fuller, Varden, and Bert Mason. 1977. "Farm Labor." *Annals of the American Academy of Political and Social Science* 429 (January): 63–80.

Galarza, Ernesto. 1977. *The Tragedy at Chualar*. Santa Barbara: McNally and Loftin.

———. 1978. *Merchants of Labor: The Mexican Bracero Story; An Account of Time-managed Migration of Mexican Farm Workers in California, 1942–1960*. Charlotte, N.C.: McNally (originally self-published, 1964).

Garcia y Griego, Manuel. 1981. "The Importation of Mexican Contract Laborers to the United States, 1941–1964." Program in U.S.-Mexican Studies, University of California San Diego, Working Paper 11.

General Accounting Office. 1988. "The H-2A Program: Protections for U.S. Farmworkers." GAO/PEMD-89-3. Washington, D.C. October 21.

———. 1997. "H-2A Guestworker Program: Changes Could Improve Services to Employers and Better Protect Workers." GAO/HEHS. 98–20. Washington, D.C.

Goldfarb, Ronald. 1981. *A Caste of Despair*. Ames: Iowa State University Press.

Grodin, Joseph. 1976. "California's Agricultural Labor Act: Early Experience." *Industrial Relations* 15 (October): 275–294.

Hayes, Sue E. 1984. "The California Agricultural Labor Relations Act and the National Labor Relations Legislation." In *Seasonal Agricultural Labor Markets in the United States*, ed. Robert Emerson, 328–369. Ames: Iowa State University Press.

Ilg, Randy E. 1995. "The Changing Face of Farm Employment." *Monthly Labor Review* 118, no. 4 (April): 3–12.

INS (Immigration and Naturalization Service). Annual. *Statistical Yearbook of the Immigration and Naturalization Service*. Washington, D.C.

Jamieson, Stuart. 1945. *Labor Unionism in American Agriculture*. Washington, D.C.: Bureau of Labor Statistics, Bulletin 836.

Jenkins, J. Craig. 1985. *The Politics of Insurgency: The Farm Worker Movement in the 1960s*. New York: Columbia University Press.

Koziara, Karen. 1980. "Agriculture." In *Collective Bargaining: The Contemporary American Experience*, ed. Gerald Somers, 263–314. Madison, Wis.: Industrial Relations Research Association.

Kushner, Sam. 1975. *Long Road to Delano*. New York: International Publishers.

Levy, Herman. 1975. "California Agricultural Labor Relations Act: La Esperanza de California Para El Futuro." *Santa Clara Lawyer* (summer): 783–816.

Levy, Jacques. 1975. *Cesar Chavez: Autobiography of La Causa*. New York: Norton.

Lieberman, Myron. 1982. *NLRB Precedent in ALRB Decisions: Legislative Intent or Administrative Fiat*. Long Beach: California State University Foundation. April.

Lipton, Kathryn L., William Edmondson, and Alden Manchester. 1998. *The Food and Fiber System: Contributing to the U.S. and World Economies*. Washington, D.C.: U.S. Department of Agriculture, Economic Research Service. Agriculture Information Bulletin No. 742. July. Available at http://www.econ.ag.gov/epubs/pdf/aib742/.

Lloyd, Jack, Philip L. Martin, and John Mamer. 1988. *The Ventura Citrus Labor Market*. Berkeley: University of California, Division of Agriculture and Natural Resources. Giannini Foundation: Giannini Information Series 88–1.

London, Joan, and Henry Anderson. 1970. *So Shall We Reap: The Story of Cesar Chavez and the Farm Workers Movement*. New York: Crowell.

Majika, Linda, and Theo Majika. 1982. *Farmworkers, Agribusiness, and the State*. Philadelphia: Temple University Press.

Majika, Theo, and Linda Majika. 1995. "Decline of the Farm Labor Movement in California: Organizational Crisis and Political Change." *Critical Sociology* 19, no. 3: 3–35.

Mamer, John, and Donald Rosedale. 1980. *The Management of Seasonal Farmworkers under Collective Bargaining*. Berkeley, Calif.: DANR Leaflet 21147. March.

Marciniak, Ed. 1950. *Toward a National Policy for Migrant Labor*. Chicago: Catholic Council on Working Life.

Martin, Philip. 1994. "Good Intentions Gone Awry: IRCA and U.S. Agriculture." *Annals of the Academy of Political and Social Science* 534 (July): 44–57.

——. 2001. "Ellis Island to The Ellis Farm: Immigration Reform and Rural America." *Choices: The Magazine of Food, Farm, and Resource Issues* 16 no. 3 (fall): 7–10.

Martin, Philip, and Daniel Egan. 1989. "The Makewhole Remedy in California Agriculture." *Industrial and Labor Relations Review* 43, no. 1 (October): 120–130.

Martin, Philip, Daniel Egan, and Stephanie Luce. 1988. "The Wages and Fringe Benefits of Unionized Farmworkers." Berkeley, Calif.: Giannini Foundation Information Report 88–1.

Martin, Philip, Wallace Huffman, Robert Emerson, J. Edward Taylor, and Refugio Rochin. 1995. "Immigration Reform and U.S. Agriculture." Berkeley, Calif.: Division of Agriculture and Natural Resources Publication 3358.

Martin, Philip, and David Martin. 1994. *The Endless Quest: Helping America's Farmworkers*. Boulder, Colo.: Westview Press.

Martin, Philip, and Alan Olmsted. 1985. "The Agricultural Mechanization Controversy." *Science* 227, no. 4687 (February 8): 601–606.

Mason, Bert. 1998. "The Raisin Grape Industry.: Mimeo. Available at http://migration.ucdavis.edu/rmn/changingface/cf_sep1998/Mason-Raisin.html.

McWilliams, Carey. 1939. *Factories in the Fields*. Boston: Little Brown.

——. 1942. *Ill Fares the Land: Migrants and Migratory Labor in the United States*. Boston: Little, Brown.

Meister, Dick, and Ann Loftis. 1977. *A Long Time Coming: The Struggle to Unionize America's Farm Workers*. New York: Macmillan.

Mines, Richard, and Michael Kearney. 1982. "The Health of Tulare County Farmworkers." Mimeo. April.

Mines, Richard, and Philip L. Martin. 1984. "Immigrant Workers and the California Citrus Industry." *Industrial Relations* 23, no. 1 (January): 139–149.

Mines, Richard, and Philip Martin. 1986. *A Profile of California Farmworkers*. Berkeley, Calif.: Giannini Foundation Information Series 86–2.

Montmarquet, James. 1985. "Philosophical Foundations for Agrarianism." *Agriculture and Human Values* 2, no. 2, (spring): 5–14.

Moore, Truman. 1965. *The Slaves We Rent*. New York: Random House.

O'Brien, Michael, Burton Cargill, and Robert Fridley. 1983. *Principles and Practices for Harvesting and Handling Fruits and Nuts*. Westport, Conn.: AVI.

Oliveira, Victor. 1989. "Trends in the Hired Farm Work Force, 1945–87." Washington, D.C.: U.S. Department of Agriculture, Economic Research Service, Agricultural Information Bulletin 561.

Olmstead, Alan, and Paul Rhode. 1997. "An Overview of the History of California Agriculture." In *California Agriculture: Issues and Challenges*, ed. Jerome Siebert, 1–28. Berkeley, Calif.: Giannini Foundation.

Padfield, Harland, and William E. Martin. 1965. *Farmers, Workers, and Machines*. Tucson: University of Arizona Press.

Parker, Carleton. 1920. "A Report to His Excellency Hiram W. Johnson, Governor of California, by the Commission of Immigration and Housing of California on the Causes and All Matters Pertaining to the So-Called Wheatland Hop Fields' Riot and Killing of August 3, 1913, and Containing Certain Recommendations as a Solution for the Problems Disclosed." In *The Casual Laborer and Other Essays*, Appendix 11, 171–199. New York. Harcourt, Brace.

Peterson, Cheryl. 1969. "The California Farm Workforce. A Profile." Sacramento. California Assembly Committee on Agriculture. April.

President's Commission of Migratory Labor. 1951. *Migratory Labor in American Agriculture*. Washington, D.C.: U.S. Government Printing Office.

Schauer, Robert, and Sennis Tyler. 1970. "The Unionization of Farm Labor." *University of California Davis Law Review* 2: 1–38.

Schilling, Elizabeth. 1992. "The ALRB in the '90s—Do Not Disturb . . . Agency Asleep." *California Journal* (March 1): 151–154.

Segur, W. H., and Varden Fuller. 1976. "California's Farm Labor Elections: An Analysis of the Initial Results." *Monthly Labor Review* (December): 25–30.

Smith, Leslie W., and Robert Coltrane. 1981. "Hired Farmworkers: Background and Trends for the Eighties." Washington, D.C.: USDA, ERS, RDR Report 32.

Sosnick, Stephen. 1978. *Hired Hands: Seasonal Workers in U.S. Agriculture*. Santa Barbara: McNally and Loftin.

Steven Street, Richard. 1996. "The FBI's Secret File on Cesar Chavez." *Southern California Quarterly* 78, no. 4: 347–384.

———. 1996–97. "First Farmworkers, First *Braceros*: Baja California Field Hands and the Origins of Farm Labor Importation in California Agriculture, 1769–1790." *California History* 75, no. 4: 306–321.

———. 1998. "Tattered Shirts and Ragged Pants: Accommodation, Protest, and the Coarse Culture of California Wheat Harvesters and Threshers, 1866–1900." *Pacific Historical Review* 67, no. 4: 573–608.

Taylor, J. Edward, and Philip L. Martin. 2001. "Human Capital: Migration and Rural Population Change." In *Handbook of Agricultural Economics*, ed. Bruce Gardener and Gordon Rausser, vol. 1. Amsterdam: Elsevier Science. Available at http://www.elsevier.nl/.

Taylor, J. Edward, Philip Martin, and Michael Fix. 1997. *Poverty amid Prosperity: Immigration and the Changing Face of Rural California*. Washington, D.C.: Urban Institute Press. Available at http://www.urban.org.

Taylor, Paul S. 1928–35. *Mexican Labor in the United States* (13 monographs). Berkeley: University of California Press. Migration Statistics (IV). 1934.

———. 1937. "Migratory Farm Labor in the United States." *Monthly Labor Review* (March): 23–26.

Taylor, Ronald B. 1975. *Chavez and the Farmworkers*. Boston: Beacon Press.

———. 1976. "California Agricultural Labor Relations." In *Proceedings of the Industrial Relations Research Association*, 29th Annual Winter Meeting. 67–72.

Thilmany, Dawn. 1994. "The Effect of Immigration Reform on Farm Labor Markets." Ph.D. Thesis, University of California Davis.

U.S. Census Bureau. 1976. *Historical Statistics of the United States: Colonial Times to 1970*. Washington, D.C.

U.S. Department of Labor. 1959. "Mexican Farm Labor Program." Consultants Report. Washington, D.C. October.

———. 1990–2001. "Findings from the National Agricultural Workers Survey (NAWS)." Washington: Office of the Assistant Secretary for Policy, Office of Program Economics. Washington, D.C. Available at http://www.dol.gov/asp/programs/agworker/naws.htm.

——. 2000. "Findings from the National Agricultural Workers Survey (NAWS): A Demographic and Employment Profile of United States Farmworkers." Office of the Assistant Secretary for Policy, Office of Program Economics, Research Report No. 8. Washington, D.C. March. Available at http://www.dol.gov/asp/programs/agworker/naws.htm.

U.S. House of Representatives. 1971. Committee on Education and Labor, Subcommittee on Agricultural Labor. "Seminar of Farm Labor Problems." Washington, D.C. June 2, 3, 10.

——. 1984. Committee on Education and Labor, Subcommittee on Labor Standards. "Hearings on Immigration Reform and Guestworkers." Washington, D.C. 11 April and 3 May.

——. 1986. Committee on the Judiciary. "Immigration Reform and Control Act of 1986, Conference Report 99th Congress," 2nd session, Report 99–1000. Washington, D.C. 14 October.

U.S. Senate. 1942. Committee on Education and Labor, "La Follette Committee Violations of Free Speech and the Rights of Labor." Senate Report 1150. Washington, D.C. March.

——. 1969–70. Committee on Labor and Public Welfare, Subcommittee on Migratory Labor. "Migrant and Seasonal Worker Powerlessness." Washington, D.C.

——. 1971–72. Committee on Labor and Public Welfare, Subcommittee on Migratory Labor. "Farmworkers in Rural America 1971–72." Washington, D.C.

——. 1979. Committee on Labor and Human Resources. "Farmworker Collective Bargaining, 1979." 96th Congress, 1st Sess. Washington, D.C.

Villarejo, Don. 2001. "California's Farm Employers: Twenty-five Years Later." Paper presented at the Agricultural Labor Relations Act at 25, Symposium, University of California Davis. October 4, 2000. Available at http://migration.ucdavis.edu/rmn/cfra.html.

Index